SECRET
WEAPONS

OSPREY
PUBLISHING

SECRET
WEAPONS

Technology, Science & the Race to Win World War II

BRIAN J. FORD

First published in Great Britain in 2011 by Osprey Publishing,
Midland House, West Way, Botley, Oxford, OX2 0PH, UK
44-02 23rd Street, Suite 219, Long Island City, NY 11101, USA

E-mail: info@ospreypublishing.com

OSPREY PUBLISHING IS PART OF THE OSPREY GROUP.

A CIP catalogue record for this book is available from the British
Library

ISBN: 978 1 84908 390 4

Page layout by: Myriam Bell Design, France
Index by Margaret Vaudrey
Typeset in Adobe Caslon Pro and Rockwell
Originated by PDQ Media, Bungay, UK
Printed in China through Worldprint Ltd.

11 12 13 14 15   10 9 8 7 6 5 4 3 2 1

Imperial War Museum Collections
Many of the photos in this book come from the Imperial War
Museum's huge collections which cover all aspects of conflict involving
Britain and the Commonwealth since the start of the 20th century.
These rich resources are available online to search, browse and buy
at www.iwmcollections.org.uk. In addition to Collections Online,
you can visit the Visitor Rooms where you can explore over 8 million
photographs, thousands of hours of moving images, the largest sound
archive of its kind in the world, thousands of diaries and letters written
by people in wartime, and a huge reference library. To make an
appointment, call (020) 7416 5320, or e-mail mail@iwm.org.uk.
Imperial War Museum www.iwm.org.uk

Osprey Publishing is supporting the Woodland Trust, the UK's leading
woodland conservation charity, by funding the dedication of trees.

www.ospreypublishing.com

Front Cover: a selection of images from the US National Archives,
the author's collection and Osprey Publishing, as well as details from
artwork by John Batchelor.

Editor's note
Conversions of units are given for general guidance.

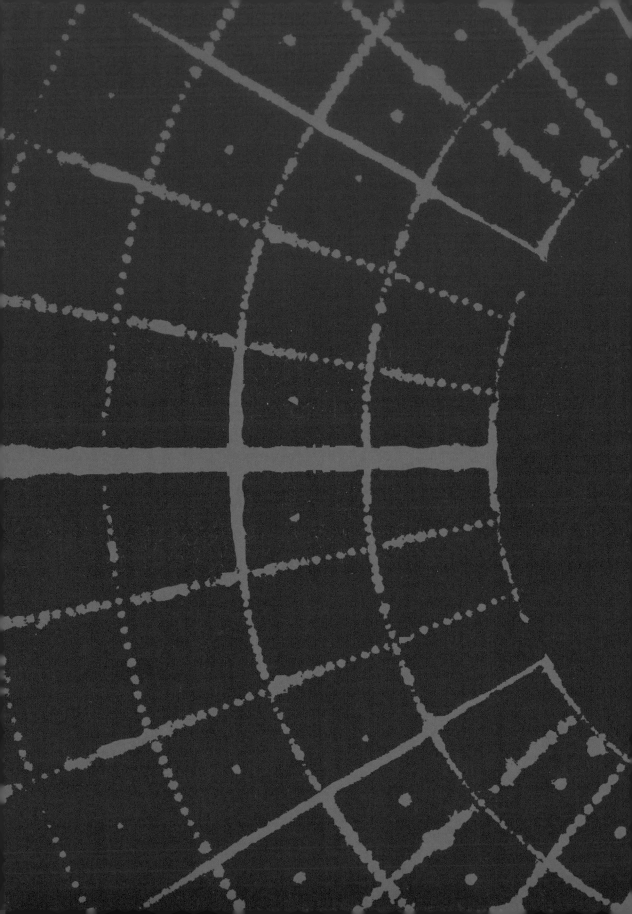

CONTENTS

INTRODUCTION

THERE HAS NEVER BEEN A RACE that can match the progress made in World War II. Computers and antibiotics went from being little-known curiosities to mainstream projects; the biplanes still popular as the war began had been superseded by jet aircraft at its end. At the beginning of the war, rockets were little more than self-propelled shells – but, by its end, they took us to the edge of space.

In the modern world, it can take five years to plan a new idea, five years to obtain permission and a further 15 years to finish the work; quarter of a century in all. During the war, a new weapon or a great building could develop from concept to reality in a matter of months. Our modern Western world is suffocating in bureaucracy and, at a time when we need new technologies to safeguard the future, we could benefit from the sense of productive urgency that flourished during World War II.

During my earliest investigations into secret weapons of World War II help was provided by many colleagues in the former West Germany – both in Berlin and the Deutsches Museum, Munich – and by Robert Friederich, Petra Kieslich and Christian Uhl as well as contacts in the Kammer für Außenhaldel in the former East Germany, where visits by the British were much less frequent. Working with me on my first books on this subject were Peter Dunbar, Sarah Kingham and John Batchelor. Indeed, John returns to work in this new book to provide many of the key illustrations. The writers on the period I have known include Barrie Pitt, Sir Basil Liddell Hart and Ralph Barker. I learned much by visiting sites ranging from the rocket launch pads in Florida where I was a guest of NASA (and watched the space shuttle being launched) to the advanced anti-aircraft launch base hidden in the bushes at Lavernock in Wales, United Kingdom. I travelled from Bletchley Park, home of the British wartime code-breakers, to tour the Argonne National Laboratory near Chicago, which arose from Enrico Fermi's top-secret Manhattan Project. Since those early years my visits have extended from the United States and Germany to North Africa, and through China and Japan to wartime sites in Guam, to Pearl Harbor, Papua New Guinea, Malaysia and Singapore.

It is impossible to acknowledge all the individuals who have advanced my understanding, but the influence of Professor R. V. Jones, Winston Churchill's Assistant Director of Intelligence, was invaluable; similarly, Professor Thomas Allibone and Professor Max Perutz gave me further insights into what went on behind the scenes. I spent many happy days with Dr George Svihla at his home in Ogden Dunes, Indiana, where we discussed his memories of working in the wartime laboratories in the United States; and with Horace Dall in Luton,

England, who was with the first scientific parties entering the German laboratories as the Allies advanced in 1945. I have consulted the facilities at major resources including the Science Museum and the Imperial War Museum in London and the libraries in New York and Washington DC. The librarians at Cardiff opened for me the reports of the Combined Intelligence Objectives Subcommittee and the British Intelligence Objectives Subcommittee, and I have been offered timely assistance at the University of Cambridge by Dr Allen Packwood, Director of the Churchill Archives Centre, and his staff. I have been advised by knowledgeable authorities ranging from Mr Rod Kirkby of Cambridge on jet aircraft and Mr John Gallehawk on Bletchley Park to Professor H. Willkomm of Kiel on wartime nuclear physics and the Rt Hon Dr Alex Hankey, whose grandfather was Baron Hankey, Chairman of the Scientific Advisory Committee of the War Cabinet under Winston Churchill. Mr Eddie Creek has kindly supplied some rare photographs for this volume, and Dr Hugh Hunt, Fellow of Trinity College, came to give the inaugural joint lecture on the bouncing bomb for Madingley Hall and the Cambridge Society for the Application of Research, of which I have the honour to be President, at the University of Cambridge.

On a personal note, I wish to express sincere gratitude to those who have done far more to assist the writing of this book than ordinarily you might expect. To Kate, for her unique insights into publishing; for the editorial skill of Emily and Margaret, and above all to Charly for her diligent professionalism and Jan for providing the essential infrastructure that every writer needs.

Differing authorities have used a variety of naming styles over the years; here we will have both the English and overseas names provided for each weapon. To bring consistency, model numbers all have a hyphen (the V2, as it was often described in Germany, is here the V-2).

The secret research of World War II brought us the first cruise missile, the birth of long-range rockets, the realities of radar and remote-control technology, earthquake bombs, supersonic planes, modern plastics and super-drugs, ballpoint pens and stealth technology. This was an astonishing, unmatched era of amazing progress in science and technology. It has lessons to teach us yet.

Brian J. Ford
Cambridge, 2011

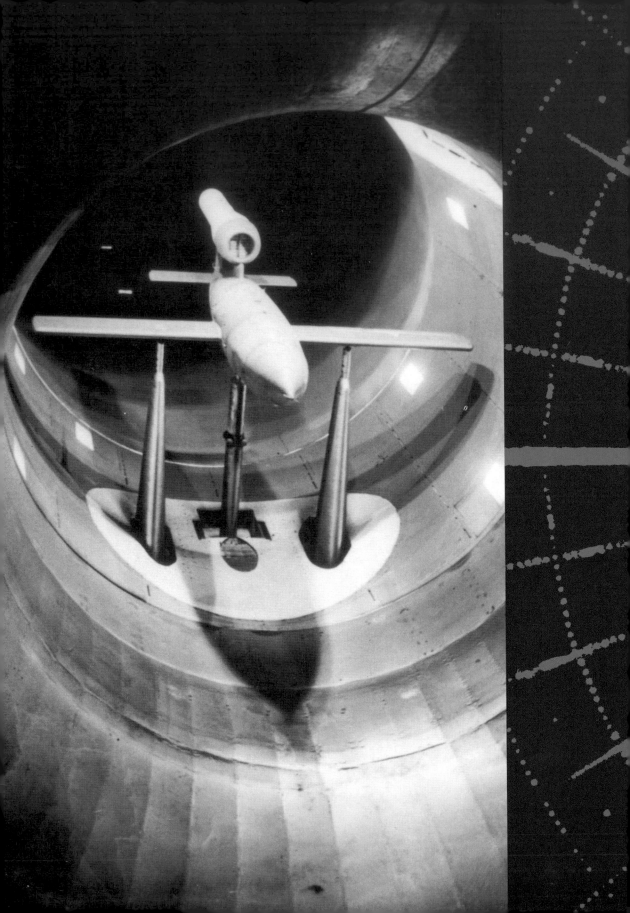

THE MAKING OF
A SECRET WAR

THE STORY OF SECRET WEAPONS is not purely a matter of history, or of specialist interest to military history enthusiasts, for it matters to us all and the legacy is all around us to this day. Wartime research gave rise to some of the most revolutionary developments and to some of the craziest ideas including the bizarre plan to change Hitler's sex by hiding hormones in his food, and another strange scheme to stick German soldiers to the ground by dropping shells filled with glue.

Tales and legends of all kinds have grown up since World War II: stories of super-bombs, deadly ray-guns and covert deals. Some sources say that the Nazis had flying saucers ready to roll and had even exploded an atomic bomb. The saga of secret science during those vital years has intrigued me since childhood – indeed the first book I wrote on the subject was published in my twenties. Yet there are still dramatic new lessons to be learned. Although we think of the United States as the home of atomic power, we should also recognize how far it developed in Germany, Britain, Russia and Japan – all of these nations had their own atomic bomb projects. 'Shock and awe' did not begin in the war with Iraq, but was born back in World War II. We will find that many of the greatest war criminals of all time were secretly pardoned and illicitly given sanctuary in exchange for continuing their work on secret weapons, but this time for the other side. Although the devastating raid on Pearl Harbor by Japan is so often spoken of as unprovoked and unexpected, it is surprising to discover that neither is true; while many daring deeds by British heroes would now be classed as war crimes. Did you know that Americans were killed by secret weapons launched from Japan during World War II? Probably not – they were secret then, and they remain secret now. Were you aware that an astronaut (as well as a satellite) was launched with V-2 rockets? Would you ever suspect that huge stocks of phosgene, the corrosive, blinding, suffocating gas that was stockpiled in World War II, are now available in industrial cities across the world? Calder Hall in Britain is famous as the world's first nuclear power station, but there was another that existed years earlier, about which few people have ever heard. Did you know that lethal secret weapons from World War II are currently threatening residential areas of the United States, or that a sound cannon developed by the Nazis was recently used to stop pirates from boarding a cruise ship? America is famous for its first nuclear reactor, but the biggest by the war's end was actually in Canada; and a form of radar, one of the most celebrated secret technologies of World War II, was in fact in use before 1914. You will have heard of the British 'bouncing bomb', but you probably don't know that the Germans also had a bouncing bomb of their own – or that *The Dam Busters* movie had a direct line of inspiration to *Star Wars*.

Books on secret weapons are traditionally seen as quirky, backward-looking, specialist volumes that appeal to historians, in the same way that strange aircraft attract plane-spotters. The subject is closer to the present day than we think. In reality, World War II gave us the science on which our modern world depends. Nothing like that pace of progress had occurred before, or has been seen since. War is a more powerful stimulus to progress than peace. The demands of the Napoleonic wars gave us canned food. It was India fighting the British that bequeathed to us the first steel rocket (invented by the Indians, not the British). The Wright brothers had military aircraft in mind when they started their experiments with flying machines. But World War II – above all – led to an unprecedented upsurge in inventiveness and innovation. After World War I, Europe and America were in a post-Victorian era where progress was steady and the major preoccupation was the preservation of social stability and the maintenance of wealth. Engineers were gentle innovators, rather than the brash adventurers of the previous century. The progress of pure science was slow and methodical, and technology proceeded at a steady pace, interspersed with revolutionary new notions in fields like radio, television, aircraft and ocean-going liners. The rocket enthusiasts were hobbyists; pioneers of jet engines were widely ignored. Development proceeded logically and progress was a methodical unravelling of realities.

SCIENTISTS WANTED

From **IAN G. FRASER, Our Parliamentary Correspondent**

THOUSANDS of scientists are wanted by the Government for war work.

Lord Hankey, chairman of the Scientific Advisory Committee of the War Cabinet, making this appeal in the Lords last night, said:—

"In these days no one man, whatever his genius, can cover more than a fraction of the immense field of science in war. We require thousands of scientists.

"We are engaged in a death struggle with an enemy who boasts with justification of his achievements in the field of science.

"Our scientists are at least as good as his, and with the aid of the scientific resources of the empire, and especially of the U.S.A., we are building up a scientific equipment that is destined to play an ever-increasing part in our war effort and in the period of reconstruction that must come thereafter."

Lord Hankey issued this appeal on behalf of Churchill's war cabinet to British scientists who could join the effort to help develop secret weapons. It featured in the *Daily Dispatch* on 3 April 1941. (Author's collection)

With the dark clouds of war approaching, science and technology took on a new and terrifying urgency. Now the pace of progress was unprecedented – and yet it was different, depending on whose side you stood. The Japanese, intent on territorial acquisition of the relatively undeveloped nations of South-East Asia, put much emphasis on planes, guns and bombs. They saw the subjects of these nations as inherently inferior, hardly worth rating as civilized humans at all. The Americans, arriving late in the battle, rushed to produce innovative aircraft and state-of-the-art shipping, and gathered together experts who were harnessing the atom to produce the most terrible and destructive weapons ever used in warfare. The French were content for decades with their Maginot line, and carried on with domestic developments without paying much heed to the international perspective. The Italians, Spanish and Russians were all developing weapons of war and stockpiling ideas as much as materiel.

Evening newspapers had a head start in publishing the day's events, and the *Evening Standard* announced the German invasion of Poland on 1 September 1939. Two days later, war was declared. (Hulton Archive/Getty Images)

Germany was different. The sole aim of her leaders following Hitler's ascension to power was the domination of Europe and, with time and good fortune, the world. Germany was surrounded by highly developed countries with a shared sense of strength and a belief in progress towards a future free from warfare, and the Nazis were well aware that they needed to overcome nations just as ingenious and as civilized as Germany herself. With the exception of Italy, whose leader Benito Mussolini had grandiose ideas of his own, all the other European nations lacked one thing, however: fanaticism. For Germany, domination was increasingly painted as a right, a destiny. And the scientific developments leading up to the war were aimed squarely at preparing for the long-term occupation of nearby nations. As war began, Hitler was emboldened by the capitulation of Czechoslovakia's allies over the Sudentenland in 1938; and when Britain declared war in 1939 as a result of the German attacks on the narrow corridor of land towards the Baltic port of Danzig, Hitler was stunned. He had never imagined that Britain would declare war in this way, and for such a small piece of territory. Then, with the bit between his teeth, he ordered the rate of progress to roar into top gear and yet – as German victory seemed assured, in the early years at least he was just as quick to withdraw support from many revolutionary and highly innovative fields of research and development, so that progress in these was nipped in the bud. At the time, Hitler optimistically concluded that these new technologies would not be required after all. Victory, he felt, would easily be his.

The situation in Britain was utterly unlike that in Germany. Britain was looking to a future without war, for the bloody lessons of World War I were vividly imprinted on the nation's collective memory. During the 1920s and '30s there was a steady decline in military expenditure, even at the risk of being unable to defend overseas

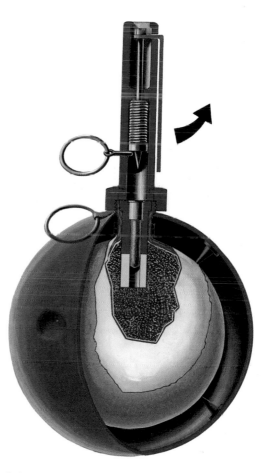

Anti-tank grenade no. 74, the 'sticky bomb', contained a strong adhesive based on birdlime. An Allied soldier would break the outer casing to release the glue and stick the bomb onto an enemy tank before triggering the fuse and running away. Although popular with troops, few successes were recorded and sometimes the bomb stuck to the solider. (John Batchelor)

territories. The large military machine was seen as a thing of the past: war was viewed as inhuman and consigned to history. The British were wrestling with a turbulent empire and the emerging mood was increasingly one of interdependence, rather than colonial domination. Whereas the focus of Germany's priorities was the development of futuristic weapons of aggression, Britain's energies during the war were primarily invested in defending herself against attack, resisting occupation and preventing Germany from producing yet more terrifying weapons of mass destruction. British scientists were intent on finding out where the German planes might be, and soon perfected radar; they wanted to follow the intimate conversations that the Nazis conducted, and so also perfected the means of cracking the codes of the Enigma encryption machines.* The British secret war began as one of defence against aggression. When Britain came up with the penetration bomb, it was not primarily to attack Germany but to demolish the Nazi fortifications within which lay their weapons; similarly, when the bouncing bomb was introduced it was to take out the factories where the munitions were manufactured. But let's keep this in proportion – the flooding of the Ruhr valley by the 'Dambusters' was seen at the time as heroic; yet it would now be considered a war crime, for thousands of innocent civilians and captured slave workers were drowned. Yet the legacy lives on. The Dambusters inspired more modern movie producers; the early computers pointed the way to today's desktop giants; our cruise missiles and guided bombs all emerged from the science and technology developed in the war.

The United States was then (as now) by far the world's richest nation, and she was quick to capitalize on the financial implications of the war. From the start, she was covertly concentrating on the possibility of building warplanes, ships and guns. In general, however, there was far less emphasis on quirky secret weaponry; America wanted to build hardware. For the United States, the major focus of secret weapons research soon became nuclear research. Crucial new developments in atomic science had arisen just at the beginning of World War II, and although the key developments took place in Europe, it was in the United States that the money was made available.

Not all of the secret weapons were large, costly, or complex; and in many ways they exemplify the various approaches of the different nations to the conduct of the conflict. Anti-tank weapons are a case in point. Early in the war, the British perfected a simple device known as the 'sticky bomb'. This was a round grenade with a time delay that could be attached to an enemy tank by a solider. In essence, it was a container of nitroglycerin in a case that was covered with industrial adhesive. It did not always work, of course, and sometimes it stuck firmly to the soldier's uniform. Records suggest that 2,500,000 were made between 1940 and 1943; but only six tanks are on record as having been destroyed by these devices.

---

* These were based on using a spinning rotor to select letters in writing a secret code. Although we think of the Enigma machines as being of German origin, their story was more complex and indeed the first design for a rotor encryption machine was invented by two Dutch naval engineers, Theo van Hengel and R. P. C. Spengler, in 1915.

The Germans adopted a different approach. They devised an anti-tank explosive weapon known as Goliath (*der Leichter Ladungsträger* or 'light explosive carrier'). It was a tiny tracked vehicle, looking like a model tank and controlled by a joystick at the end of a 2,000ft (600m) wire and packed with 220lb (100kg) of high explosive. They had little ground clearance, so often found themselves stuck on a ridge, but 7,500 were constructed starting in 1942 and they were still in use during the D-Day landings in 1944.

Futuristic technology also emerged on all sides, though predominately from the genius of Germany. In today's world, we know that a new development can cost millions, and take decades of testing and redesign before it reaches the market. Not so during World War II. Throughout those years, and the decade leading up to them, caution was thrown to the wind. Personal whim, charisma, ambition, guesswork, crazy good luck ... every motivation you could wish to cite came to the fore. A new idea could become reality within weeks. Revolutionary new concepts of earth-shattering importance could go from the drawing-board to reality in a matter of months. No period of human history has seen such incredible changes, and the results are all around us.

We like to think of the developments of that time as highly organized, well funded, carefully prepared and amazingly productive. The reality is far from the public perception, with private fads and personal rivalry causing crazy changes in policy and priorities. Step one way and you'd rule the world with astonishing new ideas; move in another direction and you could be executed on the spot. A proposal that was unwanted at one moment could become the highest priority in a changed climate of opinion. At the end of it all, many of these astonishing new advances were harnessed by the victors through illegal means – murderous criminals were hailed as heroic innovators if they could bring benefit to their hosts. Even the word of a president could be ignored if it helped promote the cause of progress.

It is sometimes said that the secret weapons of World War II were ridiculous, or expedient, or simply lucky guesswork; in fact, many of them introduced revolutionary concepts from which we benefit to this day. So much of what we now take for granted began as secret science during World War II.

THE TRIGGER FROM VERSAILLES

World War I was the birthplace of secret weapons. Small rockets were used in large numbers, and poison gas was used by both sides. That terrible conflict was brutal and disfiguring, and the victors at once laid all the blame on Germany. The Treaty of Versailles was touted as an agreement to end all wars, and the German people were relieved to see the conflict at its end. They initially joined with everyone else in wishing to see the perpetrators of warfare punished for their crimes. Yet Versailles did not bring this about. The treaty failed to identify the roots of the conflict, but instead simply blamed all the German people for the war, and demanded

1. Rhineland demilitarized.
2. Saarland under League of Nations
   administration until 1935.
3. Alsace-Lorraine returned to France.
4. Upper Silesia ceded to Poland after plebiscite.

☐ Germany in 1918
◼ Land lost by Germany as a result
of the Treaty of Versailles in 1919

0   200 miles

0   250 km

that they repay the victors unimaginable sums of money by way of reparation. Germany was even obliged in future to use her shipyards for the construction of Allied vessels. The Germans felt humiliated, not liberated.

Typical of the aftermath was the Ten Year Rule which the British government adopted in August 1919. Calculations of the budgets for the armed forces would now be made on the assumption that the 'British Empire would not be engaged in any great war during the next ten years'. As a victorious nation, Britain felt confident that Germany had been humiliated and could never again pose a problem to any other state, so military expenditure was slashed. We think of Winston Churchill as being instinctively in favour of preparedness for war, but in the years following World War I his attitudes were very different. In 1928 Churchill was Chancellor of the Exchequer, and it was his powers of eloquence that persuaded the Cabinet to agree that this Rule would remain in force until it was specifically rescinded. By 1931, Prime Minister Ramsay MacDonald thought that the international situation was becoming dangerous, and that perhaps the Ten Year Rule should be abolished. The First Sea Lord, Sir Frederick Field, warned in the same year that the British Navy was 'below the standard required for keeping open Britain's sea communications during wartime'. No port in the entire British Empire, he said, could be adequately defended, but nobody took any notice, and the Ten Year Rule remained a key component of British foreign policy.

Not until 23 March 1932 was the Ten Year Rule abandoned by the Cabinet. Even then it was countered with a cautionary statement: 'This must not be taken to justify an expanding expenditure by the Defence Services without regard to the very serious financial and economic situation' which Britain faced.

Matters were quite the reverse in Germany. Article 231 of the Treaty of Versailles forced the whole German nation to accept complete responsibility for World War I. Henceforth, the German Army (the Reichswehr) would amount to a maximum of just 100,000 persons; there could be no conscription; and the size of the Navy (the Kriegsmarine) was restricted, with absolutely no submarines being permitted. In addition, Germany could hold no poison gas, and have no airships. Instead of being a people freed from the tyranny of their leaders, the whole German population was made to feel personally culpable for the cruelty of the war. With extra money being printed to help pay reparations, the German currency spiralled into hopeless inflation, and then a global stock market crash followed. Germans who had rejoiced at the fall of the Kaiser were seeking a new leader, any leader, who could restore their morale and give them back some dignity. Germany had not even been permitted to join the new League of Nations, and had lost all her overseas territories. The humiliation of the nation – when no

---

Opposite: The land lost by Germany under the Treaty of Versailles is here shown in pink. Belgium took over Eupen and Malmedy, and Poland gained a corridor to the Baltic Sea. (The Map Studio © Osprey Publishing)

foreign troops had ever set foot on German soil throughout the course of the war – left the people vulnerable to any charismatic leader, even a diminutive Austrian painter.

The ramifications of the Treaty of Versailles were not limited to problems in Europe. The United States government refused to ratify the treaty and Kaiser Wilhelm – whom everyone assumed would be put on trial – was exiled to the Netherlands. The British Prime Minister Lloyd George was determined that the Kaiser should hang, but the American President, Woodrow Wilson, refused and argued that there were Allies they would also wish to see executed for their conduct during the war. Attempts to extradite the Kaiser and take him to court failed and, surprising as it seems, the Kaiser survived to see World War II, eventually dying in 1941. The fledgling USSR, still trying to create a new national state out of the ruins of revolution, capitalized on the sense of uncertainty by secretly offering the new German government facilities in the USSR to develop and test new weapons – in exchange for assisting the Soviets in building up their own new Army General Staff. In March 1922 German officers went to Russia to start their illicit training; in April 1922 the Junkers Company started manufacturing aircraft at Fili, near Moscow, and the German Krupp Company was soon established at Rostov-on-Don in southern Russia. At Vivupal, near the spa resort of Lipetsk, Russia, German pilots went on training courses for the future German Air Force (the Luftwaffe). By 1926, the German Army was using a Russian tank training school at Kazan and a chemical warfare institute in Samara Oblast. The Soviet Army was given the benefits of the latest German developments in military theory and weapons technology. By 1929, Germany was actively helping Soviet industry to modernize, and tank production at both the Leningrad Bolshevik Factory and the Kharkov Locomotive Company was being streamlined. Russia was not the only country to help out. Britain was also increasing her legitimate trade with Germany during this period, selling many of Britain's best designs of aircraft engines to the burgeoning German air industry. These were fitted into the existing German aircraft, while Germany's engineers examined the British engines and set out to improve them so that German manufacturers could equip future generations of warplanes. When Hitler came to power in 1933 this cooperation came to an end, but by then the secret roots of German militarism had been well-established.

Deny a nation its right to development, and it will do it covertly. Limit the size of its army, and it will raise the quality of each soldier to the highest level. Place constraints upon the size of its warships, and it will develop the most efficient, lightweight, state-of-the-art vessels in history. Tell it to eschew airships, and – who knows? – it might even opt to develop space rockets instead. A victorious nation should always seek to dignify the population of a defeated state, for they have often suffered greatly during the conflict imposed upon them by their leaders; humiliating them will never augur well for the future. In considering secret weapons in the context of World War II, we can see that their origins lay long before the outbreak of war.

SCIENCE AT SPEED

For today's citizen, the secret weapons of World War II should be seen as a mainstream matter, not a specialist subject; for they reveal how rapidly science and technology can advance. Projects that meandered indifferently for decades acquired a dramatic momentum and developed faster than ever before in history. Given a similar sense of urgency, could we not introduce ways to sequestrate carbon dioxide, capture geothermal power, produce superabundant food without despoiling the landscape and conquer diseases like malaria, HIV and tuberculosis? Rapid results provided the key to the secret development of weapons of World War II, and we have not yet learnt how to generate the same sense of urgency in peacetime.

The one exception I could cite would be the vision of a man on the moon, which President John F. Kennedy put to the American nation on 12 September 1962. He promised America that their great nation would have a man walking on the lunar surface within a decade – and the speech fired up the nation in a frenzy of support. He found, uniquely in peacetime, a common cause to bring energies together, and the rate of progress until the moon was reached paralleled the efforts made during World War II. Neil Armstrong stepped onto the moon on 21 July 1969; the whole project had been successfully telescoped into less than seven years. So – it can be done. Before, however, we reach the conclusion that it's easy to fire up innovation and the speed of progress in peacetime, we should reflect on one crucial matter: the race to the moon was performed by teams led by the German rocket engineers who invented the world's first space rocket, the V-2. The impetus we saw in the National Air and Space Administration (NASA) was a continuation of the culture of wartime Germany, harnessed this time for the purposes of peace. Even here, it was secret weapons that pointed the way ahead.

The essential lesson of history is that people never learn from the lessons of history. The secret science of World War II, and its legacy in the wars we wage today, arose from that unchangeable fact.

FLYING WEAPONS: SECRET AIRCRAFT

AIRCRAFT OF EVERY CONCEIVABLE SIZE AND SHAPE appeared during World War II. Throughout the war, and in the years immediately preceding it, both Allied and Axis forces produced novel aircraft of increasingly sophisticated design and increasingly impressive specifications, as well as incredible new missiles that paved the way to the future, as we shall see in the next chapter. Mustangs, Messerschmitts, the Zero and the legendary Spitfire are all remarkable aircraft and between them they altered the course of the war. Many planes that had been developed in peacetime were converted from civilian to military use. Thus, for example, the Douglas DC-3 airliner was modified to become the legendary Douglas C-47 Dakota, the military transport Skytrain. Over 10,000 of them were produced in California at Long Beach and Santa Monica, and also at Oklahoma City. Similarly, in Seattle, Boeing had launched their B-247, the world's first all-metal airliner, in 1933. They moved on to commence design of the larger B-322 in 1934, and in 1940 were given a contract to convert the aircraft for military use. It became the B-29 Superfortress bomber.

Although all these aircraft played a crucial role in World War II, not one of them was a secret. Only the Germany military establishment produced an astonishing range of top-secret flying devices, some of which defy the imagination, and many of which led to future technology.

THE DIRIGIBLE – BLIMPS AND AIRSHIPS

But in the years leading up to the war, it wasn't aircraft that dominated the airways, but huge dirigible airships. Some were still in use throughout World War II – but where did they begin? A dirigible is a lighter-than-air balloon which can be driven forward and steered. Those that don't have an internal skeleton to support the shape of the balloon are known as blimps; a true airship has a framework that provides its shape with fins and motors to drive it forward and steer it. They began with a French enthusiast, Lieutenant Jean Baptiste Marie Meusnier, who flew across the English Channel in 1785, in a balloon fitted with moveable wings (for propulsion) and a fan-tail (with which to steer). A design for a steam-powered dirigible featured in the 1851 Great Exhibition at the Crystal Palace in London, and in the following year Henri Giffard flew 12 miles (20km) from Paris to Trappes in a steam-driven airship. By 1884, the French were flying an airship 170ft (52m) long and lifted with 66,000ft³ (1,900m³) of hydrogen. It was powered by an electric motor running from a battery weighing 960lb (413kg). In 1896 an engineer from Croatia, David Schwarz, designed a metal-covered airship which was first flown at Tempelhof airfield, Berlin, shortly after he had died that year. His widow, Melanie Schwarz, was paid 15,000 Marks (almost $100,000 today) for the details of Schwarz's research by a retired military enthusiast who was fascinated by the idea of building a huge airship of his own.

The person who bought the plans was Count Ferdinand von Zeppelin. Although several versions were at work at the dawn of the twentieth century, including those of the French and Italians, it was the Zeppelin airships that came to dominate. Luftschiff Zeppelin LZ-1 was first flown in 1900, with the LZ-2 following in 1906. The Zeppelin airships had a frame made of light alloy girders that contained separate gas cells and were covered with fabric. They captured the public imagination, and in 1908 H. G. Wells published *The War in the Air* which described how airships could attack and obliterate entire cities. In 1912, an Italian airship was sent on reconnaissance west of Tripoli behind Turkish lines and this was the first military use of an airship. The German airships continued to be a success; by the start of World War I they had already carried 37,250 passengers on 1,600 flights lasting 3,200 flying hours and covering 90,000 miles (144,840km) without an accident. Airships would play a crucial role during this first global conflict but the technology behind them would also influence technological developments in World War II and beyond.

AIRSHIPS DURING AND AFTER WORLD WAR I

Airships were used by the Germans before World War I for reconnaissance patrols across the North Sea. This escalated on 19 January 1914 when the Germans dropped bombs on Britain from a Zeppelin, killing two civilians and injuring 16 more. Every few weeks a further raid was launched, and May 1915 saw the first bombing raid over London in which seven people died. In June 1915 Lieutenant Rex Warneford was sent on a bombing mission from Britain against the airship hangers at Evere in Belgium. The Zeppelin LZ-37 suddenly appeared, returning from a bombing raid over London, and Warneford decided to attack. He tried shooting at it with his rifle – the only gun he carried – but was driven off by the Zeppelin's machine guns. Warneford doubled back and climbed above the enemy, dropping his bombs on top of the airship. The detonations set fire to the hydrogen gas and the Zeppelin crashed in a pillar of flame. It was the first time a Zeppelin had been downed in the war.

The sight of the airships over English soil was terrifying to the population, though they did little real damage. Most of their bombs fell wide of the target, and they were vulnerable to searchlights, night fighters and cloud. When the British began to use incendiary shells the destruction of hydrogen-filled airships was easier. In 1916 four Zeppelins were brought down in the battle of Verdun, and from then on they were prey to British fighters. At the end of the war, all German airships were to be handed over to the victorious powers, but most were damaged or destroyed by the Germans. Many of the airships constructed across Europe in the following years were built from the German designs.

After the war, these machines of terror re-emerged in a more peaceful guise. The British inaugurated a round-trip airship service to New York in July 1919 with the R-34, and ten years later construction began on the R-100 and R-101. In these airships, then the largest ever built, the structure of the ship was based on a geodesic lattice, a revolutionary concept that

POLICE WARNING.

WHAT TO DO
WHEN THE
ZEPPELINS COME.

Sir Edward Henry, the Commissioner of the Metropolitan Police, has issued a series of valuable instructions and suggestions as to the action that should be taken by the ordinary householder or resident in the event of an air raid over London.

New Scotland Yard, S.W.
June 26, 1915.

In all probability if an air raid is made it will take place at a time when most people are in bed. The only intimation the public are likely to get will be the reports of the anti-aircraft guns or the noise of falling bombs.

The public are advised not to go into the street, where they might be struck by falling missiles; moreover, the streets being required for the passage of fire engines, etc., should not be obstructed by pedestrians.

In many houses there are no facilities for procuring water on the upper floors. It is suggested, therefore, that a supply of water and sand might be kept there, so that any fire breaking out on a small scale can at once be dealt with. Everyone should know the position of the fire alarm post nearest to his house.

All windows and doors on the lower floor should be closed to prevent the admission of noxious gases. An indication that poison gas is being used will be that a peculiar and irritating smell may be noticed following on the dropping of the bomb.

Gas should not be turned off at the meter at night, as this practice involves a risk of subsequent fire and of explosion from burners left on when the meter was shut off. This risk outweighs any advantage that might accrue from the gas being shut off at the time of a night raid by aircraft.

Persons purchasing portable chemical fire extinguishers should require a written guarantee that they comply with the specifications of the Board of Trade, Office of Works, Metropolitan Police, or some approved Fire Prevention Committee.

No bomb of any description should be handled unless it has shown itself to be of incendiary type. In this case it may be possible to remove it without undue risk. In all other cases a bomb should be left alone, and the police informed.

E. R. HENRY.

EXTRACT FROM
LATEST POLICE WARNING:

KEEP SAND AND WATER HANDY.

Press Bureau.

In view of the possibility of further attacks by hostile aircraft, the Commissioner of Police deems it advisable to call attention to the public warning published on June 26 recommending residents to remain under cover, and advising them for dealing with incendiary fires to keep a supply of water and sand readily available.

* * * *

(Signed) E. R. HENRY,
Commissioner of Police of the Metropolis.

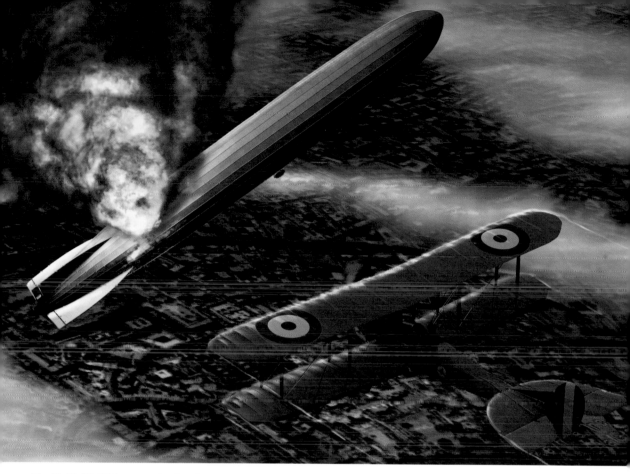

The SL-11 (SL XI) became the first German airship brought down by a British fighter on 2 September 1916. In his report 2nd Lieutenant Leefe Robinson of the Royal Flying Corps noted that he '... got behind it (by this time I was very close – 500ft or less below) and concentrated one drum on one part (underneath rear). I was then at a height of 11,500ft when attacking [the] Zeppelin. I had hardly finished the drum before I saw the part fired at glow... I quickly got out of the way of the falling blazing Zeppelin...' (Ian Palmer © Osprey Publishing.)

had been introduced by the young Barnes Wallis. Wallis (who was later to design the 'bouncing bomb', p.71) was an engineering apprentice who went on to become one of the greatest innovators in aircraft construction. His design for a lattice of light alloy girders allowed the construction of a remarkably lightweight framework. However, the haste to develop these huge aircraft led inexorably to tragedy. The R-101 was still undergoing tests and modifications when she was ordered to fly to India to carry officials to a conference; but she was not properly prepared and on 5 October 1930 she crashed in France, killing 48 of the 54 people on board. The British Air Ministry cancelled all further flights, and sold R-100 for scrap in 1931. The United States Navy ordered the British R-38 for military use but it was inadequately designed and was destroyed prior to delivery. Several semi-rigid airships were constructed in the Soviet

---

Opposite: Official advice was issued promptly when the Zeppelin raids began in World War I. This report from the *Daily News* in London was tied to an offer of 'Zeppelin Bombardment Insurance'. (Courtesy of Charles Stephenson)

Union and their SSSR-V6 set the world record for endurance with a flight of 130 hours. It eventually crashed into a mountain in 1938 with the loss of 13 of the 19 people aboard. In 1923 the Americans launched their own design of airship, the USS *Shenandoah*, which was the first to be filled with non-inflammable helium.

Germany had continued to design airships secretly in spite of the original ban imposed by the Treaty of Versailles. To help finance their development, the German designers undertook contract work for the United States, building the LZ-126, which was later named the USS *Los Angeles*, in 1924. Negotiations to end the treaty continued throughout; Germany argued that the conditions had been unilaterally imposed upon her, and so the treaty was really nothing more than a *Diktat*, or dictated peace. Hitler also argued that Part V of the treaty had called for all sides to reduce their military capability, and he showed that the Allies had ignored the ruling. In 1932 the German government announced that it would no longer observe any of the military limitations imposed by the treaty. By then, the treaty restrictions had already begun to be eased, and in fact the *Graf Zeppelin* (LZ-127) was launched in 1928. It went on to fly 990,000 miles (1,600,000km) without a single injury to any passenger, and made the first circumnavigation of the globe by air. The United States Navy built two further airships, but all were eventually lost: the USS *Shenandoah* went down in a thunderstorm in 1925, the USS *Akron* crashed off New Jersey in April 1933 and the USS *Macon* crashed off Point Sur Lightstation State Historic Park in 1935. The German airships continued to dominate until the *Hindenburg* (LZ-129) burst into flames and crashed at Lakehurst, New Jersey, while approaching the landing mast on 6 May 1937. It was made into one of the most famous disaster films of all time, and led to the end of the civilian air transport by these airships.

AIRSHIPS AND BLIMPS DURING AND AFTER WORLD WAR II

World War II had already begun before the Germans scrapped the final two Zeppelins, yet the Soviet Union did use an airship during the war. The Russian W-12 had been constructed in 1939 and was used for transporting equipment and for parachute training from 1942 to 1945. A second Soviet airship was built in 1945 and used for mine-clearance and removing wreckage from the Black Sea until it crashed in 1947. A third airship, also built in 1945, was later used for training and as an eye-catching feature at parades and major celebrations. The Russian company Augur-Ros Aerosystems Group now manufactures multi-functional airships that can carry ten passengers, and patrol airships including the Au-12 and Au-30.

Apart from the Russians, no nation used airships during World War II, though the United States had squadrons of blimps that were used for detecting submarines, mine-sweeping and transportation of equipment. These blimps were able to control the Straits of Gibraltar and patrolled the coastal waters of North America and Brazil. One was based in the hangar originally built for the *Graf Zeppelin* at Santa Cruz, Rio de Janeiro, which had closed down after the *Hindenburg* catastrophe. From 1942 until the end of World War II, the blimps of the United States protected the Atlantic fleet, making 37,554 flights with a total flying time of 378,237 hours. It is proudly claimed that over 70,000 ships in convoys were protected by blimp escorts, and only one of those dirigibles was ever brought down by the Germans.

After several decades of lack of interest since the end of World War II, development work on airships has resumed. Per Lindstrand designed the GA-42 blimp for the Goodyear Tire and Rubber Company, which was the first to use fly-by-wire flight control. He also conceived of the largest hot-air ship, the AS-300m, which was constructed in 1993 and is used for transporting botanists to the tropical rain forest canopy. The Chinese have built the CA-80 airship, launched in 2001 by the Shanghai Vantage Airship Manufacture Co., and now the Zeppelin Company has resumed construction of airships. Most are used for pleasure flights, but a Zeppelin in South Africa is being utilized in the search for potential diamond mines. Hot-air ships are being built by companies including Cameron Balloons of Bristol, England, while the European Space Agency has been investigating a high-altitude long-endurance airship and there are even plans for a high-altitude airship sponsored by the United States Army Space and Missile Defense Command. An 'orbital airship' could lift cargo into low Earth orbit; and other secret developments are now believed to be under development in the United States.

Meanwhile, the huge hangars in England where airships were constructed in the 1920s still stand near the university town of Milton Keynes in Bedfordshire. Today they have a fresh coat of paint. Inside workers are currently busily constructing payload modules, engines and fuel tanks of a revolutionary new airship – the Lockheed Martin Hybrid Air Vehicle. It will be a huge airship over 300ft (91m) in length. Once the British-built hardware has been fitted to the American-made gas envelope, this giant craft will be flown to the East Coast of the United States. There it goes on trial as a surveillance aircraft for the US Military and is destined to cruise at high altitude – up to 20,000ft (6,000m) above areas where soldiers are engaged in warfare, like Afghanistan. There it can remain on station, untouched, unmanned if necessary and watching ceaselessly what goes on beneath. When the last airship left those historic hangars in 1931 nobody would then have guessed that the hangars would be in use 70 years later, this time for the construction of a futuristic generation of airships.

GEODESIC ENGINEERING

There is one further crucial legacy of airships: the geodesic principle. Conventional aircraft structures were built with straight girders supporting panels. In geodesic designs, the shape of the body is formed from a network of struts. In the post-war years buildings based on this design flourished around the world. The large dome for the Spaceship Earth pavilion at the Epcot Center in Florida is one example; the huge domes at the Eden Project in Cornwall, United Kingdom, are another. Although associated with the name of Buckminster Fuller, the idea was first perfected by the brilliant young British designer Barnes Wallis in the 1930s. After realizing

Workers assembling the fuselages of Wellington bombers at the Vickers factory at Castle Bromwich, Birmingham. Sir Barnes Wallis's geodesic principle was the key to the design. (SSPL/Getty Images)

A dome glasshouse at Mitchell Park Horticultural Conservatory, Milwaukee, is a typical modern application of the principles of geodesic design promoted by Buckminster Fuller in the post-war years. (istock)

that he could apply this revolutionary design principle to airships, Barnes Wallis turned his attention to the design of a lightweight frame for a World War II bomber. In April 1932 the British Air Ministry placed a contract with the Vickers aircraft company for a biplane with an intimidating list of roles: low-level and dive bombing, reconnaissance, casualty evacuation and torpedo bombing. The result was the Vickers Type 253. The frame of the fuselage was designed by Barnes Wallis, who had risen to become Vickers' chief structural engineer, and he decided to make it from a geodesic lattice of light-alloy tubes. It was accepted with delight by the Air Ministry. The idea was so successful that Vickers decided privately to build a plane with similar specifications, but in the form of a monoplane. Wallis's design offered improved performance and an increased payload. This was the Type 246 experimental aircraft and it was so successful in its trials that it became the top-secret Type 287 Wellesley bomber – and was immediately ordered by the Air Ministry under conditions of high security.

During the mid-1930s the Air Ministry in London sensed the approach of war, and realized that the Wellesley bomber would no longer be suitable as a warplane. They commissioned the development of a twin-engined long-range heavy bomber, the Vickers Wellington. It was designed at Brooklands, Surrey, by Vickers's chief designer, R. K. Pierson, and the fuselage was entirely based on the geodesic design of Barnes Wallis. It was a revolution. Wallis's design gave one of the lightest yet most robust airframes ever built, and the Wellington thus had a greatly extended range. It was also remarkably resilient. There were many examples of the bombers flying safely back to base, with huge areas of the surface shot or burned away by enemy fire. In one example, Sergeant James Allen Ward won the Victoria Cross for his actions when the wing of his Wellington bomber caught fire. He climbed out of the cockpit, kicking out sections of the fabric covering and using the gaps as footholds, to climb along the wing and manually extinguish the blaze before returning to his cockpit in the howling slipstream and flying safely back to base.

However, there was one problem with the geodesic construction. It required specialized tooling and could not easily be used alongside traditional methods of manufacture. During the war it did not find widespread applications, though it did give the Wellington bomber a unique life-span and a durability that was unparalleled. Was it the best bomber of all? During the entire war, the Mosquito dropped more explosives with fewer losses than any other bomber, and the Lancaster dropped a far greater tonnage. The Wellington's strong point was its ability to return to base, even if half the fuselage was shot to ribbons. It was the geodesic construction that allowed them to survive. This idea was taken up and popularized by the American architect Richard Buckminster Fuller during the post-war years. Like Wallis, Fuller was not a university graduate; indeed, although he went to Harvard university twice, he was rusticated on both occasions. Nonetheless, his geodesic domes became world-famous and are often described as the world's first.

THE ROCKET PLANE

Many World War II aircraft were at the opposite end of the spectrum to the airship. Rockets were widely seen as useful aids to the take-off of an aircraft, but what about a plane entirely propelled by rocket power? From the beginning of World War II, the Germans worked on the design of a rocket plane that could outstrip the opposition.

THE KOMET

The Nazis conducted their work in such secrecy that the name of the prototype – the Me-163 – was the same as that given to an earlier aircraft, the two-seater Messerschmitt Bf-163 that had been designed in 1938. Every care was taken to ensure that no word of the new rocket-propelled project, code named the *Komet* (Comet), reached the outside world. The first trials were successful, and on 2 October 1941, the Me-163A V4 reached 624.2mph (1,004.5km/h) with Heini Dittmar at the controls. Another Komet pilot, Rudy Opitz, reportedly reached 702mph (1,130km/h) in July 1944, though his account has been doubted by many; in any event, nothing flew as fast again until after the war ended. The Me-163 was named the Komet by its highly innovative designer, Alexander Martin Lippisch. He had earlier envisaged a swept-winged low-powered prototype, the DFS-39, and the Komet further refined his idea. An early proposal was for the aircraft to be propeller-driven, but eventually rocket propulsion was agreed as the way ahead. It was felt that it would give the Luftwaffe a potentially crucial advantage over the Allies.

To conserve weight in flight, the Komet was designed to be launched from a trolley that was jettisoned at take-off. This immediately caused problems, as the wheels often rebounded high into the air and struck the plane itself. The rocket design was modified during tests and was eventually designed to run on hydrazine hydrate and methanol, referred to as C-Stoff,

The Delta IVc in flight. The aerodynamic findings from flying this revolutionary aircraft were to influence the design of the piston engined DFS-194 and the Me-163. (EN Archive)

burning in oxygen provided from hydrogen peroxide, T-Stoff (see table). Hydrazine was in short supply in Germany during the later years of the war and the choice of the same fuel for the V-1 flying bomb (p.99) led to a conflict of choice. Hydrazine is a dangerous liquid and explosions of the rocket planes while still on the ground were not uncommon. Eventually, protective clothing was supplied to the pilots to resist splashes of the corrosive fuel. The below table lists the liquids used by German rocket and plane designers, some of which were first used in World War I. They were designated as 'Stoffe' with code-letters to maintain secrecy and the exact nature of some of the fuels is still disputed.

A-Stoff (World War I)	chloroacetone (tear gas)
A-Stoff (World War II)	liquid oxygen (LOX)
B-Stoff	hydrazine or ethanol / water (used in the V-2)
Bn-Stoff	bromomethyl ethyl ketone (World War I tear gas)
Br-Stoff	ligroin extracted from crude gasoline
C-Stoff	57% methanol / 30% hydrazine / 13% water
E-Stoff	ethanol
K-Stoff	methyl chloroformate
M-Stoff	hydrazine or methanol and water
N-Stoff	chlorine trifluoride
R-Stoff or Tonka	57% monoxylidene oxide / 43% triethylamine
S-Stoff	90% nitric acid/10% sulfuric acid or nitric acid/ferric chloride
SV-Stoff or Salbei (sage)	85% nitric acid / 15% sulfuric acid [or] 94% fuming nitric acid / 6% dinitrogen tetroxide
T-Stoff (World War I)	xylyl bromide tear gas
T-Stoff (World War II)	80% concentrated hydrogen peroxide
SV-Stoff /Z-Stoff	sodium or potassium permanganate

For the pilot, the launch must have been an interesting experience. Films of a take-off show the aircraft racing along the runway at an alarming rate, oscillating and bumping along the grass, until it climbs from the ground and sheds its wheels, leaving them bumping erratically high into the air. The plane then turns towards the skies and – as if the mechanism has developed a fault – roars upwards at a seemingly impossible speed, climbing at more than 10,000ft (3,000m) per minute. The aircraft itself is not pleasing to the eye, being short and stubby, with projecting rivets and exposed screws. Indeed, the first time I saw one I wondered how it could fly at all; the wing area seemed surprisingly small.

But fly it did. Once aloft, the Me-163B Komet had excellent flying qualities. Lippsich designed the delta wings with leading edge slots which gave it great stability: it was resistant to stalling or spinning. The glider design did pose problems, however, since slight winds could

The Nazis released this impression of the German Bf-163 bomber. It is a montage – only a single prototype was ever built. The development of the Me-163 was kept secret by using the same model number. (Getty Images)

cause the plane to lift into the air unexpectedly when landing and it could fly along in 'ground effect' with the pilot finding it difficult to set the plane down where he wished. That apart, the delta design was supremely successful.

At launch, the plane would take off at 200mph (320km/h) and climb gently to an operating speed of 420mph (670km/h) at which point it could climb at some 70 degrees to an altitude of 39,000ft (12,000m) in just 3 minutes. The Komet could then accelerate to a final operating velocity of 596mph (959km/h) or even faster, so that it was higher, faster and more manoeuvrable than any conventional aircraft. Nothing could touch it.

In practice, the speed and agility made the Komet into a difficult machine of war. Its velocity and rate of climb meant that it reached – and passed – its would-be target in a matter of seconds. The rapid flight of the Komet meant that the pilot could hardly ever hit a slow-moving bomber. One highly ingenious answer to this was developed, the Sondergerät 500 Jägerfaust. This secret weapon was a group of five upward-pointing guns firing 2in (50mm) ammunition that was installed in each wing. They were triggered automatically – the firing mechanism was in fact actuated by a photo-electric cell. All the pilot had to do was fly beneath the intended target, and the shadow cast by the plane on the Komet would cause the guns to fire automatically, with guns pointing upwards into the belly of the target plane. It was an ingenious idea. Even so, only one aircraft was shot down by this system. But most standard Me-163s were instead fitted with two 30mm (1.18in) MARK-108 cannon, a design which was subsequently manufactured widely in Germany and beyond.

On 16 August 1944 several Me-163s attacked US Air Force B-17s. Donald Waltz, the pilot of B-17 *Towering Titan*, recalled the briefing for this mission, in which particular attention was paid to the Me-163 threat.

Our bomb group had been briefed for the previous ten days on the possibility of attack by a new German 'jet' fighter aeroplane – the Me-163. At our early morning briefing on 16 August, out Group Intelligence Officer again described the Me-163. He said the aeroplane was in early production – not too many in operation so we were 'unlikely to see the Me-163 on this Leipzig mission'.

He further indicated that if we did encounter the Me-163, we would have no problem with aircraft recognition, 'it will be the fastest aircraft any of us have ever seen'. I recall that mission being long and rough.

Donald Waltz, quoted in Ransom, S. and Cammann, H. H. *Jagdgeschwader 400*,
Osprey Publishing (2010)

The greatest problem with the Komet was the short flight time. The maximum burn of the rocket motor was only 7½ minutes which meant that the plane might seem to be a highly intimidating interceptor fighter – but could, in reality, do little damage to the enemy. Modifications were made to the engines, to give the pilot two separate rocket motors – a high-powered rocket to blast him up to operating altitude, and a smaller, less powerful rocket motor to maintain his cruising speed. These later models were to have a pressurized cockpit to protect the pilot and the maximum altitude was to be increased to 52,000ft (15,800m) which would give a powered flight time of up to 12 minutes. However, these improved models remained untested by the end of the war.

The Komet did not enter active service until 1944, and its psychological impact on the Allies was considerable. Its effect in terms of attack success was much more limited. The usual attack pattern was for the pilot to fly through the Allied bombers at high speed, reach an altitude of 35,000–39,000ft (10,000–12,000m) and then dive down to the bomber formation once more. The Komet pilot thus had just two brief opportunities to shoot at the enemy. Since he was usually in an unpressurized cockpit the pilot was fitted with a restrictive oxygen mask and, with the protective clothing, was unable to respond rapidly. In spite of all the development and the meticulous design, this aircraft was a tactical failure and many of the Komets were grounded owing to a shortage of fuel. There were 16 confirmed examples of bombers shot down by a Komet. The most successful pilot, Feldwebel Siegfried Schubert, had just three successes to his credit.

Nonetheless, the Komet rocket plane was a truly innovative design and it pointed to what lay ahead. The production version was 18ft 8in (5.7m) long, had a wingspan of 30ft 7in (9.33m) and was 9ft (2.75m) tall. Its weight was 4,200lb (1,905kg) when empty and 8,710lb (3,950kg) when fully loaded, and it had an operating range of about 25 miles (40km). Even now, designs derived from these tiny aircraft still operate. Planes like the Skybaby are popular with hobbyists – it is 5ft (1.52m) tall with a wingspan of just 7ft 2in (2.18m) and a top speed of 185mph (298km/h). The Bumble Bee II designed by Robert Starr is 8ft 10in (2.7m) long, has a wingspan of 5ft 6in (1.67m), weighs 396lb (180kg) and has a top speed of 190mph (306km/h). It seems that the little plane projects of World War II have inspired many imitators since.

A version of the Komet was also produced in Japan. Two German submarines were sent to Japan with parts and designs; one did not arrive, so the Japanese had to improvise some of the components. The Japanese version of the Me-163B Komet was the Ki-200 Shusui produced for the Imperial Japanese Army by Mitshubishi. It was equipped with two 30mm (1.18in) Ho 155-II guns. A version known as the J8M was built for the Navy which had its first flight on 7 July 1945 with Lieutenant-Commander Toyohiko Inuzuka as pilot. On returning to base, the plane clipped a building and crashed in flames, killing the pilot. On 15 August 1945 the Japanese war ended and so did the Japanese Komet.

The Komet needed an airfield from which to fly, and during the later stages of the war Allied warplanes were sent to bomb the runways so that Komets could be prevented from operating. The answer was to use a compact launch pad, like a rocket; this would be far harder to detect than a conventional launch pad, and even more difficult to destroy with bombs. As design work proceeded, the idea of a vertical take-off rocket fighter began to emerge. By the end of the war, this revolutionary idea had been realized and prototypes were already in production, nicknamed the *Natter* (Viper).

THE NATTER

In August 1944 the Chief of Development for the German Air Ministry (Reichsluftfahrtministerium), Colonel Siegfried Knemayer, was asked for new proposals for a hard-hitting plane that would be difficult to disable, and he listed the criteria that such an aircraft should satisfy. The result was the Natter. Knemayer decided to take a cheap rocket-powered aircraft that could fly near the speed of sound, fit it with armaments, and blast it from a vertical launch to attack enemy planes. A full set of control surfaces and landing gear would not be necessary, as the pilot would simply bail out and return to earth by parachute as soon as the attack was over.

Engineers developed the Bachem Ba-349 Natter (Viper), a rocket-propelled interceptor. It was launched vertically from a rig that was difficult to detect from the air. (Cody Images)

With its rocket motors, the Natter had an unprecedented climb rate. But it was not a success; there was just one test flight in 1945 and the test pilot, Lothar Sieber, was killed. (Author's collection)

THE ME-163

One of the most secret of all Germany's warplanes was the Me-163 Komet, which demonstrated the power of rocket-propelled aircraft. However, it was this very power that proved to be its undoing. Not only was it difficult to control but its velocity meant it was often impossible for the pilot to attack a slow-moving bomber. As such, its success rates were low. Nevertheless, the Me-163 had a marked effect the on Allied pilots who saw it in action.

Left: An Me-163 Komet is caught heading directly towards a Spitfire on 27 August 1944. *Jagdgeschwader* 400 was a fighter group set up to operate the Me-163s and they were scrambled to attack fighter escorts of Allied bombers. (EN Archive)

Below: In 1944 the prototype Me-163A (left) was photographed alongside the combat-ready version, the Me-163B (right). Although the wings remained essentially unaltered, the tail-plane and fuselage had been modified. (EN Archive)

This Me-163A V4 of October 1941 was one of ten prototypes built by Messerschmitt AG in Augsburg to assess the feasibility of the design. The test pilot chosen was Heini Dittmar. (Jim Laurier © Osprey Publishing)

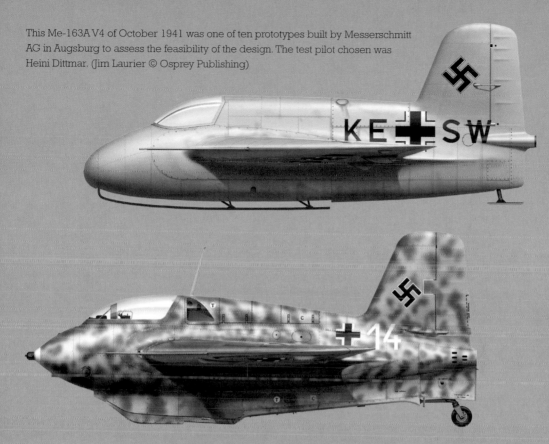

Production versions of the Me-163B were the armed and operational variants. This profile shows Me-163B 'White 14', which served with *Jagdgeschwader* 400. (Jim Laurier © Osprey Publishing)

The Messerschmitt Me-163 was powered by a Walter HWK 509-2 rocket motor. Each was towed to its launch site by a purpose-built tractor. (Cody Images)

Work began at the Bachem-Werke in Waldensee in 1944 and the result was the Ba-349 Natter, which translates as Adder or Viper. This was destined to become one of the oddities of World War II. It was intended to bring down the formations of Allied bombers that were relentlessly pounding German factories and cities in the latter years of the war. The Ba-349 followed a simple design that even semi-skilled workers could construct in less than 1,000 hours. The control surfaces were confined to the tail fins, making it easy to fly and simple to manufacture. It was powered by a Walter 109-509A rocket motor generating 3,700lb (1,700kg) of thrust and was equipped with 4 Schmidding 109-533 solid-fuel booster rockets fixed to the fuselage to assist the launch. Fully laden, the Natter weighed 4,800lb (2,177kg) of which 1,400lb (635kg) was fuel. The plane measured 21ft 3in (6.5m) in overall length and was fitted with two sets of 12 solid-fuel 2.84in (73mm) rockets to be fired in a single volley.

Flight testing of unpowered prototypes began in November 1944 at Neuburg an der Donau. The first was towed up to nearly 10,000ft (3,000m) by a Heinkel He-111 bomber and the test pilot, Erich Klöckner, reported that it handled well. In December 1944 vertical take-off tests were started at Truppenübungsplatz near Lager Heuberg yet the first manned flight in March 1945 soon ran into difficulties and the pilot, Lothar Sieber, was killed when his parachute failed to open. Problems were experienced from the start; even with the rocket boosters the velocity of the Natter when launched was too low for the control fins to work effectively, so steel vanes were fitted to deflect the rocket exhaust. They were prone to melting in the heat, so they were filled with water; although the water soon boiled away and the vanes were destroyed by the temperature of the rocket fame, the Natter had – by that time – gained enough speed to be conventionally controlled.

As the war was ending, the factory was closed down and a Dutch designer named Botheder was dispatched to take four of the Natters to a new base. Botheder was reported to have a ski chalet, the Einen Achalpe, in the nearby mountains and it was apparently agreed that this is where the teams would rendezvous after the troubles were over. In the event, he was intercepted en route to this eagle's lair by advancing American forces in May 1945 and the truth was out. Botheder explained that the remaining staff members were a test pilot named Zeubert, who had successfully flown an unpowered gliding version of the prototype, an engineer called Granzow, who was in charge of the rocket motor, and a coordinator who kept a watchful eye on the proceedings. This man's name was Schaller, and Botheder said he was convinced he was a Nazi party member put there to report back, secretly, on everything that was happening.

In total, 36 Natters were constructed during the war. Of these, 18 were used as test vehicles and two were destroyed in crashes. Ten were destroyed at the end of the war. One Natter was taken by the British, and another by the Soviet Army. Four of the surviving Natter rocket

Opposite: A test launch showed that the design of the Ba-349 Natter could fly. In the event, only 36 were ever constructed, 18 of them used in flight tests. (Cody Images)

German engineers designed this Heinkel He-111 ostensibly as an airliner, but its real purpose was to become the Luftwaffe's standard twin-engine bomber, photographed here in May 1942. The design was later further improved to provide a heavy-duty aircraft. (Apic/Getty Images)

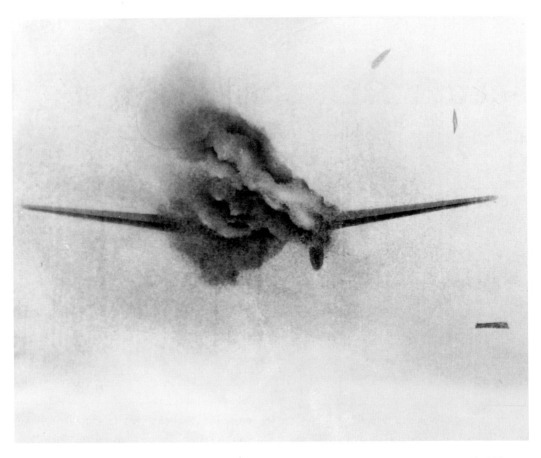

Flight-Lieutenant Adolph Gysbert Malan caught this dramatic photograph as he brought down a He-111 over Dunkirk on 21 May 1940. It was his first attack. Because he did not witness the bomber hit the ground, it was never confirmed. The young South African went on to become one of Britain's ace pilots. (IWM C 1704)

planes were taken back to the United States. One of these was test-fired, unmanned, from the Muroc Army Air Base in 1946. It was the first manned surface-to-air interceptor. Only three of the Natters have survived. There is a Ba-349A at the Deutsches Museum in Munich, now painted in the markings of one of the unmanned test aircraft. A second Natter is in the collections of the National Air & Space Museum in Washington DC. There is also a Ba-349A on show at the Planes of Fame Museum in Chino, California; this one, however, is only a wooden copy. In Japan during the last days of the Pacific War, the Mizuno aircraft company began constructing an aircraft that was based on the concept of the Natter. The Mizuno Shinryu interceptor rocket plane was the result. It would have been equipped with rockets fired from under its wings and could also have been fitted with a warhead in the nose, to be used for a suicide attack. Development was still underway at the end of the war.

And this provides us with a fascinating thought. The rate at which these new designs were realized seems extraordinary in a modern world, hide-bound by administration, bureaucracy, health and safety directives and the need to comply with regulations. From the viewpoint of wartime Germany, work began too late. Had the Axis powers begun work on their secret weapons earlier, many of these extraordinary innovations would have been proved a success and the course of the war might have turned out very differently.

PEACETIME DESIGNS IN WAR

Many of the secretly designed planes of World War II came from more conventional sources. For example, the Heinkel He-111 had been developed in peacetime in direct defiance of the Treaty of Versailles. Although claimed to be a commercial transport aircraft it had been covertly designed for easy conversion to military purposes. It became the Luftwaffe's standard twin-engined bomber and was produced in scores of different variations. Typical of the type were planes with a wingspan of 82ft (25m) and length of 52ft 6in (16m), with an operating speed of 280mph (450km/h). In 1940, 750 of the planes were under construction; the number doubled during 1942, with the result that this bomber was produced in greater numbers than any other German plane during the early years of the war. It took part in the Battle of Britain, but the superiority of the British fighters proved that its time had passed. It had poor manoeuvrability, limited operating speed, and its armaments were inferior. However, it could often remain flying even when badly damaged and so was eventually employed on many fronts during the war. As well as serving as a bomber it was useful as a transport aircraft on the Eastern, Western, Mediterranean, Middle East and North African Fronts, and was successfully used to drop torpedoes in the North Atlantic campaign. As the war ended, the He-111 re-emerged in a different guise, ensuring the design remained in use for many years. It was produced in Spain under licence by Construcciones Aeronáuticas SA, and the first of these planes flew before the war ended in May 1945. After the war, since it was no longer possible for the manufacturers to obtain the Junkers engines, they installed the Rolls-Royce Merlin 500 instead. Over 170 Merlin engines were ordered in 1953 alone. A nine-passenger transport aircraft, the 2.111T8, was to follow. Many of these planes found a use in movies about World War II, repainted to look like the original Heinkels. The Spanish planes continued in daily use until they were finally withdrawn from service in 1973.

The strangest version of the He-111 was the top-secret heavy-duty version designed to tow gliders filled with tanks, artillery and troops. It was manufactured as a pair of conjoined He-111 aircraft with a common wing upon which a fifth engine was mounted. The entire wingspan was some 125ft (38m) and the pilot flew the plane from a cockpit in the left-hand fuselage using identical, linked control levers. Towing a glider of over 35 tons, this twin aircraft was said to have flown to 30,000ft (9,100m) in 1942. The large numbers of these vast tow-trucks that would have been necessary for large-scale invasions were never produced. Certainly the handling and aerodynamics of this bastard giant would have been intimidating at the very least.

Following the success of the He-111 came the He-115, a seaplane comparable to the Sunderland Flying Boat that was produced in large numbers by the British. The He-116 was designed for long-distance cargo transportation and was used for flights to Japan; the He-117 and He-118 were tactical developments that never got off the ground and the He-119 – which could travel up to 375mph (600km/h) and was to be powered by two DB-603 engines – was never put into production.

A revolutionary high-altitude bomber was proposed as the He-274, intended to be a four-engined bomber with a number of advanced features. Development began in October 1941 and the prototypes of the new bomber were contracted for construction in France by the Société Anonyme des Usines Farman (SAUF) firm in Suresnes, near Paris. The He-274 dispensed with twin coupled engines and instead featured four independent DB-603 A-2 engines with a greater wingspan and a lengthened fuselage. The cockpit would be double-glazed and pressurized to maintain an air pressure for the crew equivalent to an altitude of 8,200ft (2,500m). The aircraft was designed to fly up to 47,000ft (14,300m), far higher than any Allied fighter. In 1937 a Bristol Type 138 high altitude monoplane had reached a world record altitude of 49,967ft (15,230m) but this was an experimental aircraft; the highest a Spitfire XIX ever flew was 44,000ft (13,400m).

As a consequence, the He-274 would require little defensive armament and the plane was designed to carry a forward-firing 13mm (0.51in) MG 131 machine gun with a further two pairs of these guns in turrets. Work on manufacture of the prototypes did not start until 1943 and the advance of Allied forces on Paris in July 1944 forced the evacuation of the German employees before the first flight had taken place. Here too, the German technology pointed to the future. After the war, the French Air Force (Armée de l'Air) finished building the first He-274 and renamed it the AAS-01A. The second prototype was flown in December 1947

AAS-01B. Both were employed as test-bed mother ships for the launch of rockets and advanced jet planes at high altitude, and were in use until they were broken up at the end of 1953.

BIRTH OF JET PLANES

These amazing aircraft clearly show that Ernst Heinkel was a leading innovator on many fronts, and the best example of this is the introduction of the jet fighter. Jet-propelled planes could have radically altered the course of the war, but they arrived on the scene too late to make a crucial difference. The origin of the aircraft jet engine dates back to July 1926, when a young British engineer named A. A. Griffith published a paper on jet turbines. The idea was followed up by Frank Whittle, then an enthusiastic Royal Air Force (RAF) recruit, but Griffith dismissed the idea of a jet plane since he was convinced that a turbine could never generate the efficiencies needed for flight. Undeterred, in January 1930 Whittle took out a patent for the first jet engine. It attracted little interest with the RAF and they placed no restrictions upon the concept. Whittle made great progress as a pilot, and yet although companies showed some interest in his proposals for a jet plane none were willing to put up the money necessary to build a prototype.

During the following year, an Italian experimenter named Secondo Campini sent a paper on jet propulsion to the Italian Royal Air Force (Regia Aeronautica Italiana) and in 1932 he demonstrated a jet-propelled boat on the Venice lagoon. In 1934 he received the agreement of the Italian Royal Air Force for the development of a jet aircraft. Campini commissioned the Caproni factory to build his prototype. On 27 August 1940 test pilot Mario De Bernardi took the plane into the air and the World Air Sports Federation (Fédération Aéronautique Internationale) recognized this at the time as the first successful flight by a jet aeroplane, until news came of the Heinkel He-178 V1. This had flown for the first time in August 1939, powered by the HeS-3B engine invented by a German designer named Hans Joachim Pabst von Ohain. As we shall see, this highly innovative aircraft would give rise to a revolution in aircraft design – one we are still experiencing today.

However, the reality is that Campini's aircraft did not have a jet turbine at all. His design featured a 670hp (500kW) Isotta Fraschini piston engine which drove an air compressor, forcing air into the combustion chamber where it mixed with a spray of fuel. Although the exhaust gases propelled the device forward, the use of a piston engine as the compressor means that it was not a jet turbine. Another Italian named Luigi Stipa also designed the Stipa-Caproni experimental aircraft in 1932, which had a ducted fan, and he also tried to claim it as the first jet aircraft. Both his plane and the Caproni-Campini used a jet of gas to propel the plane along, but neither was a pure jet turbine.

Meanwhile, in Britain, Whittle was still trying to develop his jet turbine idea, and in 1934 he was authorized to take the two-year engineering course at Peterhouse College, University of Cambridge, where he graduated with a first-class degree in Mechanical Sciences. Whittle received a note in the mail to remind him that his patent for a jet engine was due for renewal in

Air Commodore Sir Frank Whittle pictured at his desk. In front of him are models of the first British prototype jet aircraft to fly and the Meteor, the first jet to enter service with the RAF. From 1943 to 1946 Whittle was attached to Power Jets Ltd working on the development of gas turbines for jet aircraft. (IWM TR 3737)

The Gloster-Whittle E 28/39, W4041/G, piloted by Squadron-Leader J. Moloney, takes off from the Farnborough airfield. The E 28/39 was the first Allied jet aircraft and made its first official flight in May 1941, though Whittle took it briefly to the air the previous month. This prototype was presented to the Science Museum, London, in 1946. (IWM CH 14832A)

January 1935. He could not afford the £5 fee. The Air Ministry told him that it was not interested in funding the renewal either, and so the patent lapsed. However, in September 1935 Whittle was introduced to two investment bankers at O. T. Falk & Partners, Sir Maurice Bonham-Carter and Lancelot Law Whyte. Whittle explained that a reciprocating engine, with its metallic components jerking up and down, seemed to him condemned to extinction. He insisted that the smooth-running jet turbine was obviously the way ahead. Whyte felt that this was a proposal of sheer genius, and in January 1936 Power Jets Ltd was formally established.

On 12 April 1937 the Whittle jet engine ran for the first time. It was a stunning success. There was a growing sense that the jet engine had immense promise, but not until March 1938 did the Air Ministry offer any funding. This funding proved to be a mixed blessing, for the project was now subject to Ministerial bureaucracy and the Official Secrets Act made it impossible to discuss the developments as widely as before. From being a topic of growing interest, it suddenly became a matter of the utmost secrecy. Nonetheless, work proceeded on constructing a prototype jet plane, the Gloster-Whittle E 28/39, and on 7 April 1941 near Gloucester the first few hops into the air were made. Whittle himself was at the controls, but had in fact been specifically ordered not to fly the plane as the Ministry did not wish to risk both the aircraft and its designer if anything went wrong. Whittle told the senior officers that he would just take out the plane for some taxi runs, which would warm up the engine; but he accelerated along the runway and (as he later said) 'it just took off'. The next month, on 15 May, the first formal test flight took off from Cranwell at 7.40pm. The plane flew for 17 minutes at speeds of up to 340mph (545km/h). Days later, it was flying at 370mph (600km/h) up to 25,000ft (7,600m) which was better than anything a conventional fighter could achieve.

Meanwhile, under conditions of top secrecy, jet planes were already taking shape in Germany. In 1936, the gifted young engineer Hans Joachim Pabst von Ohain had taken out a patent for the use of the exhaust thrust from a gas turbine as a means of propulsion. This was six years behind Whittle's original patent. Ohain presented his ideas to Heinkel, who agreed to help develop the concept. The prototype was speedily developed and built, and Ohain successfully demonstrated his first engine in 1937. It was powered by hydrogen gas which quickly burned through the components, and was extremely simple in design, but it proved that a jet turbine could run just five months after Whittle's prototype engine. It is remarkable to think of these two gifted young men, each constructing and testing the first jet engines in the world, separately in England and Germany, and at the same time. Although Whittle had been unable to find finance for a year, plans were quickly made in Germany to construct one of these engines to power an aircraft.

Ohain had joined the staff of the Heinkel Company as a designer, and subsequent developments were rapid – in complete contrast to the lack of interest shown by the British authorities in Whittle's earlier design. As Ohain's first experimental jet engine had used hydrogen as fuel, it burned with too much heat and produced too little thrust to be

On 24 August 1939 the He-178, the world's first jet plane, made tentative hops into the air, before an official flight three days later. Based on Von Ohain's designs, it had Erich Warsitz at the controls. (Bundesarchiv Bild 141-2505)

operationally viable, so his designs for a more compact version were intended to burn conventional liquid fuels instead. The He-178 jet plane, the first to be designed in the world, was based on Ohain's third design, the HeS-3, which now burned diesel fuel. All the flight tests were carried out under conditions of total secrecy and on 27 August 1939 the first flight of the Heinkel He-178, with Erich Warsitz at the controls, was successfully completed. The entire project had been privately conducted at the expense of Heinkels, and the test flight of the German plane was two years ahead of the British.

The aircraft was a small plane with a metal fuselage of conventional configuration and construction. The jet intake was in the nose, and the plane was fitted with a tail-wheel undercarriage. The main landing gear was intended to be made retractable eventually, but was fixed in the down position throughout the flight trials. The plane proved the principle, but had a combat duration time of only 10 minutes so it was never going to be a production-line success. It inspired the design of the twin-jet He-280 which became the first prototype jet fighter in history. These remarkable designs were privately financed by Heinkels, as the German authorities were, much like the British, slow to be convinced of the merits of jet-propelled aircraft.

Although the fact is usually forgotten, the Russians were also developing a jet engine at this time. This was the brainchild of a relatively unknown engineering pioneer named Arkhip Lyulka from Kiev Oblast in Ukraine. Lyulka's first interests were in turbofans as superchargers of piston engines on the Petlyakov Pe-8 bomber. Between 1939 and 1941 Lyulka worked on what was to become the first double-jet turbofan engine in the world, which he patented in April 1941. Work began on building a prototype fighter aircraft, but as the Nazis invaded Russia, Lyulka stopped his work and evacuated to the Ural mountains.

German engineers competed to design a production-line jet aircraft. The result was the Me-262B, the most advanced fighter design of the war. It flew faster than any Allied plane and over 500 Allied aircraft were shot down by this impressive weapon of war. (Apic/Getty Images)

The Me-262 would not look out of place on a present-day airfield. It was soon fitted with accessories – external fuel-tanks to increase the range, and radar equipment, with the aerials mounted on the nose. (Cody Images)

Heinkel realized that the time had come to convince the German High Command of the importance of the jet plane, and so in 1941 a contest flight was organized in Germany between a jet-powered He-280 and a propeller-driven Focke-Wulf Fw-190 fighter. The He-280 completed four laps of the course in less time than the Fw-190 could finish three. The jet plane was designed to be light, in order to match the relatively low thrust of the jet engines, it burned kerosene, instead of the more costly aviation spirit, and it had shown jet fighters to be a success. Yet the Nazis put their weight behind a rival design for a jet aircraft designed by Messerschmitt, the Me-262 *Schwalbe* (Swallow) or *Sturmvogel* (Stormbird). In July 1944 the Me-262 came into service. It is heralded as the world's first jet fighter. In the same month the Gloster Meteor came into use, too; some people believe that the Meteor may have been in service several days before the Messerschmitt, in which case the British would take the claim. What is remarkable, however, is the astonishing synchronicity of the dates. We have seen that the German and British jet engines were being developed at exactly the same time (p.47) and each nation had the first jet fighters ready at the same time. The ideas had progressed in Germany and in Britain at exactly the same rate. Which was the better plane? There is no question about that. The Me-262 was faster and better armed than the Gloster Meteor. The new British jet could fly at 410mph (660km/h) whereas the German Me-262 flew at 560mph (900km/h). The German jet fighters were an unquestionable success, and the German pilots would claim a total of over 500 Allied aircraft shot down for the loss of 100 Me-262 fighters. In contrast, the British jets were forbidden to fly near continental Europe, in case they were

Walter Blume designed the Ar-234 *Blitz* (Lightning) in 1941 with a small company, Arado. Conceived as a high-altitude jet bomber, it introduced an automatic pilot, ejector seat and brake parachutes. It entered service in 1944 and was used for reconnaissance. (Cody Images)

brought down and revealed design secrets to the enemy. Although they helped to intercept V-1 drones heading for London, they had little military impact. The Meteor did set a world airspeed record in November 1945 at Herne Bay in the UK, when Group Captain H. J. Wilson set the world's first airspeed record by a jet aircraft. He flew a Meteor F Mk 4 at 606mph (975km/h). Macari's Café, near the beach in Herne Bay, still has a small plaque on the wall to commemorate the event. The next year the record was raised to 616mph (991km/h), also by a Gloster Meteor.

Meanwhile, engineers from the United States and Canada had been to visit Whittle. The Americans designed their own jet, based on the British research, the Bell P-59 Airacomet but it was an unsuccessful aircraft and lacked the power of the Gloster Meteor. Development work also went ahead with the National Research Council of Canada. In May 1943 their findings were published in a top-secret report entitled *Report on Development of Jet Propulsion in the United Kingdom*, which reached two important conclusions. One was the need to establish a group to study jet engines in cold conditions (this was an area of research nobody else had thought to embrace); the other was the importance of forming a Canadian jet company as quickly as possible. In March 1944 Turbo Research was formed in Toronto. At first they developed the Whittle centrifugal-flow jet engine, but they soon progressed to their own design for a new axial-flow design, the Chinook. As the war was reaching its end they began to manufacture their Orenda jet engine which had many crucial advantages: its longer combustion chambers and increased power meant that it was, at its time, the most powerful jet engine in the world. The engines sold were worth a quarter of a million Canadian dollars.

Canadian researchers went further than anyone else among the Allies in investigating the protection of pilots at high altitude, and they constructed the first experimental decompression chamber in North America to study the effects of low air pressure on pilots. The result was the first anti-G suit to prevent pilots blacking out. It was invented by Wilbur Franks and became known as the Franks Suit. It was first used in 1942 by the Royal Navy pilots covering the Allied landings in North Africa.

In Germany, meanwhile, during the closing months of the war, the Arado Company manufactured the first jet bomber, the Ar-234 *Blitz* (Lightning). It had twin engines and a single pilot, and was flown mostly for reconnaissance at altitudes around 36,000ft (11,000m) where it was impossible for it to be shadowed or intercepted. The project began late in 1940, when Arado proposed their design for a jet bomber with the designation E-370 designed by Professor Walter Blume. It was a jet-engined aircraft with a Junkers Jumo-004 engine fitted beneath each of the wings. The design weight of the aircraft was 17,600lb (8,000kg) and, to keep the weight down, there were no landing wheels. The plane ran on a three-wheeled trolley which was jettisoned after take-off, and it landed later on skids. The plane had a maximum design speed of 490mph (789 km/h) with an operating altitude of 36,100ft (11,000m) and a range of 1,240 miles (1,995km). In April 1945 this became the last German warplane ever to fly over

British soil during World War II. The Ar-234 was nicknamed the *Hecht* (Pike) and was described as a 'blitz-bomber' though in fact it never flew carrying a payload.

British fighter pilots saw a remarkable jet fighter in the closing months of the war, though there are no records of any engaging in combat. This was the Heinkel He-162 *Volksjäger* (People's Fighter), a single-seater aircraft with an H-shaped tail fin. It was built of glued wood and constructed by semi-skilled labour, and could achieve a top speed of 562mph (905km/h) at 19,690ft (6,000m). What makes this so remarkable is that it went from conception to test flight in just 90 days.

Allied aircraft responded to the arrival of these amazing new jet aircraft by bombing the runways and factories where the planes were evident, and it was this relentless barrage coupled with a shortage of fuel that ensured that the Me-262, for all its technological sophistication and success in use, had limited impact on the course of the war. Nonetheless, the German designs went on to influence developments in the United States, notably the design of the Boeing B-47 and the North American F-86, better known as the Sabre jet, which was developed with the extensive involvement of German data from the war.

AFTER THE WAR

In Russia, work on jet engines had revived in the closing months of the war. From 1944 the Soviets had evidence of the British and German developments in jet engine design, and Lyulka was encouraged to try to improve them for use in Soviet aircraft. Starting in 1945 he constructed the first Soviet jet engine, the TR-1, which passed all the required tests successfully and went on to give rise to the engines which powered the highly successful MiG fighters. They were built by a company established in December 1939 by Artem Mikoyan, a young aviation designer from Sanahin, Armenia. Many of these Russian engines were copied from Junkers and BMW

The Ar-231 was designed as a lightweight seaplane for carrying aboard a U-boat, allowing it to attack Allied shipping with minimal flying time. It was never used in the war due to its instability and lack of power. (Cody Images)

jet engines brought to Russia from Germany after the war. Then, in 1946, the new British Prime Minister Clement Attlee – keen to cement cordial relationships with the Soviet Union – arranged for an export of 40 Rolls-Royce Nene turbojet engines. It was hoped that further orders would follow, but instead the Russians simply copied the British design and constructed a pirated copy of the engine for use in the MiG-15. Rolls-Royce, with Government encouragement, sought to reclaim £207 million in license fees, but did not succeed.

Gyrogliders were used for observation in World War II and the Focke-Achgelis Fa-330 could be easily dismantled and stored in a small container on a U-boat. It was used for spotting ships at distance while being towed behind the submarine. The submarine could rapidly submerge, usually (but not always) with the kite pilot safely back on board. (EN Archive)

These MiG-15 fighters, used later in the Korean War, proved to be superior to anything in the West. The MiG-29 is the fourth-generation MiG fighter aircraft designed in the Soviet Union and was developed from the earlier designs during the 1970s by the Mikoyan Company. This aircraft entered service with the Soviet Air Force in 1983 and it remains in use to the present day by the Russian Air Force and also in several other countries.

Hans Joachim Pabst von Ohain was brought to the United States in 1947 under the top-secret Operation *Paperclip* (p.159). He joined the staff at the Wright-Patterson Air Force Base and in 1956 became Director of the Aeronautical Research Laboratory. In 1975 he was appointed to the role of Chief Scientist at the Aero Propulsion Laboratory. Ohain made innumerable contributions to American fuel technology and won many awards, including the United States Citation of Honor. Ohain eventually retired to Florida, where he died in 1998.

Meanwhile, in 1976, Whittle had divorced from his British wife Dorothy and he married an American woman, Hazel S. Hall. He emigrated to the United States and became the NAVAIR

Coastal Command aircrew at Wick, Caithness inspect a visiting Cierva Rota C-30 autogyro. Designed by Juan de la Cierva and first flown in 1933, manufacture was licensed across Europe during World War II. This propeller-driven aircraft had a top speed of 110mph (177km/h). (IWM CH 5423)

(Naval Air Systems Command) Research Professor at the Naval Academy in Annapolis, Maryland. He later wrote a book entitled *Gas Turbine Aero-Thermodynamics: With Special Reference to Aircraft Propulsion* which appeared in 1981. He came to know Ohain, and the two often gave talks together. Ohain reportedly said that if the RAF had taken Whittle's design seriously when it was originally submitted, there would have been no World War II at all. Sir Frank Whittle died in 1996 at his home in Columbia, Maryland.

SMALL WARPLANES

Not all the secret aircraft were fast, large or impressive. Small and discreet airplanes also played their part. The Arado Ar-231 was an extremely lightweight seaplane that the Germans designed as a spotter plane and it was intended to be carried aboard the U-boat Type XI B. The plane was designed with light parasol wings and was powered by a 160hp (119kW) Hirth HM 501 inline engine. The plane weighed 2,200lb (1,000kg) and had a wingspan of just 33ft (10m). It could be folded down within 6 minutes and fitted inside a tubular casing measuring 6.7ft (2m) across. Although it was an ingenious little portable aircraft, it proved to be seriously underpowered, too light to handle and unstable in flight, even when the weather was calm. With small waves causing unsteadiness in the mother submarine, it proved near-impossible to fold up the wings and store the plane away. Six prototypes were built for testing purposes, but it was never used in the war.

Submarine commanders, however, knew that some means of carrying out reconnaissance was imperative. Current limitations were imposing severe restraints upon the U-boat campaigns. The distance of vision is severely restricted through a periscope, and some means of gaining height – as in the abandoned Ar-231 – conferred a considerable advantage. Accordingly, focus was directed instead to the notion of having an observer towed along underneath some kind of kite. This would not be just a conventional kite, either, but a superbly thought-out and well-designed kite with rotary wings.

The project was put to the designers at the Focke-Achgelis Flugzeugbau (a division of Weser Flugzeugwerke) of Hoykenkamp in Lower Saxony, who were experienced in helicopter production. Since helicopters had emerged in their present-day form in 1936, their production had become routine and companies like Focke-Achgelis Flugzeugbau were well equipped to tackle the problem. The Weser Flugzeugwerke were based at the Lloyd Building in Bremen, and they acted as the government contractors for the project; all development and manufacture, however, was carried out at Hoykenkamp. The result was the Focke-Achgelis Fa-330 gyroglider, an autogyro that could be tethered to the deck of a submarine at the end of a wire cable 500ft (150m) long. A minimum airflow of 20mph (32km/h) from the movement of the submarine caused the rotors to turn at about 200rpm, lifting the glider 400ft (120m) above the sea. The observer could spy out features up to 25 miles (40km) away, rather than being able to see just 5.5 nautical miles (10km) from the top of the submarine's conning tower, and he could send back real-time reports by telephone. When observations were over, the FA-330 was hauled down, the rotors stopped by means of a hub brake, and the craft stowed away in watertight compartments aft of the conning tower. This was not a simple task and could take 20–25 minutes in rough seas.

The Fa-330 was nicknamed the *Bachstelge* (Sandpiper) and 200 were built. These little gliders were successful in use, but were disappointing as agents of warfare. There was only one instance when a sinking resulted from their use – a Greek steamer in 1943. They also posed a problem for the submarines, for they could be detected by British radar and thus inadvertently reveal the location of the submarine. Pilots of the Fa-330 were sometimes forgotten about by the captain of the submarine, which suddenly dived leaving the pilot and his craft doused in the sea. It soon became routine for the pilot to call down the line 'Haul me in!' *before* announcing that an enemy ship had been sighted. In May 1944 one of these gyrogliders was captured and examined by the Allies. Experiments were carried out by the British, but the helicopter was seen as a higher priority and the little rotary glider was never used again. Design of the Rotachute, a British single-seat gyroglider, was undertaken by an expatriate Austrian designer, Raoul Hafner. The design was modified by Dr Igor Bensen after he had seen one of the German Fa-330 gliders, and the Benson design became popular. This original Rotachute was intended to be towed behind an aircraft, and was not ready until 1946; but Benson's B-7 gyroglider was a success and later re-emerged as a sports craft. It is still popular with enthusiasts today.

The gyroglider was a form of aircraft similar to an autogyro – the essential difference being that the forward motion of an autogyro was provided by its own onboard propulsion system, whereas the gyroglider was towed by a moving vehicle. Autogyros were the invention of Juan de la Cierva, a Spanish engineer and flight enthusiast. His first successful design, the fourth with which he experimented (the C-4), flew in 1923. The aircraft had a forward propeller and engine with a rotor on a vertical mast. The C-19 was licensed to several overseas manufacturers, including Harold Pitcairn in the United States and Focke-Achgelis in Germany. Amelia Earhart flew a Pitcairn PCA-2 to a world-record world altitude of 18,415ft (5,613m) in 1931.

During the war, Germany also employed the Focke-Wulf Fw-186 and experimented with the Focke-Achgelis Fa-225 and the two-seater Flettner Fl-184. But it was the Spanish design of the La Cierva C.30A that was most successful. The United States used a version which they named the Kellet KD-1A; Britain and Canada produced their own models as the Avro 671 Rota Mark.1 and the French called theirs the Lioré-et-Olivier LeO C.30/31. The Soviets had their own design, the TsAGI (Kamov) A-7 observation autogyro. In the Pacific arena, the Japanese produced their Kayaba Ka-1 Autogyro for reconnaissance and for use as an anti-submarine observation aircraft. Although the war brought helicopters visibly into use as a crucial means of transporting men and materiel, we should also remember the small, secret 'spy in the sky' that was the autogyro. Autogyros remain popular to the present day, mostly as the aircraft of hobbyists, yet they flourished only because of the pressures of secret weapons development in the war.

FLYING WINGS

The flowering of innovation in the development of German secret weapons during the war years was especially pronounced in the field of revolutionary aeronautics. Britain was consumed with finding responses to the German onslaught, but the German High Command became fanatical about the domination of the Western world. The engineers and visionaries came up with startling, stunning concepts, and the rate at which they progressed was astonishing. Some of the ideas could never reach fulfilment. One was for the 3 x 1,000 project, intended to bomb English cities. This was the aim of Reichsmarschall Hermann Göring, and would have involved a bomber carrying 1,000kg of explosives for 1,000km at 1,000km/h, equivalent to 2,200lb of bombs for 625 miles at 625mph.

THE HORTEN BROTHERS AND THE HO-229

The birth of the 'flying wing' had been in the USA where Jack Northrop had experimented with delta-wing designs in the late 1920s. Little came of it, however, until the pressures of World War II led to new calls for revolutionary aircraft designs. Both the United States and Germany began development, but research took longer than expected. In Germany, two brilliant brothers, Walter and Reimar Horten, revived the concept during war and planned to take it to unprecedented heights. Both were members of the Hitler Youth and later of the Nazi Party. They first designed an unpowered delta-wing glider, the Ho-229, for flight testing, and its initial flight was in March 1944. After this successful test, the development was taken over by the Gothaer Waggonfabrik Company. They installed an ejector seat for the pilot, and added systems to carry air to the jet engine with which it was proposed to power the plane. Even before the aircraft had flown under jet power, Göring had an order placed for 40 of these aircraft with the designation Ho-229. Further test flights showed that the plane had superb handling qualities, though there were some tragic accidents during the test flights of prototypes. The Germans were building a twin-engined Ho-229 V3 when the Americans arrived during the liberation of Europe at the end of the war.

During the final stages of the conflict, the United States military initiated Operation *Paperclip* (p.159), a top-secret initiative by the United States intelligence agencies to capture advanced German weapons research, and keep it out of the hands of advancing Soviet troops. A Horten test glider, and the partly built Ho-229 V3, were packed up and shipped to the United States, and the Hortens – for all their active Nazi participation – were secretly taken to America and given sanctuary. Their hardware was sent to Jack Northrop.

The Horten IX (Ho-229) prototype, the first delta-wing glider, first flew in March 1944. (Cody Images)

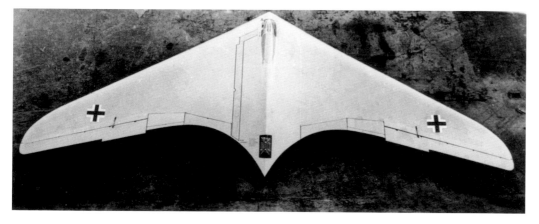

The Horten H IX V1 was used as glider to test the aerodynamics for the later jet-powered V6 prototype. This photograph was taken at Göttingen in 1944. (EN Archive)

Northrop Grumman designed the B-2 Spirit ('the Stealth Bomber') which first entered service with the USAF in December 1993. Its design owes much to the work of the Horten brothers in Nazi Germany. (US Air Force)

FLYING WINGS IN THE UNITED STATES

The first of Jack Northrop's new generation of planes, the N-1M, had taken to the air in July 1941 at Baker Dry Lake, California. These pioneering test flights showed that the design clearly had a future, though the plane's twin 65hp (48kW) Lycoming 0-145 four-cylinder engines left it low on power and the construction was too heavy. The power-plants were replaced with 120hp (88kW) six-cylinder air-cooled Franklin engines and the design was modified though, in spite of it all, the plane never went into production.

Engineering design of the first American delta-winged planes started in 1942. The aircraft would be constructed of the latest light-alloy sheet. There would be a cabin embedded in the delta wing with bunk beds for crew to sleep on during prolonged flights. Bomb bays would be fitted in each wing with seven gun turrets carrying machine guns. Yet progress was slow and the XB-35 did not make her first successful flight until June 1946 when she flew from Hawthorne, California, to Muroc Dry Lake. By May 1948 the plane was ready to start production, but the planes – powered by propeller engines – were rendered obsolete by the advent of the jet bomber. Jet engines were fitted to a few but they were not successful, though one plane, designated the YRB-49A, was tested as a reconnaissance aircraft. Although the United States Air Force had originally ordered 200 of the original B-35 planes, they proved unsatisfactory and not worth converting to jet propulsion so the entire project was peremptorily cancelled. It was a controversial decision, and Jack Northrop later stated that it was due to his refusal to accede to the wishes of Secretary of the Air Force Stuart Symington, who wanted Northrop to merge with the Convair Company. Jack Northrop insisted that unfair terms were being imposed on him, and that it was Symington who suddenly cancelled the flying wing. Northrop may have been right; Symington subsequently became President of the Convair Company when he resigned from government service shortly afterwards.

The Me-261 V3 'Adolphine' coded BJ+CR is photographed at Lechfeld prior to its 10-hour flight from Germany to Austria and back again on 16 April 1943, covering around 2,800 miles (4,500km). (EN Archive)

The Fw-200 *Kondor* (Condor) was the first plane to fly non-stop between Berlin and New York City on 10-11 August 1938, taking 24 hours and 56 minutes. During the war it was used as a long-range maritime bomber and reconnaissance aircraft. (Bundesarchiv Bild 101I-405-0555-06)

THE WORLD'S FIRST STEALTH BOMBER?

The final legacy of the Horten brothers' original design lives on, however. Their aircraft were intended not only to be aerodynamically efficient, but also to reduce the radar signature. As the British began to develop and improve radar technology, the Germans were increasingly aware of the need to defeat its penetrating gaze. The Hortens used a unique glue in their planes, rather than metal nails or rivets; the glue – a carbon composite – and the low profile meant that the aircraft were far harder to see on radar. In 2009, a full-size reproduction of the Ho-229 V3 was constructed for a television documentary. It cost $250,000 (£160,000) and took 2,500 hours to build, but its radar profile was found to be less than 40 per cent of a World War II fighter (such as the Messerschmitt Bf-109). Not only was this a revolution in design, but the plane, had it gone into production, would have been the world's first stealth bomber.

AN OLYMPIC VISION – THE ADOLPHINE

An aircraft with a greatly extended range had begun as an idea before the war and by the war's end it was envisaged as a plane that could span the world from high altitude. It is a remarkable story of both brilliance and foolhardy adventurism that far out-reached itself.

This story had its roots in 1936 in Berlin, site of the XI Olympiad. The city selected to host the next Olympics was Tokyo, Japan, and Hitler had a vision that the German team would fly direct from Germany to Japan in a record-breaking non-stop flight aboard a futuristic aircraft designed especially for the event. As it happens, plans for the Olympics were agreed at the Cairo Conference of the International Olympic Committee held in 1938 but Japan renounced the conference because of the Second Sino-Japanese War. Japan was thus stripped of her right to hold the games, which were rescheduled to be held in Helsinki, Finland. By this time, the Germans were already developing the super-plane Hitler had envisaged: work had started in 1937, when the Messerschmitt Company launched Projekt *P-1064*. It was viewed as a development of the Messerschmitt Bf-110 twin-engined heavy fighter into a reconnaissance plane that had unprecedented range. Conceived with a slender fuselage and with two engines, this was the Messerschmitt Me-261 and it was seen as spearheading German superiority in long-range flight. The Luftwaffe designated it the 8-261. Since it had the backing of the Führer, the projected aircraft was named Adolphine.

For its time, the plane was remarkably futuristic. The all-metal wings were deep and served as fuel tanks, and were fixed to a fuselage with a rectangular cross-section which had room for five

The Ju-390 was made by adding to the wings and fuselage of the Ju-90 and Ju-290 airframes. Stories circulated about it making a reconnaissance flight over the USA, but can be discounted. (Bundesarchiv Bild 141-0072)

crew, with pilot and co-pilot seated in the cockpit alongside the radio operator, and a navigational officer and engineer at the rear. The four Daimler-Benz DB-601 engines were coupled in pairs through a shared gearbox. Work was under way in 1939 and was supported from the highest levels of the Nazi power structure – but with the outbreak of World War II the 1940 Olympics were cancelled, and the project lost both urgency and direction. By August 1939, work had come to a standstill. Within a year, however, it was plain that the war would be no walkover for Germany, and the Luftwaffe began once again to involve long-distance bombers in their strategy. The Adolphine suddenly had a part in these plans, so work was resumed under conditions of urgency and the first prototype flew in December 1940.

It seemed highly promising and, with the DB-606 engines, the range was predicted to be as much as 12,000 miles (20,000km) for the production aircraft. The engines were in short supply, however. They were being produced as fast as possible, but all were needed for established, successful planes like the Heinkel He-177. The second version was flown in 1941, but Messerschmitt realized that the fuel-carrying wings posed a radical problem: there was no room in the wing structure for weapons. There was a plan for the aircraft to fly over New York, dropping propaganda leaflets, but this public relations scheme was abandoned when Allied bombing destroyed both prototypes. There was a third prototype, fitted with two DB-610 engines and with space for two further crew members. It first flew in early

The prototype Lippisch DM-1 glider was used to test the feasibility of the rocket-powered Darmstadt D-33. Although development was carried out, the aircraft never made its way into operational service. The craft shown here was taken to America after the war and used in US space research into 'lifting bodies' – which gave rise to the shuttle. (EN Archive)

German scientist and designer of the ramjet, Dr Alexander Lippisch, photographed in the USA in November 1946. (Time Life Pictures/Getty Images)

1943 and in April 1943, the Me-261 V3 flew for 10 hours over 2,790 miles (4,500km), the distance from Europe to America across the Atlantic. It was an unprecedented achievement. Three months later the prototype crash-landed, damaging the undercarriage. The plane was used for several long-distance reconnaissance missions but the need for an aircraft to catch the public attention no longer existed, and the project was finally scrapped in 1944.

CROSSING THE ATLANTIC

The idea of a plane that could cross the Atlantic had remained a continuing preoccupation of the German High Command throughout the war. The Commander-in-Chief of the Luftwaffe, Hermann Göring, often spoke of his wish to have a bomber that could curtail the 'arrogance of the Americans'. One scheme had been to use the mid-Atlantic Portuguese islands of the Azores as a stop for fuel. The Portuguese dictator António de Oliveira Salazar had allowed the Germans to obtain fuel for their U-boats and Navy vessels from São Miguel in the Azores, but in 1943 he signed leases with the British, allowing them to use the islands as a base from which to patrol the North Atlantic by air.

The other designs were all for high-specification aircraft that could fly across the Atlantic and back without touching down. Those that were hurriedly prepared were the all-new Messerschmitt Me-264, upgraded versions of the existing Focke Wulf Fw-200 known as the Fw-300 and the Ta-400, an improved version of the Junkers Ju-290 (the Ju-390) and the Heinkel He-277. Messerschmitt were quick to produce a prototype of the projected Me-264, though in the event it was the Ju-390 which was chosen to go into production. In early 1944, the second prototype Ju-390 reportedly made a trans-Atlantic flight and came within 12 miles (20km) of the coastline of the United States. Another Ju-390 is also claimed to have flown from Germany to south-west Africa (present-day Namibia) early in 1944. These reports are all post-war, however, and are impossible to substantiate.

Many German aircraft companies investigated the problem of bombing the United States of whom Junkers, Messerschmitt, Heinkel and Focke-Wulf were the principal players. Long-distance aircraft were generally seen as impossible to construct in the time-frame, so the plans involved the capture of facilities on the Azores and the use of these strategic islands as a stopping-off point in the middle of the ocean. Bombers including the Ju-290, He-277 and Me-264 would then be within reach of United States targets with a bomb payload of up to 6.5 tons. Targets were listed in detail, and included American producers of light alloys, aircraft engines and optical equipment. Other targets were Canada and an Allied base in Greenland. It was calculated that attacks on American soil would cause the United States to devote her priorities to defending herself, rather than protecting Britain. In this way, the Germans would have less resistance from the British forces and the occupation of the United Kingdom would be easier to attain. However, these detailed plans failed to bear fruit.

Concorde, the Anglo–French supersonic airliner, was based on British designs, derived from research begun in World War II. Able to carry people across the Atlantic, the concept is resonant of a jet fighter. (Getty Images)

FLYING TRIANGLES

The DM-series of delta-winged planes was a joint project of the Darmstadt and Munich Akafliegs (*Akademische Fliegergruppen*, academic flight research teams). During planning all limits were set aside and what may seem impossible today was seriously considered, such as the DM-4 with a planned wing area of 753ft^2 (70m^2) that was calculated to reach speeds of 1,000mph (1,600km/h), well above the speed of sound.

These aircraft were not the only delta-shaped planes envisaged in Germany during the war. Alexander Lippisch, the distinguished Munich-born engineer, proposed to develop a ramjet defence fighter powered by a new and highly efficient form of propulsion unit. Rather than relying on air compressed by a spinning turbine, this new design – the ramjet – used the plane's forward motion to collect and compress the air. Ramjets could operate at very high efficiency, but – because the plane must already be moving to compress the incoming air – they could not be used to propel the plane from a standing start. The ramjet only took over when the plane was already moving at speed. Lippisch named his design Projekt *P-13a*.

He persuaded the Darmstadt Akaflieg to build a full-scale flying prototype, which the company designated the Darmstadt D-33. Work was proceeding when the Akaflieg Darmstadt workshop was hit during an Allied bombing raid in September 1944, so the D-33 project was transferred to the Munich Akaflieg where the work was completed. They renamed the D-33 the Akaflieg Darmstadt/Akaflieg München DM-1. It was designed as a single-seat glider made from steel tubing and plywood that was impregnated with Bakelite, at the time a highly innovative process. The glider was discovered by United States soldiers when they arrived on site in May 1945, and the prototype was then inspected by Charles Lindbergh who arranged for it to be shipped back to the United States. The prototype was wind-tunnel tested and examined by scientists from the National Advisory Committee for Aeronautics (which later gave rise to today's NASA – National Air and Space Administration). Among the planes inspired by this German design, as by the Hortens' flying wing, were the Convair XP-92, America's first delta-wing fighter, and Convair's F-102 Delta Dagger which flew in Vietnam.

Of a similar, uncompromising delta design was the Convair F-2Y Sea Dart which was a seaplane fighter that took off on buoyant skis from the surface of a body of water.

In Britain, research into the delta-wing concept gave rise to the Handley Page HP-115 and the Fairey Delta 2 or FD2 – the first plane to fly faster than 1,000mph (1,609km/h) – and then the great Avro Vulcan bomber. These are the planes that gave much of the technical data needed in the development of Concorde, the successful supersonic passenger aircraft. Once, when flying aboard Concorde to New York, I was told by a captain that it was not useful to think of Concorde as a supersonic airliner. That didn't make sense to him – his advice was to envisage it instead as a huge supersonic jet fighter that carried passengers instead of weapons. He was right: that made far more sense.

TWO AIRCRAFT IN ONE

One novel method of reaching the United States from Germany was the proposal for a hybrid of two planes. A Heinkel He-177 would be used to transport a Dornier Do-217 bomber equipped with an extra Lorin-Staustrahltriebwerk ramjet engine until the planes were sufficiently close to the United States for the Do-217 to be released and fly on towards the target. The plane would deliver its bomb to United States territory and then be ditched in the Western Atlantic, where the pilot would be recovered by a German submarine. The design could not be realized as the distances proved to be insurmountable, so the idea was soon abandoned.

This was not the novel idea it might seem. The first planes to be carried as 'parasites' were small planes that could be released from giant airships in the 1920s. During the 1930s the Soviets experimented with the idea of carrying fighters aboard larger aircraft. The Zveno series became increasingly complex, until a Tupolev TB-3 carried three Polikarpov I-5 fighters: one mounted on each wing, and a third above the cockpit. By 1935 the Aviamatka had been flown, a TB-3/AM-34 which carried five small fighters. Some were deployed just once during the war years; in mid-1941, a Zveno flight from the Black Sea was dispatched to attack the Negru Voda bridge in Romania.

The idea of carrying a plane aboard a larger transporter also re-emerged elsewhere in Germany during World War II. The principle was nicknamed *Mistel* (Mistletoe) because of the way that a small plane could be carried, like the parasitic plant, safely attached to a larger one. The concept was that the 'parent' plane could carry the attack aircraft towards the target, so that the smaller aircraft could carry out its attack and still have a full fuel tank with which to return to base. The first of these trials earned the nickname *Huckepack* (Pick-a-Back, or Father-and-Son). The attack aircraft was to be a Focke-Wulfe Fw-190 *Würger* (Strangle) fighter that had been designed by Kurt Tank in 1938. As a fighter, this small plane became well known as a routine strike aircraft and a ground-attack plane. It would be carried aloft mounted above a Ju-88 Mark 4, a bomber based on the design of the successful Ju-88 but with more powerful engines. It flew for the first time in early 1940. The Mark 4 of the Ju-88 had

German designers attempted to increase operational range by constructing a combination of two planes. A Fw-190 is here shown fixed to the top of a Ju-88 transport plane. (Fox Photos/Getty Images)

'Mistel' aircraft ready for take-off. Later versions of the idea involved a bomber being filled with explosives and controlled from the detachable fighter, thus creating a flying bomb. (Author's collection)

a wingspan of 70ft (20m) compared to the 65ft 10.5in (18m) of the previous models, with improved streamlining and a somewhat larger cockpit offering improved visibility.

The first five of these combined Mistel aircraft were ready early in 1944 and training began in Nordhausen. Both upper and lower aircraft were initially crewed, but it was envisaged that the Ju-88 could eventually be controlled from the smaller fighter and released as an unmanned 'flying bomb'. Once the Allied invasion of the Normandy coast began, the unit moved from Nordhausen to St Dizier with a squadron of 12 of the combined aircraft. They were used with some effect; the crashing of an unmanned fully laden Ju-88 was extremely unnerving for the British, and this curious combined aircraft went on to fly further successful missions.

THE ULTIMATE AIRCRAFT

For extreme long-distance raids, there remained one top-secret German proposal of immense potential. It was for the 'antipodal bomber', a stratospheric aircraft that could span the world. It was the brainchild of one of the greatest German visionaries, yet also one of the least well known. This was Eugen Sänger, born in Pressnitz, now in the Czech Republic, who had studied civil engineering at the Technical Universities of Graz and Vienna. As a student, Sänger had been captivated by Hermann Oberth's book *Die Rakete zu den Planetenräumen* (*The Rocket into Planetary Space*, p.114) and indeed we will come across both Oberth and Sänger again later in this book when we look more specifically at rocket-powered weapons. It was Oberth's book that inspired Sänger to change from studying civil engineering to a career in aeronautics and as a first step he joined the Society for Space Travel (p.115) in order to learn more from Oberth. The subject of Sänger's thesis was originally intended to be rocket-powered flight, but this was rejected by the university as being unrealistic. Instead he was instructed to submit a relatively mundane report on the statics of wing trusses. His original work was not lost, however; and Sänger went on to publish it under the title *Raketenflugtechnik* (*Rocket Flight Technology*) in 1933, and followed this with several magazine articles on rocket-powered flight. They appeared in an Austrian magazine *Flug* (*Flight*) and soon came to the

Austrian engineers Eugen Sänger and Irene Bredt describing the skip-flight method of their proposed antipodal bomber. (Time Life Pictures/Getty Images)

attention of the German Air Ministry, who could envisage Sänger's ideas as one way to build a bomber that could attack the United States from an airfield in Germany.

One of Sänger's dreams was for his great antipodal bomber – a long-range sub-orbital aircraft, launched by rockets, that could travel around the world through the stratosphere and deliver a payload to the opposite ends of the earth. Sänger called his craft the *Silbervogel* (Silver Bird) and worked on the design with a brilliant young mathematician named Irene Bredt, of Vienna, Austria, whom he later married. Sänger also designed the rockets so they could generate a thrust of 225,000lb-ft (0.3 meganewton metres). The silver bird was known as the *RaBo* (*Raketenbomber* or Rocket Bomber) and it would be launched by rocket sled from a 2-mile (3km) launch-track at about 1,200mph (2,000km/h). It would then fire its own onboard rocket motors and climb to an altitude of 90 miles (145km) reaching a velocity of 13,700mph (22,100km/h). The craft would then slowly descend in a sub-orbital trajectory until it entered the upper atmosphere and, as its wings and body generated lift, it would bounce back into space before slowly descending again. After several 'hops', it would be at the opposite pole of the earth. It was calculated to be able to deliver a 8,800lb (4,000kg) bomb to the United States and then fly on to land in the Pacific where the Japanese would ensure it was recovered for the Germans. The complete flight would be 12–15,000 miles (19–24,000km) in length.

It was an adventurous and futuristic scheme – too futuristic for the Luftwaffe, who brought development to a halt as early as 1942. As we have seen, they preferred to invest in proven aircraft technology. Sänger was assigned to carry on research at the German Gliding Research Institute (Deutsche Forschungsanstalt für Segelflug) where he made important developments in ramjet design. He remained an authority on rockets, and came to prominence again when German rocketry was reaching its height.

The end of the project was not the end of the idea. After the war, calculations proved that the antipodal bomber would not have worked – the heat generated by the 'hops' into the upper atmosphere would have caused far greater heating than the Germans had realized, destroying the craft. Even so, the Soviets tried to tempt Sänger to move to Russia and continue his research there, but he declined the offer and instead continued his research in France,

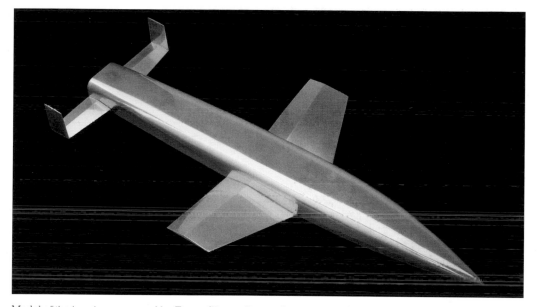

Model of the bomber proposed by Eugen Sänger. Research was stopped by the Nazi authorities in 1943, and after the war Sänger worked for the French. (SSPL/Getty Images)

where he founded the French Astronautical Federation (Fédération Astronautique) in 1949. He spent his later years back in Germany, working on a ramjet-powered spacecraft that was never realized. He also pioneered the idea of using photons from the sun for long-distance space propulsion, and introduced the still-popular concept of the solar sail.

But the importance of the lifting properties of a body that is descending into the upper atmosphere still stands today. Sänger's work and his wife's calculations proved significant in the design of the North American X-15 rocket plane, the X-20 Dyna-Soar and eventually in the design of the Space Shuttle. In October 1985 the Messerschmitt-Bölkow-Blohm (MBB) Organization renewed studies of the Sänger system as the core of a two-stage spacecraft with horizontal take-off. The first stage would propel the plane to high speed and would then be jettisoned, allowing the second stage to fire and carry it further towards space. In my view, this would make great sense, and I have extolled the widely unrecognized ingenuity of Sänger in the television series *Weird Weapons of World War II* for the History Channel. My view is that the present method of launching a rocket is excessively wasteful of fuel, for the energy is used to support the mass of the rocket as it gathers velocity. Launching the rocket on wheels, running on a ramp that later curves upwards to launch the rocket aloft, is a clear design advantage; for then it is the track which supports the weight, rather than the rocket thrust. It would be possible for the rocket to achieve high launch speeds by running horizontally before its path turned upwards, conserving onboard fuel for the entry into space. Who knows? Those secret ideas from World War II may yet find realization.

FLYING WEAPONS: BOMBS AND MISSILES

AS WE HAVE SEEN, there were impressive and powerful developments in aircraft technology in World War II. However, the description 'flying weapons' is not restricted to aircraft. Many of the strangest secret devices of the war were airborne weapons, and some of them were of an incredibly advanced design.

THE QUEST FOR A SUPER BOMB

Barnes Wallis was a crisp and authoritative figure with a warm, avuncular manner when I met him in the 1970s at the BBC in London. His proposal as World War II enveloped Europe was to construct increasingly massive bombs. Wallis argued that the best way to bring the German war machine to its knees was to disrupt its capacity for weapons production, and he had in mind the huge factories in the Ruhr. He realized that the Nazis would seek to construct massively reinforced concrete bunkers that would be impregnable to conventional explosives, and proposed huge bombs that would bring about the desired level of destruction. Wallis decided on a 10-ton bomb that would be dropped from high altitude and demolish the most heavily reinforced construction by penetrating deep inside the ground before it detonated and erupted from beneath. In 1940 he revealed his proposal for a 22,400lb (10,200kg) bomb that could even bring down the massive dams on which German industry relied.

The Air Ministry conceded that the idea was viable, but it failed because there was no aircraft large enough to carry such a weapon. Barnes Wallis responded by designing just such an aircraft, the Victory bomber. It was designed to be 96ft (23m) long with a wingspan of 172ft (52.4m), designed to fly at an altitude of 34,000ft (10,000m) at a cruising speed of 352mph (566km/h). This was an astonishing concept: the American B-245 Liberator in comparison cruised at 214mph (344km/h) at a maximum altitude of 28,000ft (8,534m). Barnes Wallis's new aircraft would carry a gun turret with four weapons, but it was otherwise undefended since it would easily out-fly any other aircraft in existence. Nonetheless, in May 1941 the project was rejected. The Air Ministry concluded that the bomber would have only one purpose, and expensive fixed-mission projects were not something the British government wished to support. Furthermore, it was calculated that the aircraft was so revolutionary that it was unlikely to be operational before the end of the war.

The refusal of the Air Ministry to give the go-ahead to the Victory bomber left Barnes Wallis with the ambition of finding alternative ways to destroy the German factories in the Ruhr. This had been an aim of British Intelligence since about 1937, and sketchy plans to bomb the dams above the factories were in mind prior to the outbreak of hostilities. The central focus was the Möhne dam, which was known to be well defended, but which Barnes Wallis knew could be destroyed with his proposed 10-ton bomb, if only there was a plane to carry it. The only feasible alternative was to use large torpedoes that could detonate against the dam wall itself, but the Germans were aware of the risk and had the dams of the Ruhr well protected by heavy-duty submerged nets. Wallis walked along the sea-shore one day, skipping stones across the surface, and suddenly thought of the notion of designing a bomb that would similarly ricochet across the water in the reservoirs – above the protective nets – and impact on the concrete dam itself. His proposal was for a cylindrical bomb, spinning backwards to the direction of travel, which would be dropped from a low-flying aircraft. The backward spin – coupled with the forward speed of the bomb – would cause it to bounce across the surface. If it struck the dam wall, the backwards spin would cause the bomb to hug close to the dam as it sank, and a pressure-sensitive hydrostatic fuse would detonate it at the optimum depth. The backspin would also slow the forward motion of the bomb with each skip, so that it would fall behind the aircraft and reduce the chances of damaging the low-flying plane that had dropped it.

The Royal Air Force was sceptical at first, but Barnes Wallis persisted and produced movie films of his successful experiments. In early June 1942 he experimented with a mine suspended on scaffolding to test the effect of underwater detonations. He destroyed the disused Nant-Y-Gro dam near Rhayader, in central Wales, with a submerged 279lb (127kg) mine, to help ascertain the way a dam might behave under attack. Dummy versions of the bombs were then dropped from a modified de Havilland Mosquito B Mark IV aircraft off Chesil Beach, near Weymouth Bay in southern England, but they burst apart on hitting the water and Wallis asked Wing Commander Guy Gibson if they could be launched from a lower altitude – 50ft instead of 120ft (15m instead of 36m). Gibson agreed and there were subsequent tests of dummies on the dams in the Elan Valley, Wales. In February 1943 the Air Ministry finally accepted the scheme and it was resolved to bomb the dams of the Ruhr in springtime, when the water in the reservoirs was at its highest. The mission was code named Operation *Chastise* and was given to No. 617 Squadron flying out of RAF Scampton, Lincolnshire, with Gibson as the leader. The Lancaster bombers carried out extensive training and numerous dummy runs, until they were accustomed to flying over the kind of landscape that they would encounter on the raid and made several successful practice runs along the Upper Derwent Valley in Derbyshire. This was dangerous work; the flying was under a full moon at night, no more than 60ft (18m) above the surface and they knew that the

Dr Barnes Wallis, who pioneered the 'bouncing bomb' and geodesic engineering. (IWM HU 92132)

THE DAMBUSTERS

Operation *Chastise* was the RAF attack on the dams of the Ruhr valley, concentrating on the Möhne dam. The Dambusters raid has since become a legend, immortalized in film. The operation was developed by Barnes Wallis for the RAF. The raid was typical of the British approach to the war – attacks on German industrial production. The death by drowning of thousands of prisoners and civilians led to a change in the Geneva Convention to prohibit such raids in future.

London's *The Daily Telegraph* proclaimed the success of the Dambusters raid on the front page of 18 May 1943. Plans to bomb the Ruhr dams had in fact been first drawn up in 1938. (Author's collection)

Code-named 'Upkeep' this bouncing bomb – in reality a depth-charge – is preserved at Newark Air Museum. Upkeep contained 6,600lb (2,994kg) of Torpex high explosive which detonated 30ft (9m) below the water's surface. Prior to launch it was given a backspin of 500 rpm, which caused it to ricochet across the water. (Author's collection)

Prior to Operation *Chastise*, No. 617 Squadron practised dropping the Upkeep weapon at the Reculver bombing range on the Kent coast. Observers keep watch as the bomb bounces toward the shoreline. Barnes Wallis, on the extreme left of the group, seems to be urging the weapon on to success. (IWM FLM 2343)

The dramatic results of the successful raid are shown in this photograph, discovered in the German archives after the war. This was the Möhne Dam in North Rhine-Westphalia. (Keystone/Getty Images)

British aerial reconnaissance showed the breach in the Möhne Dam caused by the raid on 16 May 1943. This spectacular feat of precision bombing had tremendous propaganda value to the Allied war effort, although its practical effects were limited. (IWM CH 9687)

target would be some 400 miles (640km) away from their base. The pilots became proficient at straight and level flight only some 30ft (less than 10m) above the ground – little more than the height of a house.

The bombers were mechanically adapted to carry the weapons and were fitted with electric motors to set them spinning, prior to the drop. Barnes Wallis knew that it was vital for the bombs to be launched a precise distance from the dam wall, or they would simply skip over the top. To facilitate this he designed a simple Y-shaped wooden sight which the bomb aimer would use to line up the two ends of the dam. Paired downward pointing lights were carefully positioned, so that the two beams met when the plane was at exactly the correct height above the surface of the water. With the dam in the bomb-aimer's sights, and the beams correctly aligned, the bomber was certain to fly within the very narrow tolerances that the mission demanded. As the teams kept practising, many of them worked out their own ways to adapt the apparatus to suit their own preferences. One answer was to tie string on struts on the windscreen, pulling it back like the elastic on a catapult, to give the range of the towers at either end of the dam.

The attack finally began on 16 May 1943. The outward flight maintained very low levels throughout. Several planes were lost, including one that crashed into high tension cables at 11.50pm, 2.5 miles (4km) north-east of Rees in the Lower Rhine area of Germany. This was the consequence of the low-level approach, of course, as was the experience of another Lancaster that actually skimmed the surface of the Zuider Zee in the Netherlands, ripping the bomb from its brackets and spraying seawater into the fuselage before the pilot managed to recover. Gibson dropped his bomb first, but the aim was poor and it fell away from the target. A second aircraft was hit by flak and the bomb overshot the target, blowing up beneath the Lancaster that had dropped it. Gibson thereafter flew to draw fire as other Lancasters dropped their bombs, until eventually one struck home and the Möhne dam collapsed with a roar. In contrast, the Eder dam was not well defended: the Germans had assumed it would be impossible to attack as it was situated in a deep valley. Pilots made repeated passes until they were confident that the dam could be mined, and only then dropped their bombs. The Eder dam was eventually breached and – with both dams destroyed – the German factories downstream were severely damaged. The nearby Sorpe dam lay in a winding valley that was unsuitable for the bouncing bombs, and was instead attacked by dropping the bombs as conventional inertial weapons; even though it was hit, it was not significantly damaged by the raids. As a result of the raid, hydroelectric power generation from the dams was interrupted, and a considerable propaganda victory was scored. The supremacy of British secret weapons research was widely celebrated in the UK, though the Nazis also claimed success in minimizing the interruption to power generation, and in the fact that the British could not bring down the Sorpe dam.

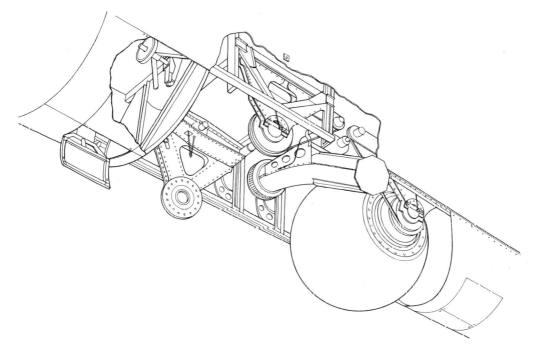

The cylindrical 'bouncing bomb' is well known but there was an alternative design code-named Highball. This was a spherical bomb intended for use against enemy shipping. It weighed 1,280lb (581kg) including 600lb (272kg) of Torpex explosive and it was slung below a Mosquito B-IV bomber. Problems with timing, and also with releasing the bomb, were not solved until 1944. At Choctawhatchee Bay, Florida, an American version (renamed the baseball bomb) rebounded and destroyed the American launch plane. (John Batchelor)

AFTER THE DAMBUSTERS

Although the raids were seen as an astonishing and heroic success in Britain, there were tragic civilian losses. At least 1,650 people died in the subsequent floods, most of them Allied prisoners and forced labourers held in Nazi prison camps. At least 500 were female Soviet prisoners. This raid was one of the incidents which led to Article 56 of the amendment to the Geneva Convention agreed in 1977, which outlawed attacks on dams 'if such attack may cause the release of dangerous forces from the works or installations and consequent severe losses among the civilian population'. What was regarded at the time as a heroic act of immense difficulty would now be categorized as a war crime against helpless civilians. Nonetheless, it is difficult to see how the Ruhr could have been disabled otherwise, especially when viewed under the pressures of a world war. When news of the civilian losses became known there was much distress in London and Barnes Wallis was medicated as he was otherwise unable to sleep. The Allies did not follow up the raids; conventional high-level bombing would have deterred the Germans from restoring the dams to use, but no plans for this were ever brought into play. Although Barnes Wallis wrote that Germany had been dealt a blow from which it would take years to recover, by 27 June that same year full water output had been restored, and

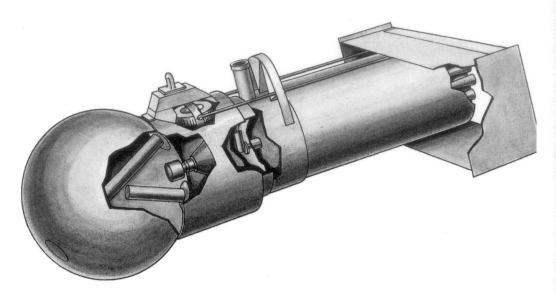

After the British raids over Germany by the Dambusters, the Germans attempted to construct a version of their own known as *Kurt*, weighing 850lb (385kg). They missed the fact that the British weapon had backspin, and fitted theirs with a rocket that detached when it hit the water. The bomb then ricocheted a further 500 yards (460m) until it collided with its target, when it would sink and explode. Kurt was never used in warfare and was cancelled in 1944. (John Batchelor)

the hydroelectric plant was back to generating power. The greatest damage was actually to the domestic residences and prison camps, and also to German agriculture. Farms and livestock were washed away and took years to recover.

And the long-term repercussions? There were smaller versions of bouncing bombs planned by the British, for use against shipping. The Highball bomb was fitted to a cradle underneath a Mosquito B-IV, though it never came into service. Although bouncing bombs did not become a feature of post-war military strategy, the legend of the Dambusters raid was perpetuated in books and films. The 1955 black and white British movie *The Dam Busters* became, and remains, one of the most successful films about the war. *

THE GERMAN BOUNCING BOMB

There was an immediate response to the bomb by the Germans. After the Lancaster crashed from hitting high-tension power lines, the intact mine was removed from the wrecked plane

---

* This film itself had spin-offs, for extracts were even included in the Pink Floyd movie *The Wall*. It was even more influential in scenes from the Steven Spielberg movie *Star Wars Episode IV: A New Hope*. Extracts from the soundtracks of each film have even been matched to videos of the other and devotees can find them on YouTube:
'Dam Wars': the images from *The Dam Busters* matched to soundtrack extracts from *Star Wars*:
http://www.youtube.com/watch?v=_NMfBKrdErY
'Star Wars a la The Dam Busters': this less expertly runs the *The Dam Busters* soundtrack over *Star Wars* footage:
http://www.youtube.com/watch?v=-q47GIgmQWo

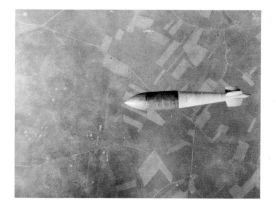

A 12,000lb (5,400kg) MC 'Tallboy' bomb is dropped from Avro Lancaster B Mark I, JB139 of No. 617 Squadron onto the V-1 store at Watten, France in July 1944. (IWM CH 15380)

RAF Grand Slam earthquake bombs photographed in June 1945. So valuable were these weapons that, if a bomber was not able to deliver it during a raid, the Grand Slam had to be returned to base intact, rather than being jettisoned in the sea. (Keystone-France/Getty Images)

An RAF officer inspects the damage inflicted by a Grand Slam bomb which pierced the reinforced concrete roof of the German submarine pens at Farge, north of Bremen in Germany. This was the result of a daylight raid mounted by 18 Avro Lancasters of No. 617 Squadron on 27 March 1945, in which two direct hits by Grand Slams led to the collapse of the partially completed roof. (IWM CL 2607)

The Rheinmetall-Borsig Company designed the *Rheintochter* (Rhine Maiden) surface-to-air missile in 1942. It was an ingenious design with a range similar to that of the *Enzian* (Gentian) and *Schmetterling* (Butterfly) missiles although it attained only half their operational altitude. This was a two-stage rocket 20ft 8in (6.3m) long, 1ft 9in (0.54m) in diameter and with a top speed of 671mph (1,080km/h). It was never used in warfare and production was cancelled in December 1944. (John Batchelor)

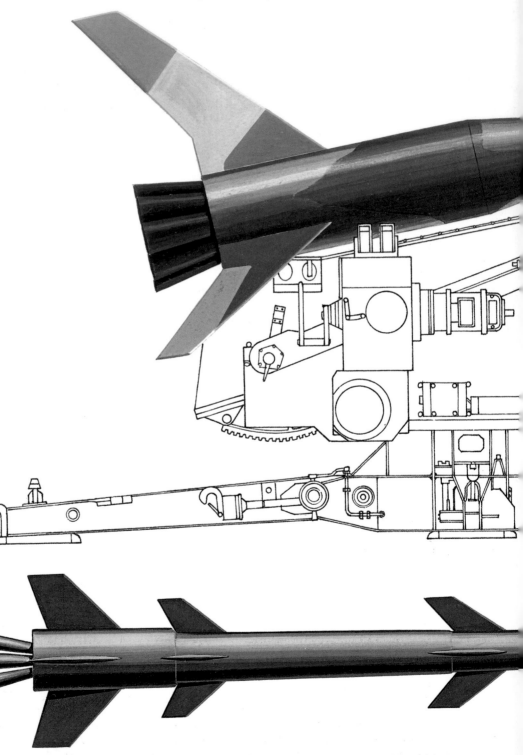

bomb, used with devastating effect against a deep underground control room near Kanggye. Bunker buster bombs were also dropped at the Ali Al Salem Air Base, Kuwait, in 1991 as part of Operation *Desert Storm*. At the outbreak of the First Gulf War none of the NATO forces possessed such a weapon, so some of the original Barnes Wallis bombs were brought out of museums and used as templates for the construction of 2-ton bombs. They were laser guided by the United States forces and proved highly effective.

During the late 1990s a nuclear bomb was being designed by the United States for use in tactical warfare. Known as the Robust Nuclear Earth Penetrator it underwent extensive design and development even though the use of nuclear weapons was prohibited by international agreement. Work on the project continued until it was finally cancelled by the Senate in 2005. Meanwhile, in 2007 the Boeing Company announced that they had carried out successful tests of their Massive Ordnance Penetrator (MOP) weapon at the White Sands Missile Range, New Mexico. This bomb, also known as the Big Blu and Direct Hard Target Strike Weapon, is a 30,000lb (14,000kg) penetration bomb designed to be delivered by a B-52 Stratofortress or a B-2 stealth bomber against heavily protected subterranean targets. This is a project for the United States Threat Reduction Agency, and is designed to hit the ground at supersonic speeds so that it can penetrate deeply prior to detonation. Most of the mass is in the casing, not the explosive component. All of his stems from the work of Barnes Wallis during World War II, so once again the legacy of these secret weapons remains with us to this day.

FLYING MISSILES

Carrying artillery and ammunition to the war front is a time-consuming and tedious business. Far better, the Germans realized, for the weapons to take themselves to the front. From the start of the war – and indeed in the Spanish Civil War, which was a prelude to World War II – the Germans began to look at ways of carrying explosives by plane, and dive-bombing soon became an early strategy in planning an attack. But the bombers were vulnerable, and losses were soon rising fast. So the Germans turned to designs for planes without pilots. These ideas could be far-reaching, because – since there was no crew whose lives could be put at risk – the planes themselves would be expendable. Nothing need be omitted in the search for an answer.

RHINE MAIDEN AND RHINE MESSENGER

By 1942, Rheinmetall-Borsig AG had risen to the challenge, and announced the design for their *Rheintochter* (Rhine Maiden) surface-to-air missile. It was a remarkable device, a two-stage surface-to-air vehicle which was named from Wagner's famed *Ring* cycle. The Rheintochter was designed with a cylindrical fuselage bearing four rounded steering fins operated by servo-mechanisms. Four large swept-back fins on the first stage kept the flight of this solid-fuel rocket-powered device stable in flight. A later modification substituted a liquid fuel engine, but even this did not provide the desired performance and – although many were launched – the project was never fully operational, and it was finally cancelled in December 1944.

In 1943 development was announced of the successor to the Rheintochter – it was the *Rheinbote* (Rhine Messenger) and was designed by the Rheinmetall-Borsig Company. This was a design for a slender 37ft (11.4m) rocket that could deliver a modest payload over distances up to 125 miles (200km). The solid propellant was to be diglycol dinitrate and the missile would be a four-stage rocket: the first stage would launch the main rocket from the ground before being discarded; the second and third stages would fire in succession, carrying the payload aloft, and the final fourth stage would fire it into its maximum altitude where it was set on its course to the target.

However, there was a major problem with accuracy. Each of the four stages was stabilized by four fins at the aft end of the rocket, and the stages were ignited in turn as the fuel charge from the previous stage reached the end of its burn. This was clearly a rocket of limited appeal, for it consumed 2 tons of steel in manufacture, with all the concomitant requirement for energy, it demanded more than half a ton of fuel propellant, yet it could deliver no more than a 44lb (20kg) explosive to its target. It produced no fragment damage and could make a crater no more than 5ft (1.5m) across. Other projects – like Herbert Alois Wagner's design for the *Schmetterling* (Butterfly) – seemed to offer far more promise and informed opinion was that the rocket was militarily valueless. This cut no ice with the High Command; the weapon could be simply understood and a four-stage device was simply too good to miss. Hitler and General Hans Kammler (who reported to Reichsführer Heinrich Himmler directly) immediately ordered production of this worthless missile. Tests were carried out, but it proved impossible to calculate the accuracy because the impact craters were so small that they could not be found.

The single advantage of the design was that stages could be removed, if the distance to be covered was reduced. Rheinbote looked spectacular, and over 200 were used against the strategically important Belgian port of Antwerp. They caused limited pockets of damage in unpredictable areas of the city, but this missile was of little use to anyone – and existed only because of the Führer's capricious decision.

ERA OF THE GLIDE MISSILE

We are all familiar with glide missiles. Although the term has the ring of modernity about it, and sounds like a state-of-the-art weapon of the twenty-first century, it is a concept that was in fact born back in World War I. It was in October 1914 that Wilhelm von Siemens proposed a revolutionary new concept that was to become the torpedo glider. In principle, it was a conventional torpedo with a primitive unmanned glider fixed above. The glider was fitted with flares to enable its course to be tracked by the attacker, and was controlled by fine wires spooled out by the controller. Siemens-Schuckertwerke had already experimented with radio-controlled attack boats, the *Fernlenkboote* (FL-boats) and flight testing of the proposed guided aerial torpedo began in 1915. It was intended to glide the device on course towards the target, where the glider would become detached on a signal from the operator, and the torpedo would be dropped into the sea to home in on its target. The device was just ready for production at the very end of World War I, but was not used in warfare.

With the re-emergence of pilotless planes in World War II, a reliable guidance system was now urgently needed. Infrared, the heat radiation given off by an engine, could be detected and this offered the best way for a missile to home in on an enemy aircraft. Like light, infrared travels for immense distances and in straight lines. The Germans soon realized that a steering system that homed in on the infrared given off by an engine could follow an enemy aircarft for miles.

The first in the world to use infrared tracking equipment was a missile named the *Enzian* (named after *Gentiana clusii*, the gentian flower). As we have discovered (p.31) the first rocket fighter, the Messerschmitt Me-163 Komet, posed practical problems for the pilot. It had a short flight time and high speed up to 596mph (959km/h) at 39,000ft (12,000m) which made it difficult for the crew to find and attack their target in time. Designers at Messerschmitt decided

---

Aluminium was in short supply during the war, so the Messerschmitt Company designed their Enzian missile with a framework of wood. The result was a lightweight rocket that could travel to the altitude of Allied bombers and explode a half-ton bomb in front of an aircraft. Problems were experienced with the power-plant, and not until 1945 was the design up to specification. The radio guidance system was later adapted by the Americans for their Sidewinder missile. (John Batchelor)

A prototype test flight of the Enzian anti-aircraft rocket developed by Messerschmitt at their Oberammergau research centre. This missile was the first in the world to use infrared guidance systems. (EN Archive)

to build a similar aircraft that could carry a huge payload to its target, and would dispense with the need for a pilot aboard. The Enzian would be launched from a sloping ramp with the aid of four booster rockets to attain a maximum speed of 600mph (almost 1,000km/h). It would be 12ft (4m) long and weigh 4,350lb (about 2,000kg) with a range of some 18 miles (30km).

Rather than risk losing a pilot, it was proposed to control the flight of Enzian from the ground. The operator would fly the Enzian in front of an enemy bomber and it would then detonate with great destructive force. The plan was for a bomb with a lethal radius of about 150ft (45m) which could be detonated by means of a proximity fuse. Work began in September 1943 and by May 1944 some 60 airframes had been manufactured. The remaining problem was the lack of a suitable rocket motor. Since work on the Rheintochter missile was proceeding smoothly, this engine was selected for the Enzian and modification began to produce a series of the motors for test flights. These trials proceeded well, though the proximity fuse proved problematic. At this point a remarkably simple new device, code named Madrid, was developed. It featured a light-sensitive photoelectric cell fixed in front of a steerable mirror; a series of vanes masked the cell and the signal from the target – a shadow – was always kept in the middle. The steering system in the Enzian followed the shadow in the mirror and made corresponding adjustments to the trajectory, so the target was bound to be followed. As the tide of war turned increasingly against the Germans, it was realized that there was no time to perfect the system, and for this reason the device never came into use. After the war, with the developers transported to the United States under Operation *Paperclip*, the work proceeded and the design was eventually perfected. It was put in use by the United States Navy as the guidance system for their AIM-9 Sidewinder missile. This is the most widely used air-to-air missile in the West, and it is said that it will remain in use for many decades to come – yet it arose from German technology in World War II.

FLYING FRITZ

During the Spanish Civil War of 1936–39, bombs were designed to penetrate steel which proved effective against shipping, but the Luftwaffe soon discovered how difficult it was to hit a moving vessel squarely. The idea began to form of a radio-controlled bomb that could be steered on course during its free fall, and the first experiments began as early as 1938. In 1939 the first experimental bombs were designed with tail-fins and guided with radio-controlled spoilers.

These could allow the bomb aimer to control the trajectory and maximize the chances of hitting the target. The Ruhrstahl Company, already expert at design and production of bombs, was brought in to move development towards the production stage. The result was the successful Fritz-X bomb, which was controlled by spoilers fitted to the four tail fins. It was tested in various configurations, and the cruciform tail unit proved to be most adaptable, and was eventually used for other controllable weapons of war.

In the early tests of the Fritz-X the carrier was a Heinkel He-111 and some of the He-177 aircraft were adapted to carry the weapon, though they never became operational. When the Fritz-X entered operational service it was aboard the Dornier Do-217 bomber. In July 1943 the first Fritz-X was launched in a raid against Augusta in Sicily. The following month, six

The Fritz-X (PC 1400 X) 3,500lb (1,588kg) remote-controlled bomb could be fitted under the fuselage of a number of Luftwaffe aircraft, but when it went into operation, it was carried by the Dornier Do-217. It was particularly effective when used to track moving targets, such as Allied shipping. (EN Archive)

of the bombers attacked the Italian fleet, which was sailing across the Mediterranean towards Malta as the Italians had signed their armistice with the Allies. This infamous Armistizio di Cassibile had been signed after the Allied successes in North Africa in 1943, after which the Allies landed in Italy, occupied Sicily and even bombed Rome. It was agreed that the Italian naval ships would transfer to Malta and the Germans became determined that they should not become available for use by the Allies. And so, on 9 September 1943, the battleship *Roma* was attacked by Fritz-X guided bombs dropped by the Dornier bombers. Her magazines exploded in a catastrophic blast with the death of 1,255 crew. Among them was Admiral Carlo Bergamini. Although *Roma*'s sister ship *Italia* was hit she managed to limp into port in Valetta, Malta.

Two days later a German Fritz-X attack was directed against a convoy of United States Navy vessels including the USS *Savannah*, one of America's top light cruisers. Observers spotted a Dornier bomber flying towards the USS *Philadelphia*. A bomb aimed at the ship narrowly missed, and exploded about 50ft (15m) away. The *Savannah* immediately increased her speed to 20 knots (37km/h) and then saw a second Do-217 K-2 attacking out of the sun from an altitude of 18,700ft (5,700m). The gunners opened fire, but the plane was not hit and the Fritz-X could be seen flying towards the American ship, leaving a trail of smoke from its flares as it flew. Its steel-piercing design ensured the bomb struck the ship and passed

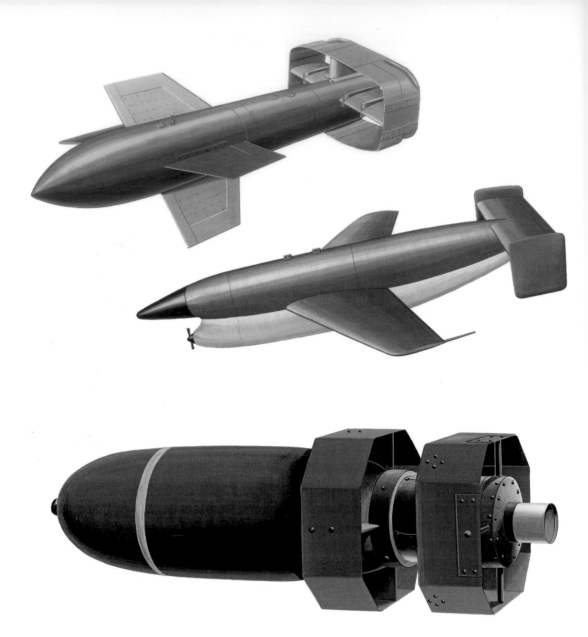

Top: 'Fritz' was the nickname for several weapons. The Ruhrstahl SD-1400 was known as the Fritz-X. Launched from high altitude, it gathered speed as it descended and was radio-controlled to strike ships and break through layers of decks, to explode in the interior where it would cause maximum damage. Several Allied ships were severely damaged by this weapon, notably the USS *Savannah*, HMS *Warspite* and HMS *Uganda*. (John Batchelor)

Middle: Most versions of this Hs-298 air-to-air missile were produced with rounded tail fins, though this variant had a rectangular assembly. Powered by a Schmidding solid-fuel 109-543 rocket motor and launched from Ju-88 and Do-217 bombers, it could have reached 426mph (685km/h) to deliver a 100lb (45kg) warhead under radio control. This weapon was never used in battle, for it was superseded by the X-4 Kramer missile. (John Batchelor)

Bottom: After the success of the German Fritz-X bombs against Allied shipping in 1943, the United States developed the VB series of guided bombs. They were known as Azon bombs (from azimuth-only – they could steer from side to side, but not up and down). Later versions had improved guidance systems, and were known as Razon bombs (Range plus azimuth-only). Some 15,000 were built during 1944, and they were successfully used to destroy enemy bridges. (John Batchelor)

Right: The R4M rocket – from the German Rakete (rocket), 4-Kilogramm, Minenkopf (mine-head) – was nicknamed the *Orkan* (Hurricane) missile. It weighed 8.5lb (3.85kg), measured 32in (812mm) in length and 2.16in (55mm) in diameter. It was developed in 1945 and a few were fitted to Me-262 and Fw-190s aircraft. It was highly effective and in April 1945 a squadron of Me-262 jets are reported to have brought down 30 American B-17 bombers in a single mission. (John Batchelor)

Below: The American Lark was a highly successful surface-to-air missile. Development began in the autumn of 1944 at the Fairchild Company, and 100 Larks were ordered from Consolidated-Vultee in June 1945. The Lark had a range of 34 miles (55km) and its velocity was 650mph (1,046km/h). It carried a 100lb (45kg) warhead detonated by a proximity fuse. The missile was 14ft (4.2m) long, with a wingspan of 5ft 2in (1.6m) and weighed 1,120lb (598kg). It was used into the 1950s. (John Batchelor)

straight through three decks before exploding deep inside the vessel. The blast tore a hole in the keel and ripped along the port side of the ship. Fires started in the magazines and for half an hour a continuous series of explosions prevented fire-fighters from tackling the blaze. Nearly 200 sailors were killed in the attack. The crew responded brilliantly, sealing off flooded compartments and correcting the ship's list to port. After 8 hours of frantic activity, her boilers were relit and the ship set off to steam to Malta for emergency repairs. Four days later, four sailors were found to have survived trapped behind water-tight doors and sealed inside. After returning to the United States, it took eight months to repair the damage caused by this single guided bomb.

Next to be attacked was the British cruiser HMS *Uganda* which was struck by a Fritz-X near Salerno on 13 September 1943. The guided bomb hit at full speed and penetrated through seven decks before exploding, blowing out a section of keel. Later the battleship HMS *Warspite* was hit, the Fritz-X penetrating six decks and detonating in a boiler room.

At first, the attacks were thought to be administered by conventional weapons but the angular trajectory revealed by the trailing smoke soon revealed the fact that the bombs were radio-controlled. The German system involved a Kehl transmitter, operated by the attacking pilot, and a receiver aboard the bomb. This system had been designed for use on the Hs-293 (addressed below) and there was a choice of 18 Kehl/Strassburg frequencies from which to choose the command connection. As soon as the radio control had been recognized by the Allies, radio-frequency jamming began. It was not a success. The frequency was rarely selected correctly; also other simultaneously attacking aircraft would chose disparate frequencies and the defences could use only one at a time. They were quickly overwhelmed.

In time, examples of unexploded Fritz-X missiles were obtained by the Allied scientists and the control mechanism was examined closely and became better understood. After several months, the British designed and constructed their Type 650 transmitter, which worked on the common frequency of 3MHz which was subsequently used as the basic communications frequency for all transmissions to the bombs. This worked for all attacks, and did not rely on finding the command frequency for each individual weapon. Due to the Allies' increasingly efficient counter-measures, the Fritz-X missile was no longer of use to the Germans by the time of the Normandy landings – though its career earlier in World War II was highly successful.

The Fritz-X needed adequate height to function as a weapon capable of piercing a ship's steel decks. Its minimum release altitude was 13,000ft (4,000m) and the minimum flight distance was about 3 miles (5km) from the target. In practice, the chosen altitude was 18,000ft (5,500m). This posed a problem for the pilot of the bomber that delivered it: the plane could easily fly beyond the flight-path of the missile, losing visual contact. Pilots tended to go into a slow climb, thus reducing speed over the ground, so that they remained within sight of the missile and could steer it on its way. The Allies discovered this, of course; it meant that the bomber was now a sitting target for the anti-aircraft gunners. When this ruse worked, it worked well; pilots had a very high rate of success and the attacks on bombers that had launched a Fritz-X bomb became easier with time.

HS-293

Since the vulnerability of the pilot had been recognized early in the war, the German engineers had set out to find an answer. And, as the Fritz-X was being developed as a controlled missile, research was directed to a flying weapon that could regulate itself rather than being steered by a pilot. In 1939 the Gustav Schwartz Propellerwerke produced designs for a glide bomb. It did not have real-time radio control, so the bomber that delivered it did not have to stay on location. Instead, it had its own onboard autopilot that flew it straight and level towards the target. This was the brainchild of Professor Herbert Wagner, chief designer at the Henschel Company, who immediately took up the project. Wagner was an Austrian aeronautical designer who was awarded his doctorate by the University of Berlin when aged 23. He decided to fit the production version with a HWK-109 rocket that could provide 1,320lb (600kg) of thrust for 10 seconds. Unpowered glider versions were first dropped from He-111 aircraft, and powered test runs had been successfully completed before the end of 1940. The finished version was the Hs-293, designed to carry a 1,100lb (500kg) bomb.

A course set by a fixed autopilot proved to be a limitation, and so a radio-controlled system was also tried. This was the highly successful 18-channel Kehl/Strassburg that had also been fitted to the Fritz-X bomb discussed earlier. Unlike the Fritz-X, the shell was contained in a conventional steel housing – this was not a steel-piercing missile. But the Hs-293 was susceptible to the increasingly sophisticated jamming techniques of the Allies, conducted not only by the British but by the Americans and Canadians as well. A particularly successful example was the MAS jammer which could intercept the signals and take over control of the Hs-293 and send it crashing into the sea. Even so, from 1942 to the end of the war, more than 1,000 Hs-293s missiles were manufactured and these glide bombs were a remarkably successful weapon of war.

AZON STRIKES BACK

The only Allied version of a radio-controlled missile appeared late in the war. This was the American Azon guided missile. It had an octagonal assembly of fins at the tail, allowing its navigational position above the ground – its azimuth – to be remotely controlled (the code name was derived from AZimuth ONly; its official designation was the VB-1, standing for 'vertical bomb') and it carried a 1,000lb (450kg) bomb. As in the case of the Fritz-X, a bright flare was fixed to the tail so that its trajectory could be followed by the crew of the delivery aircraft. Others followed; the range extended through to the VB-13 Tarzon which was was a sophisticated glide bomb that was being constructed as World War II ended, and went on to be used in the Korean War (1950–53).

The design was originally proposed by two American engineers, Major Henry Rand and Thomas O'Donnell of the United States 458th Bombardment Group, as a means of attacking the Burma railway and was dropped from a B-24 Liberator which was specially modified for the weapon. Few were used during the war. It was the German bombs that proved the principle, and the Allied version came too late to make a difference. The version produced by the Germans established that a radio-controlled glide bomb was a viable weapon, and it has remained a mainstay of present-day warfare.

THE Hs-293 AND Hs-294

John Batchelor's art shows how secret weapons were designed in various guises as development proceeded. Various versions of the Hs-293 are shown; they gave rise to the Hs-294 (central image). These were glide missiles that were dropped by He-111 aircraft and radio-controlled towards their determined targets. These weapons were susceptible to jamming by Allied radar.

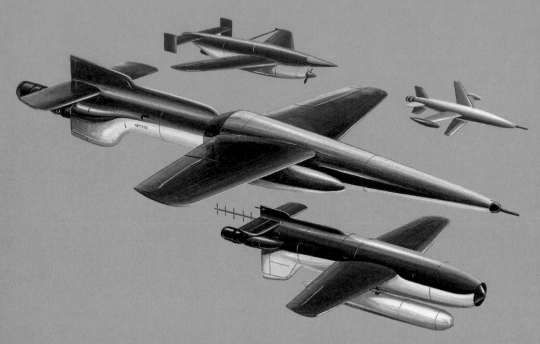

Of the various designs of the Hs-293, the version below was most widely used. The missiles were launched from about 4,900ft (1,500m) and had a range of several miles, controlled by radio from the mother plane. Dozens of Allied ships were destroyed by these secret weapons, which were the world's first guided missiles. Although Allied engineers devised ways of jamming the radio signals that controlled them, they remained in service throughout World War II. (John Batchelor)

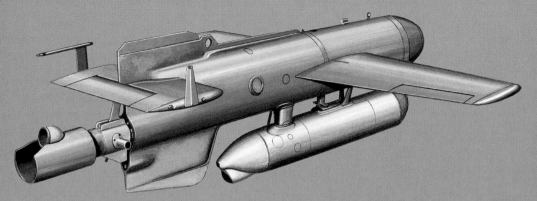

Henschel und Sohn first designed an Hs-293 missile in 1939 for use against Allied ships. After tests with gliders, a liquid-fuel rocket was fitted in 1940 to give 1,300lb (590kg) of thrust and the missile went into production during the remainder of the war, with continued modifications and improvements to the design. With a top speed of 580mph (933km/h) and a length of 12ft 6in (3.82m) the Hs-293 produced a long line of successful attacks, the last one in December 1944. (John Batchelor)

The Henschel Hs-294 missiles were aerial torpedoes, based on the successes of the Hs-293. The Hs-294 first appeared in 1943 and was flown towards the target ship before diving into the sea, breaking off the wings, and proceeding under the surface as a torpedo. Its explosive charge was triggered by the same proximity fuse as those fitted to conventional torpedoes. Although this design was successful in combat, nothing like it is currently in production. (John Batchelor)

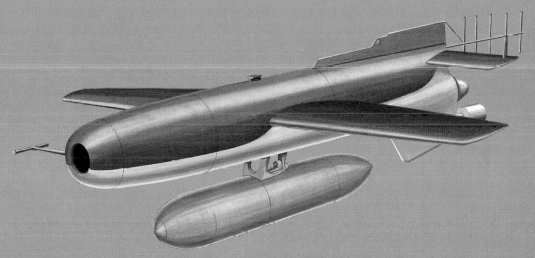

The conspicuous antenna on the tail of this missile was a television aerial necessitated because it was guided with the aid of an on-board television camera. Its Walter HWK 109-507B liquid-fuel rocket engine created 1,300lb (590kg) of thrust, giving it a maximum speed of 280mph (451km/h) and it could deliver a 650lb (295kg) explosive charge over a range of 7.5 miles (12km). (John Batchelor)

THE X-4

Guided by wire that unspooled as it flew, the X-4 8-344 air-to-air missile was designed by Max Kramer at Ruhrstahl in 1943. It was powered by a BMW 109-548 rocket engine and carried a warhead containing 44lb (20kg) of high explosive with a destructive range of 25ft (7.6m). This missile had a top speed of 716mph (1,152km/h) and the control cable was 3.4 miles (5.5km) long. Although roughly 1,000 were built, the Kramer missile was never used in the war. (John Batchelor)

Simpler rocket weapons were also produced by the Germans. Their R4M missiles were air-to-air weapons that could be fired from pods beneath the wings of Fw-190 and Me-262 aircraft; they were used to break up groups of American bombers in the closing months of the conflict.

The United States began developing sophisticated guided rockets late in the war, and some of their designs were remarkably futuristic. The Consolidated-Vultee Aircraft Corporation designed and built the Lark missile, a surface-to-air device designed to be launched from the decks of ships with solid propellant booster rockets. Its range was up to 40 miles (65km) and it delivered an explosive payload weighing 100lb (45kg). Work on the project began in 1944, but it was not ready for use in World War II. During 1946–50 it was used to refine missile systems and was the first American surface-to-air missile to bring down a test drone in flight.

THE PIKE AND THE FIRE-LILY

From the start of the war, the Rheinmetall-Borsig Company had carried out design work on the *Hecht* (Pike) anti-aircraft missile. The Hecht-2700 was conceived as an 8ft (2.5m) long missile weighing 300lb (136kg), fitted with four stabilizing fins, and designed to fly at about 500mph (800 km/h). Within two years the project was ended and no missiles of this type were ever constructed.

But the ideas lived on and gave rise to the *Feuerlilie* (Fire Lily), on which Göring's German Research Institute for Aviation (Deutsche Forschungsanstalt für Luftfahrt) began work in

Originally known as the Hs-297, the Schmetterling missile was first designed in 1941 and revived in March 1943 as the Hs-117 missile. It was constructed of magnesium/aluminium alloy, wood and steel and was powered by a BMW 109-558 rocket motor. The Schmetterling was launched with the aid of two Schmidding 109-553 booster rockets and had a maximum velocity of 650mph (1,046km/h), almost breaking the sound barrier. Deployment was in March 1945, too late to have any effect on the war. (John Batchelor)

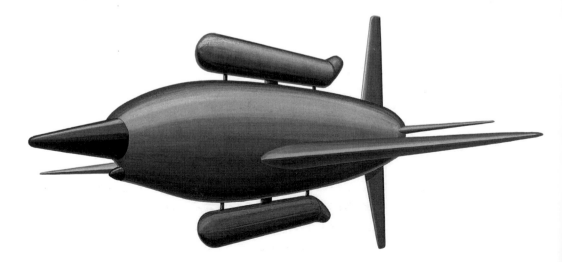

1940. The first version attempted was the Feuerlilie (4.4 F), a scaled-down model designed to prove the principle. From this arose the F-25, produced jointly by the German Gliding Research Institute (Deutsche Forschungsanstalt für Segelflug) and the Post Office Research Department (Reichspost-Forschungsamt). Initial problems with the remote-control system were overcome by early 1943 and wind-tunnel tests proceeded according to plan. Further difficulties were experienced in developing the propulsion system, and it was not until 1943 that the first test firing was attempted at Leba, Poland, on the Baltic Sea. Within a year there had been four tests, though none of them was truly satisfactory.

By now, interest was focusing on the successor – the F-55. This was to be a radio-controlled two-stage device with a solid-fuel first stage and a supersonic liquid-fuel second stage. It would be launched somewhat like a plane, with a sloping ramp for take-off. The Ardelt Company in Breslau was given the contract for the production of five test rockets in January 1943, but problems with both the propulsion unit and the remote-control system persisted. The initial order for 25 missiles was reduced to just 11 late in 1944, and early the following year it was agreed to use the control units designed for the successful Hs-293 which were known to be reliable. Decision making continued to be unpredictable, however, and early in 1945 the entire project was scrapped.

THE BUTTERFLY

No sooner had Professor Herbert Wagner seen his design for the Henschel Hs-293 successfully realized, than he proposed a new missile concept to the German Air Ministry. Wagner could see a tremendous future for guided missiles, and his new invention was the Hs-117 – the *Schmetterling* (Butterfly). This would be the next stage after the Hs-293. The idea was that two people would fly what was, in essence, a miniature exploding aircraft. The pilot would fly a Junkers Ju-188, Ju-388 or Dornier Do-217 that would be specially modified to launch the missile, while the other crewman would be solely concerned with steering it towards its target.

Schmetterling was a great advance; rather than being steered as it glided down to its target, this missile could fly wherever the controller desired and would attack an enemy 3 miles (5km) away, even if it was at an altitude far higher than the delivery aircraft. Today's cruise missiles exploit exactly this kind of technology to the full. It was a brilliant insight, and history has shown how timely Wagner's ingenious concept was.

Even so, it did not impress the Nazis. Hitler was convinced that he would be victorious, and he felt that his government had invested more than enough in the development of novel guided missiles. Work was scaled down and development soon stopped. The High Command changed its mind in 1943, when the large-scale attacks on Germany began to turn the tide. Hitler now wanted everything he could throw back at the Allies, so the Schmetterling was suddenly revived after all, and with the greatest urgency. During 1944 many of the test firings

The Wasserfall surface-to-air guided missile was essentially an anti-aircraft rocket. Its most obvious relation is the V-2 rocket, but unlike that missile it was fitted with a radio guidance system. (Bundesarchiv bild 141-1898)

of prototypes revealed design problems that were methodically rectified, and by the end of the year production was set to start. The order was placed in December, with the missiles scheduled to enter service in March 1945, but by February it was clear that time was running out, and the orders were finally cancelled for good.

WASSERFALL FERNGELENKTE FLAKRAKETE

This futuristic *Wasserfall Ferngelenkte Flakrakete* surface-to-air guided missile – in English: the waterfall remote-controlled anti-aircraft rocket – was designed and developed at Peenemünde on the Baltic coast. In some ways it was similar to the V-2 (p.136) – for example, it was designed to have four tail fins but was also fitted with four near the middle-point of the body to aid control in flight. However, it was one-quarter the size, measuring 26ft (7.9m) tall, with an effective range of 17 miles (27km). And, unlike its famous larger cousin, it could be radio-controlled throughout its flight so it was not a ballistic missile. Another crucial difference was that the V-2, like modern space rockets, was charged with liquid oxygen immediately prior to launch, whereas the Wasserfall was intended to rely on fuels held in store until needed in action, and could then be launched with little notice. In reality, the Wasserfall was intended to stand ready for periods of up to a month and fire on command, so the fuel chosen for the new rocket motor was to be a mixture of vinyl isobutyl ether and SV-Stoff which comprised 94 per cent fuming nitric acid and 6 per cent dinitrogen tetroxide. These were stored in tanks alongside the missile, and were forced in at speed by nitrogen under pressure.

It was the missile's Rheinland guidance system that was particularly ingenious. This used a simple radar unit to track the target, and a transponder on the missile that was tracked by a direction finder at the launch pad. The operator would see the two spots on the screen and home the missile on the target so that the two spots merged. The rocket exhaust could be diverted from side to side by four graphite vanes placed within the exhaust gas – the same system eventually used for the V-2 – in order to establish it in controllable flight. From then on, as the graphite burned away, four ailerons on the tail fins were used to control the trajectory. Like the earlier examples we have already encountered, the radio control was achieved using the proven 18-channel Kehl/Strassburg system. A later modification was designed, in which the missile would itself home in on a radar beam that was pointed at the target (by the operator) and picked up by transponders on the Wasserfall.

The first proposals had been to equip the rocket with a 220lb (100kg) warhead but it was soon recognized that only a direct hit – on a vulnerable target – would make this worthwhile; later proposals were for a 660lb (300kg) liquid explosive payload. It was planned that this would create a relatively large sphere of damage within a squadron of bombers, and bring down a number of enemy planes. This was a weapon for which there was a clear demand, and

The idea for a guided weapon steered through an on-board television camera was envisaged in the US in 1941 by the RCA Company. The result was the so-called Bat Bomb, which could deliver a 1,000lb (454kg) warhead. Later designs were launched from 25,000ft (7,600m), travelled up to 240mph (390km/h), and successfully destroyed Japanese shipping in 1945. (John Batchelor)

John and Joseph Kennedy pictured in their naval uniforms. Joe Kennedy was killed when a B-24 Liberator, filled with explosives as a flying bomb, detonated prematurely in 1944. (Hulton Archive/Getty Images)

the design work began in 1941. Within a year the details of the final specifications had been agreed and the first flight tests started in March 1943. There were setbacks because of the Allied bombings under Operation *Hydra* (p.150) and scarce resources were diverted away from Wasserfall development for a time. Not until February 1945 was there a successful firing that reached a speed of 1,740mph (2,800km/h) in vertical flight. There were some 35 test launches before Peenemünde was finally evacuated as the Allies advanced in February 1945.

The Wasserfall was never deployed; but it represented an advanced kind of remote-control missile and paved the way for later developments. After the war, prototypes were taken back to the United States and test firing took place with a new name – the Wasserfall W-10 was now the American Hermes A-1 Missile. Several modifications to the design were made until the cancellation of the project. By then the A-3 was ready for testing, the project had cost tens of millions of dollars, and it was 1954!

THE AMERICAN FLYING BOMB

The Americans had no super-bomb to match Barnes Wallis's Tallboy, but developed an idea that they hoped would provide an alternative approach. During 1944, the development of a reliable remote guidance system gave rise to a particularly economical proposal – old airplanes, which had come to the end of their useful lives, would be filled with explosives and remotely flown into enemy targets. This was code named Operation *Aphrodite* and was developed under conditions of total secrecy by the United States Eighth Air Force. They took old B-17 and PB4Y bombers that were still flying, but no longer repairable, and stripped out all their surplus equipment, loading them to capacity with explosives.

Simple television cameras were fitted so that the view from the cockpit could be followed from an accompanying CQ-17 mother ship. Each aircraft, packed with twice as much high explosive as it had ever carried as a bomber, was to be taken up by a pilot and his co-pilot who would then bail out, leaving the rest of the flight in the control of the mother-ship pilot who steered the old bomber over the target. The Americans saw these as an alternative to the

Tallboy bombs manufactured for the Royal Air Force, though they lacked the penetrating power and proved to be less useful. The operation was not considered worthwhile, due to a failure to incorporate the most modern technology. It ran from August to December 1944 but few of the missions were successful.

Operation *Anvil* was a similar scheme of the United States Navy over the North Sea between Britain and Germany. They converted their old B-24 bombers to become flying bombs, and had the control handled by an accompanying Ventura PV-1 aircraft. The first mission in August 1944 ended in disaster when the plane exploded in mid-air with a tremendous blast. The two crewmen, Navy lieutenants Wilford J. Willy and Joseph P. Kennedy Jr, were blown to pieces. The young Joe Kennedy was being groomed for the American presidency, and his tragic death meant that his younger brother John Fitzgerald Kennedy took his place. The second mission inflicted damage to German establishments in Heligoland, but missed its intended target and so the scheme was discontinued.

At the same time, a batch of surplus B-24D/J Liberator bombers was converted into radio-controlled flying bombs which were to be used against the fortified installations on Pacific islands held by the Japanese. In the same way as Operation *Aphrodite*, these bombers would be stripped of unnecessary equipment and packed with explosives before being flown to operational altitude by two crew, who would then bail out to safety. Each of these flying weapons contained 25,000lb (11,300kg) of high-explosive Torpex, but the Japanese campaign was never launched.

ENTER THE BUZZ-BOMB

The idea of a pilotless airplane had first been raised in 1937 when the German Air Ministry issued a contract to the Fieseler Company to supply a radio-controlled flying drone for use as a target. They manufactured prototypes of what became the Fi-157, a low-wing monoplane made of wood and intended to be launched from beneath a bomber. They also manufactured a single Fi-158, a piloted version, intended to try out guidance systems. All of the prototypes were failures, and all crashed out of control. Another approach to the problem had been investigated by Fritz Gosslau at Argus Motoren GmbH and they began to develop a drone at the Argus-Flugmotorenwerke in Berlin-Reinickendorf during the same year. Their design was the As-292 and it was designated Flakzielgerät 43 (Flak-Target Apparatus 43). It first flew as a test version in June 1937 and by May 1939 it was successfully tested with remote-control guidance. Arrangements were then made to install cameras and in October 1939 they were obtaining useful reconnaissance photographs. By the end of 1939 an order for 100 of the planes had been placed, and deliveries began in 1942.

As World War II erupted, one of the first decisions of the German Air Ministry was to investigate the design and development of a pilotless aircraft that could deliver an explosive payload weighing 2,200lb (1,000kg) over a distance of 310 miles (500km). Fritz Gosslau at

THE V-1

The Fi-103 V-1 remains one of the most recognizable weapons of World War II, and marked a new era in autopilot cruise missiles. They caused terror across the United Kingdom, particularly in the south, as the Nazis launched at least 100 of these new weapons each day throughout July 1944.

During the war both sides were always trying to discover the other's secret weapons. When a V-1 fell into American hands in 1944, the US were quick to create their own copy, the JB-2. This shows a model under test in a wind tunnel. (NARA)

A V-1 caught in mid-air as it falls on Piccadilly on 22 June 1944, early in the missile attacks on London. (NARA)

First conceived in 1935, and powered by a simple pulse jet, this highly successful cruise missile was first launched in December 1942. It weighed 4,750lb (2,150kg), was 27ft 3¾in long (8.32m) and had a wingspan of 17ft 6in (5.37m). More than 8,000 were launched during the war, destroying 1,270,000 homes and killing 22,900 people. (John Batchelor)

A nose view of a V-1 'doodlebug' installed on its launching platform. The background of this photograph was obscured by German censors. (Keystone/Getty Images)

This scene depicts a night launch of an Fi-103 A-1 over the North Sea by an He-111H-22 of the Luftwaffe bomber wing *Kampfgeschwader* 3. The Heinkel banks away, since the launches were visible over a distance and could attract the attention of RAF Mosquito night fighters. (Jim Laurier © Osprey Publishing)

Argus went into a joint venture with Arado Flugzeugwerke and Lorentz AG to develop the project as a private venture. In April 1940 they announced their provisional design, only to learn within a month that the Air Ministry did not want this weapon after all. The war was going well for Germany, there seemed little opportunity for the weapon to be used in combat operations, and they were not convinced that the little pilotless plane could be safely controlled by radio. But work did not stop, for Gosslau could see the promise of his invention and was determined to have something ready when the tide turned. The engineers at Argus had come up with a design for a pulse jet motor and Gosslau proposed to use two as the propulsion units for his flying machine.

The pulse jet is a simple device. It takes the form of a tubular jet pipe which is closed at the front end by an array of what look like vanes of a Venetian blind. A mist of fuel is injected into the tube and ignited with a spark plug. As it ignites, the vanes slam shut as the fuel explodes and a pulse of hot exhaust is emitted from the rear end of the tube. In flight, this pushes it forward at speed. The lack of air inside the tube, exhausted by the combustion, now causes the burning to cease; the pressure of the air against the vanes blows them open, so a new charge of fresh air rushes in, the new charge of fuel ignites, a further explosion of fuel/air mixture occurs, the vanes snap shut again and so the flight proceeds. The sound is that of a series of muffled fuel explosions repeated 50 times a second and is like a lawnmower engine that needs repair or a small car with a blown gasket. The term 'buzz-bomb' was an inevitable coinage for a weapon that produces a sound like that. In Germany it was nicknamed (at Hitler's instigation) the *Maikäfer* (Cockchafer or June Bug).

As work proceeded, it was agreed to cut down the number of pulse jet motors from two to one, and since Argus were not specialists in airframe construction the assistance of Robert Lusser, technical director at Heinkel, was brought in. In June 1942 General-Fieldmarshal Gerhard Milch gave the authorization of the Ministry for development to proceed as a top priority and in secret. By the end of that year an unpowered version was already being flight-tested. Powered versions posed the problem of starting, since a pulse jet relies on the forward movement of the device to keep going – the jet has to fly at a minimum speed of 150mph (240km/h) to maintain operation. Launching was done by flooding the tube with acetylene and setting fire to it from an external battery. The whole craft was then launched from a ramp and – once at speed – it just kept flying. The ramps were powered by hydrogen peroxide (T-Stoff) and potassium permanganate (Z-Stoff) which generated a burst of gas that accelerated the bomb to a launch speed of 360mph (580km/h).

Once aloft, the V-1, as the missile was commonly known, was guided by a simple autopilot invented by the Askania Company in Berlin. An inertial pendulum was attached to a stabilized gyrocompass and the flaps were controlled by compressed air from two large round tanks pressurized to 150atm (15,000kPa) prior to the launch. The same pressure was also used to feed the fuel into the motor. The early V-1 missiles sent towards London were fitted with small radio transmitters to allow their progress to be monitored. A small propeller on the nose of the craft was fixed to an odometer which counted the revolutions – every 30 rotations of the propeller caused the counter to go down by 1. The initial setting was made to match the distance that the pilotless plane was intended to fly; when it had counted down to zero it was above the destination and had reached the planned target. At this point explosive bolts fired within the control mechanism and the V-1 was set to dive into the target. Many people have thought that the odometer shut off the fuel supply, as the V-1 fell silent as it began to fall. That's not the case – the silence was due to the fact that the sudden drop in the nose prevented the fuel from getting through. The type of V-1 flown later in the war had this fault corrected, so the motor continued to run until the craft hit the ground.

And so the buzz-bomb entered the annals of secret weapons history. The Fieseler Fi-103 V-1 was a flying bomb weighing 4,750lb (2,150kg) and measuring 27ft 3¾in (8.32m) long, 17ft 6in (5.37m) wide from wing tip to wing tip and just 4ft 8in (1.42m) tall. It carried 1,870lb (850kg) of the explosive Amatol-39 and was powered by an Argus As 109-014 pulse jet over a maximum range of 150 miles (250km) and an operating speed of 400mph (640km/h) at an altitude between 2,000 and 3,000ft (600–900m). The buzz-bomb was one of the crudest, cheapest and simplest secret weapons ever developed – and yet it remains one of the best known.

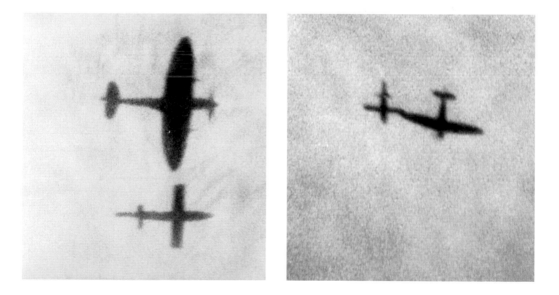

An RAF Supermarine Spitfire edging into position in order to tilt the wing of a V-1 flying bomb to alter its course. The second photograph shows the Spitfire making contact. This was known as 'tipping' a V-1, which required remarkable skill and courage on the part of the pilot. (IWM CH 16280 and IWM CH 16281)

This was Hitler's first weapon of retaliation, and was also the world's first successful cruise missile. Known in full to the Germans as the Vergeltungswaffe-1, and nicknamed by the British 'the doodlebug', it was designed at Peenemünde by the Luftwaffe during World War II as a terror weapon with which to attack major cities – the principal target being London. The very first V-1 was launched towards London on 13 June 1944 and hit a railway bridge

Top: 'Little Joe', the KAN-1 missile, was developed by the United States in response to the Kamikaze attacks launched by the Japanese. It was the first surface-to-air guided missile produced by the Americans, and was designed rapidly in 1945 while the more complex Lark (p.94) was still under development. Using existing take-off rockets, it weighed 1,210lb (550kg), was 11ft 4in (3.45m) long and 22.7in (58cm) in diameter. It was cancelled in 1946. (John Batchelor)

Bottom: The Aeronca GB-1 glide bomb was introduced by the US in 1943. Apart from a steel bar through the wings, the body and twin spars were constructed from wood. A Boeing B-17 could carry two of these weapons, one slung beneath each wing. Although these glide bombs could carry a 2,000lb (907kg) bomb, they were hard to steer and had little effect on the war. (John Batchelor)

on Grove Road, Mile End, killing eight residents. It was just one week after the Allied landings had begun on the Normandy beaches. Within a month, more than 100 of the V-1 weapons were being dispatched to rain down on London every day. Roughly 30,000 V-1s were manufactured, each taking 350 man-hours and costing 4 per cent as much as a V-2

THE PILOTS

Despite the advanced technology, there were problems with the V-1s that couldn't have been foreseen. A German pilot recalled the problems they came up against:

> Because there were no launch sites left in France and Belgium, the V-1 rockets were struggling to reach central London, so in October [1944] we began to fly with them. The main problem with them was the wind. If we didn't judge the wind right we missed London. Also, many of our V-1s got shot down by English flak. We had to climb to 500 metres before we could let go of the V-1, that is if the English fighters didn't get us first... By the time the V-1 came in, we still had a little hope that we could win the war, but not much, as the Allied air power was so superior.

> Ernst Eberling, Imperial War Museum Sound 11389

As the numbers of V-1s over England increased, the RAF pilots sought alternative methods to deal with them, rather than relying on anti-aircraft fire. Of the first 144 missiles that reached the coast in the first V-1 attack, seven were downed by British fighter pilots. The Hawker Tempest was discovered to be the best aircraft for shooting down the rockets due to its speed and 20mm cannon, but by late June pilots discovered that they could also 'tip' the V-1 over by flying alongside and banking their aircraft – the missile could not cope with the change of direction, and so would fall to the ground. Squadron-Leader Berry was the most successful at downing a doodlebug, claiming 60 V-1 rockets:

> There is a new kind of battle going on in the skies over London – Spitfires versus the German Flying Bombs... Mind you, I can say from personal experience that the Doodle Bug doesn't go down easily... You have to aim at the propulsion unit – that's the long stove-pipe, as we call it, on the tail. If your range and aim are dead on, you can see pieces flying off the stove-pip. The big white flame at the end goes out, and down goes the bomb.

> Squadron-Leader Joseph Berry, BBC radio interview

This V-1 was one of many that prematurely crashed in the French countryside shortly after launch. The fuselage has split open, exposing one of its two pressurized air bottles. (NARA)

rocket. Altogether 9,521 doodlebugs landed in Britain before the final launch site was occupied by the Allies in October 1944. The remaining weapons available to the Germans were then trained on Antwerp, which received 2,448 attacks until March 1945 when the Allies captured the final launch ramp. The V-1s killed a total of 22,892 people and almost every one of them was a civilian. This was a sustained terror bombing, a cruel and vindictive campaign against a defiant enemy.

The British were at a loss as to how to defend themselves against the relentless attacks. They began to use barrage balloons that were large hydrogen-filled blimps, such as those discussed earlier in this book, with lines of steel cables hanging down in a long array. These were intended to intercept flying bombs as they approached, but the leading edge of the V-1 was able to cut the cables and only about 300 buzz-bombs were claimed to have been brought down by the barrage balloons. The Allies also began to use simple analogue computers to calculate the aim of anti-aircraft guns in June 1944. Just 17 per cent of the flying bombs were brought down by gunfire during their first week on the south coast, but with the assistance of the simple computers this rose to 60 per cent by 23 August and 74 per cent by the end of that month. On the best day, 82 per cent of the V-1s launched were destroyed by Allied guns.

Aircraft were relatively ineffective against the V-1. The fighters that were fast enough to catch them included the Hawker Tempest, the Mustang and the Griffon-engined Spitfire XIV. On several occasions – but not many – a V-1 was brought down by being tipped off-balance by the wing of a fighter flying alongside. In the closing months of war, the Gloster Meteor jet fighter was rushed into service with 616 Squadron to catch and disable V-1s. Some 13 of the buzz-bombs were shot out of the sky by this new British jet fighter.

In 1944 there were discussions on how to mislead the Germans about the results of their V-1 attacks. The obvious way to feed false information would be to report the weapons as overshooting the target; the Germans (if they believed the reports) would adjust their flight times to compensate and have the weapons falling in Kent, rather than on the capital. This was not considered realistic. The sites of impact were being reported by the newspapers, large and small, to which the Germans could have access through neutral nations. Instead it was decided to feed information about all the genuine hits to the north of London. The cumulative effect might be that the Germans would conclude they were overshooting the capital – and the reports would be confirmed by those they saw in the newspapers.

This ruse seems to have worked, and post-war calculations held that the number of fatalities had been reduced by half as a result. Nonetheless, it was a V-1 that made the last enemy attack on British soil in the war, when the final missile hit Datchworth, Hertfordshire, on 29 March 1945.

The pulse jet was brought into other designs, too; one was for an attack vessel filled with explosives and a prototype was built from a *Sprengboot* – a wooden craft crammed with high explosive – with a pulse jet screwed to the top. In didn't work, and such craft were experimentally fitted with conventional piston engines from then on. Pulse jets were also used by the Japanese. An Argus pulse jet was taken to Japan by sea in 1943 and the Kawanishi Baika was the result, though it existed only as a design and was never constructed. The Japanese also proposed building the Mizuno Shinryu, a kamikaze plane powered by pulse jet, though it, too, was never built. Post-war France manufactured versions of their own (modified from the German blueprints) to use as target drones under the designation CT-10 – some of which were later sold on to Britain and the United States.

The Soviets brought back components of the V-1 when they occupied Blizna, Poland. The version produced in Russia was the Izdeliye-10 and test launches were made at a range in Tashkent. They also considered the mass-production of a piloted version but these plans were abandoned when their chief test pilot died in the crash of a modified Izdeliye-10. They continued to work on modifying the V-1 design into the 1950s, by which time onboard television monitoring was offering radical new ideas for cruise missile design.

The United States began work on their version of a V-1 before the war ended. In 1944 they shipped parts of recovered V-1 missiles to America from Britain and by September they had built their own version, a prototype Republic-Ford JB-2 known as the Loon. The design was almost identical to the German V-1 but with a slightly increased wing area, the JB-2 having 61ft^2 (5.6m^2) compared to 55ft^2 (5.1m^2) for the original V-1. The wingspan was an extra 2.5in (6.4cm) wider and the entire fuselage was 2ft (0.6m) longer. The original intention was to use these German-designed missiles against Japan as a key component of what was code named Operation *Downfall*. A Navy version, the KGW-1, was also designed and ready. Plans were in place to produce 1,000 of these missiles per month, and an order for 75,000 was planned, but by the war's end none had ever been fired in action by the United States. Within a few years research had been transferred to more modern projects, but the influence of the V-1 remains with us. It was the world's first successful cruise missile and those that have followed owe much to the original German research. Today's cruise missiles are equipped with sophisticated navigational and communications technology, and can be monitored and controlled over a vast distance. Thanks to the internet and satellites, the operator need no longer be even on the same continent. But, when we consider today's weaponry, it is a simple matter to think back to how it started, and to imagine the threatening growl of an approaching V-1 in World War II. From that to the cruise missile of today is a leap in time – but not in principle.

THE ROCKET

GERMANY BEGAN HER RE-EMERGENCE from the shadows of World War I as the established disciplines – after stopping dead in their tracks as that war ended – began slowly to recover. The industry of Germany had already shown its pre-eminence in fields such as chemical engineering, particularly in drugs and dyes, and in manufacture, where names like Mercedes, Daimler, Benz and Diesel remain to this day as hallmarks of German excellence and innovation. These crucial fields had fostered an elevated cultural position for engineering in German society. To be addressed as an engineer in Germany is on a par with being a surgeon or a film director. In many Western societies an engineer is the person who replaces the drive belt in your washing machine or overcharges you for what should have been a routine service on your car. For Germans, the problem solving that engineers use and the mental disciplines of the design process are among the greatest and most admirable of traits. This is as true today as it was in a previous century.

A sense of reassertion was the inevitable rebound against the disgrace imposed by the Treaty of Versailles. Throughout the Weimar Republic, which flourished between 1919 and Hitler's coming to power in 1933, Germany had lived within the humiliating constraints of Versailles. There were lists of restrictions on the machinery of war; but they served only to optimize the German effort in the post-World War I years. The German Army was set at a maximum limit of 100,000 soldiers and so, because of this burdensome constraint, the authorities had to ensure that every single member of the forces was of the highest possible quality. In consequence, although the German Army was one of the smallest, it soon became by far the most highly qualified and efficient army in the world. There were strict limits on artillery and on gun manufacture, so enormous emphasis was now being placed on maximizing every aspect of development in these fields. Because there was little military interest in rocketry during World War I, rockets were omitted entirely from the provisions in the Treaty of Versailles. This curious fact was to underpin the progress towards World War II, and to mould the conduct of all future wars. Whoever was responsible for this omission gave a massive impetus to the study of rockets and, eventually, to the landing of a man on the moon. The story of the rocket epitomizes the development of modern warfare, and the unexpected legacy of ill-thought-out restrictions imposed by victorious nations on the vanquished foe.

The young German elite of the Weimar Republic were not simply thinking of Germany's current role, but were looking to the future. All around the world, there was a sense of rebirth. In an era when the brutality of world war seemed to have been conclusively ended, brave new horizons opened up. The Tsar and his family had been eliminated in Russia and the reign of the Kaiser had been ended in Germany. In this resurgent nation of Germany it was felt that dreams could perhaps become reality. The greatest dream of all was that humans could leave the earth and travel into space – and suddenly even this seemed to be on the verge of possibility in the minds of many. The twentieth century marked the time when space rockets emerged from being the hallmark of futuristic fiction into the full glare of reality, and it was the pressures of World War II that were harnessed to bring it about. German rocketry during World War II did more than any other single aspect to shape the post-war world and its story is rich in resonances of the national culture, and of the time. It is timely to look for the origins of this great new adventure, and we can also see how resurgence was greeted differently in Germany to how it was received elsewhere. There are lessons here to learn. No wonder the word that we use for this sense of time is not English, but German: *Zeitgeist*.

FIRST ROCKETS

No reader will be surprised that the origins of rockets as agents of warfare lay in China. There have been occasional references to 'fireworks' in antiquity, though nobody can be sure whether these connote anything more than the use of incendiary devices. Gunpowder was long in the making, and we can be certain that alchemists had experimented with inflammable powders for centuries before explosives were perfected. The discovery of black powder is agreed to have been in ninth-century China, and emerged from experiments by Taoist philosophers. Rockets were an inevitable consequence. The first rockets were made by packing black powder into stems of bamboo, and the Mongol ruler Genghis Khan and his son Ögedei used them successfully against Europeans in the thirteenth century. And so rockets were being used in warfare 700 years ago.

Yet it was in India that the first metal rockets were designed and built. The British East India Company fought for decades to subdue the kingdom of Mysore and in 1792 rockets made of iron were designed and built for the rulers of Mysore, Haider Ali and his son Tipu Sultan. The metal casing was some 8in (20cm) long and gave these rockets a range of over half a mile (about 2km) and they so surprised the British that attempts were made to copy them. Examples were sent back to the Royal Arsenal at Woolwich, London, where Sir William Congreve developed the design and introduced the (better-known) Congreve rocket which was successful in the Napoleonic wars. Although the Congreve rocket deserves a place in the history of rocketry, it was the Indian craftsmen who had produced the first successful iron rockets. They were launched in their thousands and deserve a conspicuous place in military history.

These rockets were stabilized by having a rod protruding from the rear, just like today's firework rockets launched from a bottle. In 1844 a self-taught British inventor, William Hale, improved the design so that the thrust was slightly vectored to produce spin along the axis of travel like a rifle bullet. The flight path was stabilized by this design change and the stick was no longer needed. The largest Congreve rockets had weighed up to 32lb (15kg) and Hale's design allowed this to be doubled to 60lb (about 28kg). These were used by the Americans during the Mexican–American War of 1846–48 and the British Army also used Hale rockets during the Crimean War of 1853–56.

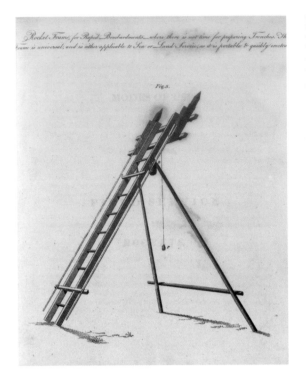

Sir William Congreve published this plate in *A Concise Account of the Origin and Progress of the Rocket System* in 1810. Congreve successfully demonstrated a solid-fuel rocket in 1805 based on designs by Indian engineers. (SSPL/Getty Images)

EARLY RUSSIAN AND FRENCH ROCKETRY

It was in the early years of the twentieth century that matters began to develop in several countries. A Russian high school mathematics teacher named Konstantin Tsiolkovsky published a paper entitled *The Exploration of Cosmic Space by Means of Reaction Devices* which was the first scientific work on rocketry. He proposed the use of liquid hydrogen and oxygen as propellants and calculated the maximum exhaust velocity they could generate. The publication date of this far-sighted book was 1903.

Knowing nothing of his Russian predecessor, a French aviator named Robert Esnault-Pelterie delivered a lecture to the French Physics Society (Societé Française de Physique) in 1912 entitled 'Consideration of the Results of the Unlimited Lightening of Motors' in which he included similar calculations on the output of rocket engines, and even advocated nuclear power (from half a ton of radium) as an energy source for long-distance space travel. Esnault-Pelterie was later in contact with Romanian-born Hermann Oberth, who was destined to become one of Germany's greatest authorities on military rockets.

THE FIRST AMERICAN ROCKET

It was also in 1912 that the American enthusiast Robert Goddard began his study of rockets. He proposed a small combustion chamber as the best source of power and even outlined the use of multi-stage rockets. Goddard was a highly enterprising visionary and ensured that his ideas were patented in 1914. He patented two inventions. The first was for a rocket using liquid fuel; the second was for a two- or even a three-stage rocket propelled by solid fuel. Two years later he compiled a paper on rocketry at Clark College in Worcester, Massachusetts. In 1919 the Smithsonian Institution published this paper as a modest book entitled *A Method of Reaching Extreme Altitudes*. In the following year Goddard was published in the prestigious science journal *Nature* where he began with these propitious words:

Konstantin Tsiolkovsky, Russian pioneer in rocketry and space research. During the 1920s he expanded on his theories of multi-stage rockets and of the flight of jet engines. (Photo by SSPL/Getty Images)

The French aviation pioneer Robert-Albert-Charles Esnault-Pelterie had ideas about rocket engines and nuclear power that were ahead of his time. (Popperfoto/Getty Images)

It is the purpose of the present article to state the general principles and possibilities of the method of reaching great altitudes with multiple charge rockets, from which the exploded gases are ejected with high efficiency. *

Goddard spent time over the next few years perfecting his design for a rocket with liquid fuel and his first successful rocket flight took place on 16 March 1926 at Auburn, Massachusetts. It flew from a 6ft (1.8m) gantry on a short, explosive flight that lasted no more than 3 or 4 seconds; but it proved that the concept worked. Within three years his improved specifications gave steadily improving results – his small rockets could now travel some 200ft (70m) at speeds of up to 60mph (about 95km/h). In 1930 he logged an altitude of 2,000ft (6,000m) and a velocity of 500mph (800km/h). This was truly astonishing progress.

Little general interest was shown in Goddard's work at the time, and what comments were published had an unenthusiastic tone. Goddard never had the satisfaction of seeing his

---

* Goddard, Robert H., 'A Method of Reaching Extreme Altitudes', *Nature* 105: 809–811, 1920.

Liquid-fuelled rockets were pioneered by Dr Robert H. Goddard at Auburn, Massachusetts. This small device was fired in March 1926 and he recorded: 'It rose 41ft & went 184ft in 2.5 secs, after the lower half of the nozzle burned off.' By 1937 his rockets had reached 9,000ft (2,700m). (Author's collection)

views take root. Those who knew of his work regarded him largely as a crank.

One of Goddard's most influential inventions was a portable rocket-powered shell that could be launched by a soldier. With a colleague, Clarence Hickman, Goddard had given a successful demonstration of his invention at the United States Army Signal Corps at the Aberdeen Proving Ground, Maryland, in November 1918. The demonstration was a complete success, but the war ended two days later and the proposal did not develop further. It was revived in World War II, and went on to evolve into the bazooka (p.136), which became one of the best-known rocket-powered devices in history.

Goddard had declared his private beliefs in the class oration which he gave on graduating back in 1904. 'It has often proved true that the dream of yesterday is the hope of today,' he said, 'and the reality of tomorrow.' The twentieth century, and the remarkable events of World War II, would prove how true those words would be.

ROCKET VISIONARIES

Rockets had been used during World War I, first by the French. In April 1916, Le Prieur rockets fired from the struts of a Nieuport fighter had brought down the German Zeppelin LC-77 full of blazing hydrogen. Later in the conflict a Belgian flyer, Willy Coppens, and a British pilot, Albert Ball, used small experimental rockets against German balloons. Nothing came of either event, and incendiary shells were found to be more effective.

During the 1920s there were enthusiasts studying rocketry in Russia, France and the United States, but there was little sense of common purpose. In Germany, however, the burgeoning sense of nationalism began to catch the popular imagination. Hermann Oberth was one of the greatest visionaries. He was a medical student at Munich and in 1922 he wrote to Goddard in America to request reprints of his writings on rocketry. Oberth was writing a book which in 1923 was published as *Die Rakete zu den Planetenräumen* (*The Rocket into Interplanetary Space*) in which he emphasized how much he had been impressed by Goddard's writings, which he cited, but went on to write that his book had not in any way plagiarized his American forebear. But interest was suddenly growing in Germany. The very next year Max Valier published *Der Vorstross in Weltraum* (*The Drive to Outer Space*) and a year after that Walter Hohmann published his book entitled *Die Erreichbarkeit der Himmelskörper* (*The Attainability of Celestial Bodies*). This volume was so technically detailed that it was still being consulted decades later by NASA. In 1926 Willy Ley published his popular book *Die Fahrt ins Weltall* (*Journey into Space*) and in July 1927 a group of amateur rocketry enthusiasts – engineers, scientists, doctors, students – met at a restaurant in Breslau to launch the Society for Space Travel (Verein für Raumschiffahrt, known as the VfR), with Hermann Oberth at its heart. It is worth noting that this was an association, not a university department. Although rockets were suddenly fashionable, they remained a subject for amateurs.

THE GERMAN SOCIETY FOR SPACE TRAVEL

Within a few weeks of its launch in June 1927, the Society for Space Travel recruited a new member: the young Wernher von Braun, who was destined to become the most influential

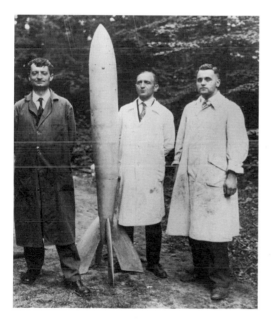

Romanian-born Hermann Oberth, left, stands alongside his rocket with two assistants in 1930. He claimed the rocket could deliver mail to New York from Berlin in 24 minutes and rise 62 miles (100km) into the stratosphere. (Getty Images)

Hermann Oberth was regarded as one of the fathers of modern astronautics. He experimented on weightlessness and designed a long-range liquid-propelled rocket. In 1941 he was assistant to the German rocket engineer Von Braun. (SSPL/Getty Images)

rocket designer of all. Membership of the Society – mostly young scientists and engineers – soon rose to about 500 and they inaugurated a regular magazine, *Die Rakete* (*The Rocket*). Von Braun was among the group (others were Walter Hohmann, Klaus Riedel, Eugen Sänger, Rudolf Nebel and Max Valier as well as Hermann Oberth and Willy Ley) who were popularizing the science of rockets. Valier organized tests of rockets attached to cars, gliders, railway trucks and even sledges. The first tests took place at a former ammunition dump at Reinickendorf, which soon earned the nickname *Raketenflugplatz* (Rocket Airfield) and today is the site of Tegel Airport.

By 1930 the Society for Space Travel was so well established that its members set up a permanent office in Berlin and agreed a design for a rocket motor powered by gasoline and liquid oxygen. This was the Mirak-1. It had its combustion chamber surrounded by the liquid oxygen tank. The liquid fuel was supplied from a hollow tail stick acting as a storage reservoir. The 'head' of the rocket was 1ft (30cm) in length; the tail measured about 3ft (1m) long. The first experimental firing was successful, but the oxygen tank exploded on the second test.

Max Valier pictured here in his rocket car, designed in 1929. He experimented with rocket vehicles and died when an alcohol-fuelled rocket car exploded in 1930. (Bundesarchiv Bild 1020-01350)

THE ROCKET

Early in 1931, Karl Poggensee launched his design for a solid-fuel rocket near Berlin. He fitted it with cameras, a speedometer and an altimeter which showed that it reached 1,500ft (450m) before landing by parachute. The first German rocket with liquid fuel was launched in the same year by Johannes Winkler and Hugo Huckel who were independent enthusiasts and not members of the Society. Their choice of fuel was liquid oxygen and methane burned in a rocket some 2ft (60cm) long. Just as had happened with the Mirak-1, the first test near Dessau was successful (the rocket reached 1,000ft, about 300m) but the second test launch in East Prussia failed when fire burst from the rocket and it crashed after reaching an altitude of 10ft (just over 3m). In April 1931 Reinhold Tiling tested a series of four solid-fuel rockets at Osnabrück. One detonated at 500ft (about 150m) but the others were successfully fired – one reaching 6,600ft (2,000m) at a maximum speed of 700mph (1,100km/h). One of his later rockets was reckoned to have reached 11,500ft (3,505m).

Research by the Society for Space Travel was moving ahead. Their new design of rockets was proposed by Willy Ley who called them Repulsors. It is a revealing choice of name. Earlier rockets had been given neutral names, or (like the Huckel/Winkler rockets) were named after their inventors. 'Repulsor' sounds much more like a military device and perhaps Willy Ley was already thinking of using military money to further his research. Like the Mirak rockets, the Repulsor burned a combination of liquid oxygen and gasoline but the combustion chamber was cooled by water in a double-walled metal jacket, rather than being cooled by the liquid oxygen. This was an inherently safer design. In May 1931 two of the Repulsor rockets reached a height of 200ft (61m). With the development of the Repulsor-3, an altitude of 2,000ft (610m) was reached and later in 1931 Repulsor-4 rockets were reportedly reaching a mile into the sky. Although rocketry was internationally regarded with indifference – and was usually dismissed, even ridiculed, whenever it emerged – in Germany it was allowing fresh new minds to find satisfaction.

In 1932 the Society for Space Travel first came to the attention of the authorities. This was not because the enthusiasts were seen as brilliant young men, but because there had been complaints about the rocket tests from people living in the area due to the noise. The Society's members had no specific authorization to carry out testing, and there was a growing fear about the increasing influence of Hitler. Hitler had begun to issue directives that restricted the activities of all organizations that had significant ties to the outside world as his influence began to grow. Members became increasingly nervous and began to drift away. In a period of economic collapse, the Society could not manage to meet its financial obligations without the membership income and later in 1933 the Society for Space Travel finally closed down. It is surprising to realize that world's first ever rocketry organization – the results of which were to revolutionize warfare – was shut down largely because of pressure from the authorities.

CIVILIAN RESEARCH CONTINUES

Even after the demise of the Society for Space Travel, some members were able to continue their activities. Some of the senior staff within the German Army had been persuaded that rocketry might yet prove to be important and as early as 1931 they had allowed Society members to conduct a test launch at the army proving ground at Kummersdorf. The rocket they authorized for the launch was a Repulsor. Its name doubtless endeared it to the military Carl Becker. As soon as he saw that the Kummersdorf people were supporting rocket development, Wernher von Braun asked permission to continue his experiments as part of his doctoral thesis on rocket propulsion. His luck was in, and he was authorized to continue to use the Kummersdorf facility. Despite the collapse of the Society Von Braun's private passion was saved.

Meanwhile an engineer named Franz Mengering, who worked for the City of Magdeburg, had become a devotee of the writings of Peter Bender. Bender propounded the *Hohlweltlehr* (hollow world doctrine) which held that – instead of being a globe – the world was a hollow sphere. Instead of flying the long way round to Australasia, Bender asserted that it would be quicker to fly straight up in the air. In this way a rocket could easily hit New Zealand. Mengering was convinced that it would be easy to prove, using a small rocket with a message from Germany. If Bender's theory was correct, then the missile would land near the South Island of New Zealand. Franz Mengering even managed to persuade the authorities at Magdeburg to fund some trial experiments. Rudolf Nebel, one of the founders of the Society for Space Travel, successfully applied for a grant of 25,000 Reichsmarks to fund the design of the rocket. Nebel had joined the Nazi Party and ingratiated himself with the authorities and stated his ambition to fly a man in a rocket 1km (over half a mile) above the earth's surface, from where he would descend by parachute. The rocket would be designed with his partner Herbert Schäfer. They proposed to launch their rocket in June 1933 as part of a major fair promoting the city of Magdeburg. The idea was to adapt the Repulsor design, with a volunteer secured inside in a torpedo-shaped fairing below the motor. The fuels would be stored in two long tubes trailing behind the rocket. It would be 25ft (7.6m) tall and a 14ft (4.6m) unmanned prototype would be used to prove that the idea worked.

In June 1933 they attempted their first launch of a test rocket at nearby Wolmirstedt, but it did not even leave the 30ft (10m) launch tower. The only successful flight was from Lindwerder Island in one of the numerous lakes that surround Berlin. It is reported to have reached 3,000ft (1,000m) before crashing to the ground only 300ft (100m) from the launch pad, which must have been a highly stimulating experience for the panicking launch crew. Some further tests were conducted from a boat moored in Lake Schwielow in August 1933, but the results were a disappointment with some of the rockets looping uncontrollably across the sky. Eventually, the whole Magdeburg Project was closed down and Nebel received just 3,200 Reichsmarks of the promised grant for his efforts.

THE NAZI ROCKETS

The chief of the Army Ordnance Bureau (the Heereswaffenamt), Colonel Carl Becker, was an expert on ballistics. In 1926 he had drafted a short paragraph on military rockets for the *Army Textbook of Ballistics* and in 1929 he issued instructions to contact any amateur rocket societies whose enthusiasts might have useful insights into how rockets could perhaps be developed. Becker was aware that rockets had not been referred to in the Treaty of Versailles, and he knew that there could be no restriction on further research into this potentially important area of ballistics. In the following year, Captain (later Major-General) Walter Dörnberger joined Becker's office to start work on a possible new solid-fuel rocket with a range of up to 5 miles (8km).

Bureaucracy was quick to play a part. It was decided that the proposals for solid-fuel rockets could best be advanced if there was an official development and testing facility, and the result was the establishment of the Army Ordnance Bureau's Research and Development Department (the Heereswaffenamt-Prüfwesen, conveniently known for short as the Wa Prüf) at Versuchsstelle Kummersdorf-West. This would become a development laboratory and a testing site for missiles. The Heereswaffenamt-Prüfwesen had been established in 1919 as the Reichwaffenamt (RWA), and adopted the name Heereswaffenamt (HWA) in 1922. As the Nazi Party began to assert its position and Germany began to move to a warlike posture during the 1930s, the task of overseeing the rearmament was handed over to the Army Acceptance Organization (the Heeresabnahmestelle, abbreviated to the Abnahme), a subsidiary of the Army Ordnance Bureau. Whether those involved ever understood it all is far from clear.

For a while, Dörnberger covertly provided funds for the Society for Space Travel but this stopped when he encountered a conflict between his interests in military rocketry, and the enthusiasts' focus solely on space flight. However his engineers were pragmatists, and research on the solid-fuel rockets quickly showed that their applications would always be limited.

Hugo Schneider AG of Leipzig produced the *Fliegerfaust* (Lucky Flyer), this ground-to-air rocket launcher, in 1944. The production version had eight chambers and was 3ft 3in (150cm) long, weighing 14lb (6.5kg). The rockets were fired from alternate barrels in a timed sequence, to avoid the rocket exhaust from the first firing interfering with those that followed. Ten thousand were ordered, but only 60 were ever used. It never entered service. (John Batchelor)

Dörnberger soon realized that they were heading nowhere. He knew that he had to speak again with the enthusiasts. Many of them had academic interests in the technology of liquid-fuel rocket development. He was also aware that building rockets is a costly affair and the Society for Space Travel was always short of funds. When in 1932 Von Braun was offered the chance to become a professional rocket developer, rather than amateur enthusiast, he was delighted to accept. His ambitions to develop bigger and better rockets were suddenly within reach, while Dörnberger knew that he was establishing a new facility that would lead him to military pre-eminence. At the time Von Braun joined there was little official enthusiasm for rocketry, but the increased military tensions allowed the Kummersdorf administration to claim a steadily expanding budget. By 1936 the total number of staff was 60, and by the outbreak of war it was almost 300. They were the cream of German rocket enthusiasts and were a new breed; so too were the weapons they were starting to develop.

Dörnberger and Von Braun had very different personal priorities. Dörnberger could envisage the crucial influence of missiles in the military arena, while Von Braun always wanted more than anything else in the world – to build bigger and better rockets. When the Nazis swept to power in 1933, Dörnberger sensed that the ultimate quest was military supremacy, and he knew that the new generation of rocketry enthusiasts could offer untold benefits to the army of an expansionist state. These new weapons could lead Germany towards world domination. For Von Braun it was different. It was the majesty of the space rocket that lured him on. Dörnberger could see that his military career offered the chance of spectacular professional success, whereas Von Braun recognized that the growing might of the German military machine could be tapped for all the funding, all the technical support and all the security that his private passions demanded.

BUILDING THE A-1 AND A-2

Under Dörnberger, the research institute at Kummersdorf had established itself as a major facility for the development and testing of a number of rocket-assisted take-off units for aircraft, using solid fuel. Von Braun found himself responsible for conducting the tests under Major Wolfram von Richthofen and Ernst Heinkel. Under Dörnberger's leadership, the team designed and built their first liquid-fuel Aggregate-1 (A-1) rocket. It was powered by liquid oxygen and alcohol. The fuel and oxidant were forced into the combustion chamber by pressure from a liquid-nitrogen tank and the rocket could develop a thrust of about 660lb (300kg). A heavy gyroscope was installed in the nose cone to stabilize the rocket during

---

Opposite: His arm raised and in a plaster cast from a motoring accident, Von Braun was here photographed in May 1945 by American officials. This photo is of interest as it also shows Major-General Walter Dörnberger, Commander of the Army Peenemünde Centre; Lieutenant-Colonel Herbert Axter, chief of the military staff at Peenemünde; and Hans Lindenberg, the rocket combustion chamber designer. (NARA)

flight. Tests showed that the design of the A-1 was flawed. The small liquid oxygen tank concealed within its alcohol fuel tank was prone to failure, with catastrophic consequences. Furthermore, the gyroscope was too far from the middle of the rocket to stabilize it effectively. As a result, the A-1 was abandoned.

The A-2, which soon followed, had alcohol and liquid oxygen tanks that were safely separated from each other, and the gyroscope was located near the middle of the rocket between the two fuel tanks. In December 1934 the first two A-2 rockets were ready. They were dubbed Max and Moritz after cartoon characters in German comics. The cartoons had first emerged in 1865 from the pen of the German caricaturist Wilhelm Busch, who is said to have had a profound influence on the then-new comic strip industry in the United States. The two rockets bearing the affectionate nicknames were launched from Borkum, an island off the Dutch coast in the Baltic Sea. Both reached about 6,500ft (2,000m) and the military authorities were pleased with the results. In 1935, Carl Becker (now a General) put together a proposal to Hitler in which he advocated the development of a large long-range rocket for the bombardment of enemy territory. It would, he impressed upon the Führer, offer a highly intimidating weapon against any future enemy of the Reich. Hitler considered the proposal, and rejected it out of hand. There was no future for large rockets in the German military, concluded the Führer. When they wanted to dominate a nation, they would use political power or military might to do so. Army missiles need not feature in his plans.

SÄNGER JOINS THE TEAM

Nevertheless, Eugen Sänger, whose proposals for the 'antipodal bomber' we have already encountered (p.65), was thought of by the engineering fraternity as a leading figure in rocket development and was invited to join the research teams at the Air Force Research Centre at Trauen (between Berlin and Bremen) to investigate the improvement of rocket motor design. Eschewing highly volatile fuels, and determining to work with more prosaic ingredients, Sänger designed a liquid-fuel rocket motor that ran on ordinary diesel oil and liquid oxygen. He soon had engines running on a static bench for half an hour, at the time an incredible feat. Other specialists were assigned to develop specific areas – telemetry (control systems), fuel combinations and so on – so that the rocket designers had an increasingly detailed knowledge base on which to rely. The majority of these research workers had no idea that they were jointly working on mechanisms that might eventually be used in giant rockets; they were brought in for a specific research project, and secrecy over its eventual purpose was strictly maintained. To the military strategists, and even (at the time) to the German High Command, rockets remained a curiosity and were still seen as being more useful for delivering small payloads, or for assisting the take-off of planes from aircraft carriers. The engineers were aware that they needed to keep the research moving ahead, even if their Führer could not see the point; and so plans for monster rockets were soon to emerge.

PEENEMÜNDE IS BORN

Public protests about the noise and danger from the test firings at Kummersdorf meant there was a clear need for a new facility, well away from large populations and with plenty of space for testing larger rockets. In 1935 the decision was taken to find a new, remote location and enquiries began. During the Christmas holidays that followed, Von Braun accepted an invitation to spend some time with friends near the coast of the Baltic Sea. They lived at Anklam, between Stettin and Straslund, by the Peene River. There was an island named Usedom nearby, with just a few inhabitants living on an isolated, rural existence; the Baltic island of Greifswalder Oie lay on the horizon, and beyond that stretched the open Baltic – it was the perfect location for a rocket base. Von Braun reported back to Dörnberger, who asked for more details and later went to inspect the area personally. It was quickly resolved to transfer the research to this new base at the mouth of the Peene River – in German, Peenemünde.

By April 1937 the rocket organization was relocated to its new top-secret base at Peenemünde. This was destined to become the birthplace of modern rocketry, and since 1992 it has been part of the Military Research Centre (Heeresversuchsanstalt Peenemünde) an Anchor Point of the European Route of Industrial Heritage. The staff at the Army Experimental Station at Peenemünde (Heeresversuchsstelle Peenemünde) set out to improve upon the successful A-2 rocket and design a successor, the A-3. The result was a 1,650lb (750kg), 21ft (7m) long rocket burning liquid oxygen and alcohol fuel. By the end of 1937 the Peenemünde team had developed and were ready to test the prototypes. The first failed, and so did the test launches that followed. To the engineers it was obvious that the urgent rush to launch had been too swift. Early problems with the rocket had shown that the tail fins needed to be redesigned; and even when this had been done new problems were emerging. The propulsion system of the A-3 was a success but its inertial guidance system still did not function correctly and further work was initiated to solve this technical problem.

An A-3 rocket mounted at Kummersdorf on stand no. 3. This was the largest at Kummersdorf and could be moved along the rails that can be seen in the photograph. (Science Photo Library)

Hitler is cheered by crowds on a visit to the Sudetenland in 1938. His view on the need for rockets fluctuated wildly during the war. In the early 1940s he felt the tide of the conflict was moving to benefit Germany and so he would have little need for costly technology. (Getty Images)

A new approach was needed – in future, every aspect would be bench tested separately and proved to work, prior to being incorporated into the final design. And so a revised policy was drawn up, in the remote vastness of Peenemünde. The German researchers laid their plans, confident that their secret location gave them the chance to make progress, away from prying eyes.

In 1938, Germany began encroaching upon the territory of nearby nations. The occupation of the Sudetenland was at first resisted, but by the end of the year the situation had been accepted by the major powers and Hitler's expansionism suddenly seemed irresistible. Hitler was encouraged to think again about rocketry and began to recognize the need for an effective ballistic weapon. The Army Ordnance Department decided that the Peenemünde teams should proceed to design a ballistic missile. It should have a range of up to 200 miles (about 320km) and deliver a 1-ton explosive warhead. It was agreed that there were constraints upon the size of the weapon, which would need to fit onto existing railways and move safely through tunnels and cuttings. It would also need to be transportable by truck along existing roadways. The new weapon was designated the A-4, but a more modestly proportioned prototype that could fall between the A-3 and the A-4 was designated the A-5. Although the A-5 was designed to be similar to the A-3, it had a more robust construction and employed a simpler, more reliable guidance system. The A-5 was designed to have the exterior appearance of the proposed A-4 rocket but on a smaller scale.

The excited sense of German expansionism was increasingly apparent to her citizens and the feeling in the research laboratories was one of an expanding future. The advent of war had seemed inevitable for some time so that the actual declaration, announced in London at 11.15am on 3 September 1939, had little effect on the teams. The A-5 tests proceeded and rocket development moved steadily ahead right through 1939. Missiles were successfully fired and many were recovered by parachute and launched again. From the start, the A-5 rockets could reach an altitude of 7.5 miles (12km). The era of the long-range rocket was coming closer by the day. However, for many years, Hitler had seen his military destiny in the invasion and subjugation of nations. His personal preferences were not so much for weapons that descended on a distant enemy from the sky, but for hordes of well-disciplined troops that would occupy and subdue a nation. Hitler had seen his troops walk across great swathes of Europe, he had seen the reports of the successful Blitzkrieg over London, and he again began to be less concerned by rocketry, seeing it as something he might not need after all.

ENGLISH EYES

The British were very strong at gathering intelligence and they were already discovering what was happening at Peenemünde. A confidential document on activity there had been sent anonymously to London by a German physicist. This was the so-called 'Oslo Report'. It was one of the most important documents of its kind ever recorded. Its author was Hans Ferdinand Mayer who earned his doctorate in physics from the University of Heidelberg in 1920. He became Director of the Siemens Communication Research Laboratory in Germany in 1936 and was able to travel widely. He had many contacts across the whole of military research in Germany, and was an inveterate gossip. Most of the flow of information, though, was one-way; and – as Mayer became increasingly concerned about the Nazi threat – he realized that something had to be done to attempt to stem its flow.

The crucial event for Mayer was the invasion of Poland on 1 September 1939 by Nazi troops. Mayer knew the time had come to act, and arranged a business trip to Oslo for the following month. On 30 October 1939 he arrived in Oslo, Norway, and checked in at the Hotel Bristol. He borrowed an office typewriter from the hotel, and over the next few days he started to type out a seven-page document which set down everything he knew about German military plans. It is an astonishing document. On 1 November he mailed the first introductory section to the military authorities in London. If they were interested in the full report, he would send it by mail, he said; confirmation of the British response was to be in the form of a subtle change to the wording of the German-language transmission for the BBC's overseas service. Mayer said it should begin with the words: '*Hallo, hier ist London*'. He listened to the broadcast, and heard the coded words. Satisfied that his work was

An aerial shot of the important site at Peenemünde. Polish resistance fighters informed contacts in London that Nazi rockets were being tested at Peenemünde and in March 1943 British aerial reconnaissance brought back crucial pictures. (Author's collection)

wanted, he completed the rest of the report and mailed it to London, along with a sample of a new proximity fuse that he had secretly obtained from Germany.

Mayer was reported to the Nazi authorities as listening to the BBC, and he was accused of uttering anti-Nazi sentiments, so he was arrested by the Gestapo in 1943 and was imprisoned in concentration camps until the war ended; but the Germans never knew about his Oslo Report. Indeed, its very existence was not revealed until 1947. At the end of the war, Mayer was taken to the United States as part of the top-secret Operation *Paperclip*, intended to give the Americans the benefit of German wartime research (p.159). After a time at Cornell University, he returned to Germany, as Director of the Siemens & Halske research department in Munich for communications technology until 1962. He died there in 1980.

In London his report was dismissed as an invention, deliberately planted by the Nazis to confuse the British authorities. But then it came to attention of a brilliant young physicist, R. V. Jones, recently appointed Churchill's head of scientific intelligence. He felt that the breadth and coherence of the document was a sign of its reliability; all the scientific details checked out and he was convinced that it could not possibly be a work of fiction, planted to deceive. Jones was a key figure in the development of radar, and noted that the Germans were also trying to bring radio direction finding (RDF) into use. Jones vehemently argued against the accusation that the information was planted. If the Germans were doing this, he maintained, they wouldn't wish to give the game away. And if they weren't, their failing to have done so would be an obvious admission of failure. Only a 'genuinely disaffected' person would write thus, argued Jones, if he wished to reveal everything he knew.

The British Admiralty were not impressed and they continued to maintain that the Oslo Report was a work of fiction. They argued that no single person could have such a broad knowledge of so many different fields. In Britain, as in the United States, and even in Nazi Germany, cooperation and contact between the Army and Navy were virtually non-existent. They saw themselves as rivals, not comrades. But Jones knew that a socially well-connected person could have friends in many places, and insisted that the Oslo Report must be true. In one paragraph it claimed that 'wireless controlled rocket gliders' were being developed at Peenemünde, and so were what Mayer described as 'rocket shells' 30in (80cm) in diameter. Today we cannot tell which the 'rocket gliders' might have been. Drones had been developed, but work on the prototypes of the V-1 was still in the future. The 'rocket shells' would have been the A-3 rocket, which had a diameter of 27in (68cm) – a reasonable estimate.

PEENEMÜNDE CURTAILED

In May 1940, just as the teams at Peenemünde were close to designing a monster rocket, Hitler convinced himself that events were moving his way, and the war would soon be over. The British Expeditionary Force that had been dispatched to fight the German Army had been quickly defeated. The Allies had retreated, becoming marooned around Dunkirk on the coast near the border between France and Belgium. They had abandoned their heavy artillery, and feared destruction by the Luftwaffe and the German Army. But, seeing that fighting had virtually ended, Field Marshall Gerd von Rundstedt, Chief of the General Staff, called a halt to hostilities. The lull in action provided a chance for the soldiers to be rescued and, in London, Churchill instructed everyone available with a ship or boat to bring home the troops. Almost 1,000 vessels set off for the coast of the continent, and 338,226 soldiers (123,000 of them French) were brought safely back to Britain by sea. A further 40,000 Allied soldiers remained on the continent; many continued fighting the Germans, some were captured, others made their own way home – some even travelling through neutral Spain to find a way back to England.

Hitler heard reports of the British retreat with immense satisfaction and sensed that they were a spent force. He now began to convince himself that hostilities would be over in a year or so, and he ordered that work should stop on all projects that could not be completed by the time the war was likely to end. Development at Peenemünde was curtailed; and for the next year the very future of German rocketry was under threat.

ROCKET DEVELOPMENT BEYOND GERMANY

A fascination with rockets was shared by many private individuals and armed forces around the world, including the USSR, the United States and Britain.

RUSSIAN ROCKET DEVELOPMENT

The capricious influence of personal ambitions was felt in Russia, as in Germany. Although Russian research into rockets is often overlooked, Russia had the first rocketry society. In 1924 in Moscow, Fridrikh Tsander proposed the formation of a Society for the Study of Interplanetary Travel and it was constituted under the aegis of the Military Science Division of the N. E. Zhukovsky Air Force Academy.

British troops, evacuated from Dunkirk in May 1940, wait at Dover for disembarkation. After this victory, Hitler felt that Germany would soon win the war. (IWM H 1628)

Marshal Mikhail Nikolayevich Tukhachevsky was a leading member of the Bolshevik party and patron of the Soviet Jet Propulsion Research Institute. He was suddenly classified as an 'enemy of the people' by Stalin, and was summarily executed. (Getty Images)

This was essentially a discussion group, and was soon renamed the Society for the Study of Interplanetary Communication.

Among the other societies that formed in the 1930s was the Group for the Study of Reaction Motion in Moscow (MosGIRD) and a similar group in Leningrad (LenGIRD). Sergei Korolev was a key member of MosGIRD and in due course he became senior designer of the Soviet space rockets. Tsander spear-headed the design of a pioneering experimental projectile, the GIRD-X rocket.

The Jet Propulsion Research Institute (RNII) was created in September 1933 through the merger of the Gas Dynamics Laboratory (GDL) in Leningrad – now St Petersburg – and MosGIRD in Moscow. Ivan Kleimenov, the former chief at the GDL, was assigned to lead the RNII which began work on liquid-fuel ballistic missiles.

A photograph on p.131 shows engineer A. I. Polyarny holding an experimental R-06 rocket prior to its successful launch in 1937. It reached an altitude of over 13,000ft (4,000m).

During the following year, the RNII was renamed NII-3. The initiative was short-lived, however, for a tragedy was about to happen. In June 1937, Soviet citizens heard the shocking news that Marshall Mikhail Nikolayevich Tukhachevsky, a leading member of the Bolshevik party, had been dramatically executed by order of Stalin as an 'enemy of the people'. Tukhachevsky was a patron of NII-3, and the Institute's director and his deputy were soon executed, while leading engineers Sergei Korolev and Valentin Glushko were given long prison terms. Research on liquid-fuel rockets was abandoned, and NII-3 could henceforth produce only unguided short-range Katyusha rockets. Just as Hitler had curtailed rocket research in Germany in 1940, Stalin's personal paranoia had destroyed Russia's high-technology rocketry research. The most successful missile the Russians perfected was the Katyusha rocket which was launched in batches from trucks, tractors, trains and tanks. The launchers were also installed on ships. The early production-line Katyusha was officially designated the M-13 and was 71in (180cm) long, 5.2in (13cm) in diameter and weighed 92lb (42kg). The propellant was a simple solid charge of nitrocellulose with a single nozzle surrounded by four stabilising fins. A warhead of 48lb (22kg) could be propelled up to 3.4 miles (5.4km). The impact of the

Katyusha was in the mass delivery – a battery of several launchers would deliver more than 4 tons of high explosive as rockets rained down across a 10 acre (4 hectare) area. Although it then took time to reload and re-set the launcher, the effect of the bombardment was devastating – and the characteristic sound of so many rockets roaring through the air simultaneously was highly demoralising to the enemy.

ROCKETS IN JAPAN

In Japan there was a clear recognition of the potential importance of rockets, but relatively little that the Japanese scientists could do about it. Japan is a nation that lacks natural resources, and at the time had limited industrial experience. Like many centralized states, it had a cumbersome bureaucracy and a tendency for rival organizations to seek to outdo each other.

In the early years of World War II, both the Imperial Japanese Army and Navy were looking at developing 8in (20cm) rockets. The Army's 8in rocket was a spin-stabilized projectile equipped with six vents to impart both spin and propulsion. It was designed to be launched from a Type 4 Rocket Launcher, in reality a mortar. By contrast, the Japanese Navy developed their own rival version. Their 8in rocket was designed to be launched from simple wooden troughs or even from holes in the ground.

The Japanese also developed the Type 10 Rocket Motor which was a simple propulsion unit intended as a launch facility for aerial bombs. They later produced a rocket 18in (44.7cm) in diameter; it was an unsophisticated projectile that was used in action on Iwo Jima and had a maximum range of over a mile (2,000m). Although it was inaccurate, it delivered a warhead of 400lb (180kg). Interestingly, this rocket was also spin-stabilized. This rotation around the axis had the potential to stabilize a rocket in flight, just as the Congreve rocket had in a previous century.

The Imperial Japanese Army focused their efforts on developing an air-to-surface missile while the Navy concentrated on the design of surface-to-air missiles. The Army decided to develop their Igo missile, while the Navy's project was the *Funryu* (raging dragon) rocket.

The Igo-1-A was a winged cruise missile constructed by Mitsubishi from wood and metal. It was 16ft (5.77m) long, and had a wingspan of 10ft 9in (3.6m). It had a launch weight of 3,080lb (1,400kg) and could deliver a 1,760lb (800kg) warhead at a velocity of 340mph (550km/h). The rocket motor was a Mitsubishi Tokuro-1 Type 3 which fired for just 75 seconds. There was also an Igo-1-B produced by Kawasaki which was of similar design but delivered a somewhat smaller payload. Both versions of the Igo-1 were launched from an aircraft at about 5,000ft (1,500m) some 6 miles (about 10km) from the target. An onboard altimeter established the missile on a straight and level path and it was then radio-controlled by the pilot to the target. The missiles left no smoke trail and it was difficult for the aircraft pilot to aim them accurately. The rockets were fitted with a tail light for use at night – but under these conditions, although the pilots could see the drone, they now had difficulty in seeing the target. The final refinement of the Igo rocket was the Igo-1-C, developed by the

Seen here at the battle for Kursk are Soviet Katyusha rocket launchers in position. The Katyusha was the most successful Soviet secret weapon, and launched rockets in batches. The effect of this mass delivery was highly intimidating. (Hulton Archive/Getty Images)

A modern version of the Soviet Katyusha rocket. During the war, launchers like these were developed for installation on ships, trains, tractors and trucks. (istock)

Aeronautical Research Institute of Tokyo Imperial University. Rather than being guided by radio, the Igo-1-C was ingeniously designed to home in on the shockwaves produced by ships when they fired their guns.

Meanwhile the Navy were developing their Funryu rockets, and planned to produce four versions. Like their Igo counterparts, they would be radio-controlled to the target. In the event, only the Igo-1-A and Igo-1-B went into production, and none was ever fired at the enemy.

Air-to-ground missiles were not seriously considered by the Japanese until March 1944. The Army continued to prefer spin-stabilized rockets, while the Navy wanted devices stabilized by fins. Had the two services combined forces, an optimized design could well have been agreed but, as it was, the age old rivalry persisted and each service pressed ahead with their own ideas. The air-to-ground missiles were to be fitted to the Kawanishi N1K-J *Shiden* (Violet Lightning)

Left: The Russian consortium of amateur rocketry enthusiasts (Gruppa Izucheniya Reaktivhogo Dvizheniya, GIRD) was headed by a brilliant young designer, Fridrikh Tsander. Leonid Konstinovich Korneev (right of the rocket in this picture) supervised the launch of their GIRD-X rocket. (Author's collection)

Bottom left: Russian engineer A. I. Polyarny is holding a R-06 rocket, which reached an altitude of 2.5 miles (4km) in 1937. The altitudes attained by these Russian rockets remained world records until broken by the German V-2 in 1945. (Author's collection)

Bottom right: Japanese troops began to use these rockets against the Allies in 1944. This, the Type 4 launcher, was equipped with a tube 8in (20.3cm) in diameter and 6ft 3.5in (192cm) long. The rocket was fired by pulling a cord measuring 25ft (7.62m) long to keep the operator at a safe distance. (Author's collection)

aircraft which were to be specially modified to carry six of the rockets ready to attack the fleet of ships that the Japanese believed to be on its way to invade the homeland. In the event, the aircraft never achieved full operational status before the war's dramatic end. Japanese plans to fire off a salvo of rockets were never achieved; instead each rocket was launched singly, in the manner of firing off a mortar, and so little useful benefit was ever achieved.

BRITISH ROCKETRY

British interest in rockets was far more modest than that in Germany. At the beginning of the war, small 3in (7.6cm) diameter rockets powered by cordite were all that were available. By the end of 1940, a larger 8in (20cm) version had been developed that could be fired in volleys of 128 rockets from a rack known as a 'projector'. There were many practical problems, and the organization of such a rocket battery had to be worked out from first principles, since there was no practical experience from which to work. On 20 May 1940, in the back room of a public house at Aberporth in Wales, a meeting was convened by the local Ordnance Director and it was decided to try using these batteries of rockets as a routine measure against enemy aircraft. Within weeks a firm in Greenwich, London, named G. A. Harbey had been contracted to mass produce the 'projector' racks and by September over 1,000 had been manufactured.

The following month, Churchill's son-in-law Duncan Sandys (then a major) organized a rocket section to defend the strategic port of Cardiff with 3in rockets, and the first German plane was brought down on 7 April 1941. By the end of 1941 there were three such facilities, known as 'Z-batteries', in existence. Two were at Cardiff, and the third was at Aberporth where there is to this day a missile testing range. The UP-3 rocket, as it was then known, was further improved and eventually emerged as a 6ft (1.8m) rocket with a lethal radius of up to 70ft (21m). By December 1942 there were 91 batteries in existence, despite enemy raids which twice razed the factory producing the rocket fuses. A modification of this rocket was produced as an operational surface-to-air missile capable of reaching 1,000mph (1,600km/h). Although the Army showed little interest in these missiles, the Navy began production of six-unit 'Mattress' projectors for use at sea. They were used in the landings in Sicily and mainland Italy which were to ensue. After further tests at Sennybridge (also in Wales) the Army began to change its mind and a Land Mattress projector was produced which went into service with Canadian troops when they fought for the Rhine and Scheldt rivers. Towards the end of the war, the Stooge rocket was unveiled. It was designed specifically to attack enemy aircraft, particularly (as it happens) the Japanese suicide squads. This was a 740lb (335kg) 10ft (3m) radio-guided missile with a range of up to 8 miles (13km). It had a top speed of 500mph (800km/h) and delivered a 220lb (100kg) warhead. The British rocket had come of age.

Not all the rocket trials were a success. In 1942 a rocket-assisted take-off was due to be demonstrated on a Stirling bomber. A clutch of senior RAF officials were in attendance, one

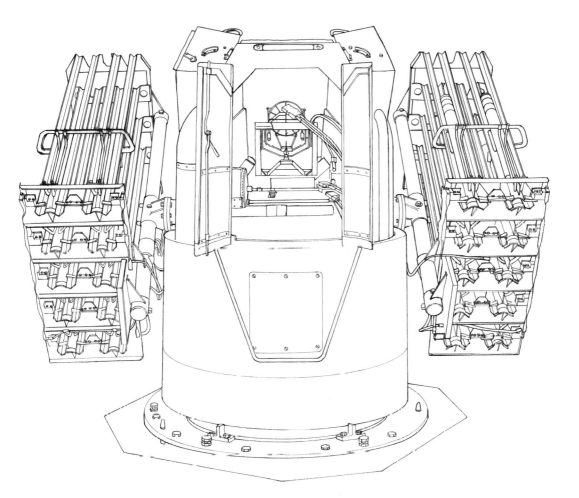

Above: Made from pressed steel, this inexpensively manufactured rocket launcher was developed (like the less successful Panjandrum, p.232) by the British Directorate of Miscellaneous Weapons Development in 1943. This body was originally known as the Inspectorate of Anti-Aircraft Weapons and Devices, IAAWD, and the initials inspired the irreverent interpretation of the 'Instigator of Anti-Aircraft Wheezes and Dodges'. (John Batchelor)

Right:Home Guard soldiers load an anti-aircraft rocket at a Z-battery on Merseyside, on 6 July 1942. The first Z-batteries were used as the front line of British defence and were used to fortify strategic positions. British civilians were trained in many roles as part of the Home Guard and their responsibilities included manning these anti-aircraft stations. (IWM H 21135)

SPANISH ROCKETS IN WAR

Small solid-fuel rockets were used during the Spanish Civil War of 1936–39. The Spanish authorities modified rockets designed for use in ocean rescue missions for delivering propaganda leaflets behind enemy lines. The sea-rescue rocket nose cones were designed to open at a predetermined altitude to release a payload of the propaganda leaflets, which were printed on an especially thin paper to help conserve weight. The rockets were reliable, and easily manufactured; yet they were in principle little different from those used in the Napoleonic era. As the omission of rockets from the restrictions imposed by the Treaty of Versailles reminds us, the rocket was yet to be recognized as a major weapon of war – only the German enthusiasts had this futuristic vision.

of them reporting directly to Churchill. Expectations were high – if successful this would allow heavy bombers to take off from small airfields, even when fully laden. Twenty-four rockets were secured beneath the wings, and a variable rheostat – a device that could progressively increase electrical current – had been installed to fire the rockets in strict sequence as the throttles were opened. On a given signal, the plane roared into life and suddenly, as it began to move forward, there was a shattering explosion and the air filled with rockets and parts of the aircraft. The rockets had fired too closely together, exerting stresses that the aircraft had never been designed to withstand. When the smoke cleared, the wreckage of the plane was left stranded on the runway, its wings and engines pointing in all directions. The pilot, miraculously, walked through the smoke unharmed – just weeks before, his previous bomber had cashed in flames, and he had walked away from that, too. He was Squadron-Leader Harold Huxtable, one of the luckiest pilots of World War II.

Even the most successful of the British forays into rocketry were no match for the Germans in terms of high-technology development. The British designs were intended mainly as weapons of defence, and there had been no interest shown in offensive weapons of a large scale.

AMERICAN ROCKETRY

Like the British, the Americans largely relied on solid-fuel rockets during the early years of World War II. The first truly successful American rocket of the war arose from the vestiges of research carried out by Robert Goddard at the end of World War I and was also one of the smallest – the bazooka. Development had been driven largely by the need to find an answer to the otherwise insurmountable problem of recoil, which occured when an armour-piercing shell was fired from a transportable gun. So fierce was the equal-and-opposite reaction that it seemed impossible to design a suitable weapon that could be moved around by soldiers on the battlefield. As Goddard had demonstrated in 1918, a rocket-propelled missile would overcome the difficulty since the motive force is generated during flight and is not due to the massive reaction of an exploding cartridge. In 1942 Clarence Hickman, Goddard's former colleague, resumed experiments at the George Washington University in Washington DC, and Lieutenant Edward Uhl – who was later credited with being 'The Father of the Bazooka' – developed a launcher tube that could be put into production. After almost a quarter-century in the doldrums, Goddard's invention was suddenly a high priority.

As a result a 21in (53cm) rocket weighing 3.5lb (1.5kg) was put into production. It contained 1.6lb (720g) of Pentolite high explosive and was fired from a launch tube which could be carried by a soldier and fired from shoulder-height during battle. Designated the M9, and originally nicknamed 'the stovepipe', the device acquired its better-known name during an

Royal Artillerymen at a Z-battery are loading 4in (10cm) anti-aircraft rockets into a mobile launcher on 18 June 1941. (IWM H 10791)

early test, when a major asked what the device was. When told, he laughed: 'It looks more like Bob Burns' Bazooka!' Burns had been a popular vaudeville performer in the 1930s, and featured a tubular brass instrument in his act which he called the 'bazooka'. The name stuck.

During the early years of World War II the weapon was used by American troops and bazookas were also supplied to Soviet forces. In 1942 some were captured by the Germans from Russian soldiers and later from Americans in North Africa and the secret was out. One survey failed to find any soldier – after many bazookas had been fired – who had reported the destruction of a single enemy tank, and so the weapon was withdrawn. The bazooka was improved and reintroduced later in the war, but continued to pose problems of its own. The smoke trail led the enemy to the exact position of the person who had launched the missile, and the soldiers were always in mortal danger when they rose to launch the weapon. The rockets proved to be unreliable, and in the later years of the war the new German tanks had thicker steel plating that was impervious to bazooka attack.

In the end they seemed to be best employed against enemy positions, rather than as anti-tank weapons, and General Dwight Eisenhower was to describe the bazooka as 'one of the four Tools of Victory' (along with the jeep, the Dakota and the atomic bomb). The design was subsequently improved further and bazookas went on to be used in Korea and Vietnam. Their precise value in World War II remains uncertain, though the bazooka was certainly a powerful device in the hands of a soldier and did much to reassure American infantrymen faced with battling German tanks and stubborn defenders.

TERROR FROM THE SKY

In their early years at Peenemünde, the German rocket researchers had no difficulty in attracting the funds they needed. Money was printed in large amounts and military expenditure for the Army now seemed to have no limits.

THE FIRST V-2

Von Braun was in his element at Peenemünde, and the design of the great A-4 rocket proceeded apace. It was to be based on the successful design of the A-5, with a redesigned control system and updated construction (p.124). The A-5 had reached an altitude of 35,000ft (10,000m) in tests during 1938, and the A-4 was designed with the benefit of the results of these pioneering tests. But things changed when Hitler began to anticipate an early end to hostilities, with Germany reigning supreme across Western Europe, and as a result research at Peenemünde was

---

Opposite: An A-4 rocket takes off perfectly from Test Stand VII at Peenemünde in the spring of 1943. The success of the A-4 benefited from the trials of the A-5 prototype, and once it was fine-tuned it was designated the V-2. (NARA)

An American soldier instructs recruits in the use of the bazooka on 3 November 1943. Although it began as a secret weapon, the bazooka has become one of the most famous and instantly recognizable weapons of the war. (IWM NA 8376)

The bazooka in war during the mid-1940s: a World War II paratrooper from the 101st Airborne Division boards a C-47 airplane, carrying his bazooka. (PhotoQuest/Getty Images)

Vaudeville performer Bob Burns performing with his tubular musical instrument, which he called his 'bazooka'. After a US Major exclaimed that the 'stovepipe' weapon looked like this instrument, it was quickly renamed the 'bazooka'. (Time Life Pictures/Getty Images)

BOMROC was the abbreviation the US military gave to these 5in (13cm) bombardment rockets. The Naval Bureau of Ordnance proposed a new generation of the rockets in May 1943 and development was undertaken by the California Institute of Technology. The first design was for a 3.5in rocket, but they went on to produce a family of 5in missiles with a range of high-explosive warheads. (John Batchelor)

reduced. In a scaled-down programme of research, the engineers contented themselves by designing improved servo-control systems and new, high-throughput fuel pumps were systematically developed. Rocket development had essentially been put on hold.

Within two years the tide was turning, and the need for rocket research began to re-emerge. Work on the A-4 picked up again and on 13 June 1942 the first of the new monster rockets was ready for test firing. The rocket was checked and re-checked. Meticulous records were maintained of every aspect of its functioning. It stood 46ft 1.5in (14.05m) tall, weighed 12 tons, and was fuelled with methyl alcohol (methanol). The oxidant, liquid oxygen, was pumped in just prior to launch. The pumps were run up to speed, ignition achieved and the rocket rose unsteadily from its launch pad. In a billowing cloud of smoke and steam it began to climb, rapidly gaining speed, and then – at just the wrong moment – the propellant pump motor failed. The rocket staggered for a moment and crashed back onto the launch pad, disintegrating in a huge explosion. The technicians were terrified and were lucky to escape.

On 16 August 1942 a second A-4 was tested. Once again, the fuel motor pump stopped working but this time it failed later in the flight, after the rocket had already passed through the sound barrier. The third test was a complete success. It took place on 3 October 1942 and this rocket was fired out along the coast of Pomerania. The engine burned for over a minute, boosting the rocket to a maximum altitude of 50 miles (80km). It fell to earth 119.3 miles (192km) from the launch pad. The age of the space rocket had arrived, and the ballistic missile was a reality. The design of the A-4 rocket could now be fine tuned and – given time – the complex design could be optimized for mass production. The Nazis now had their new *Vergeltungswaffe* ('retaliatory' or 'reprisal' weapon). The term was important; although Hitler saw these as weapons of mass destruction, he hoped that the world – instead of seeing him as the aggressor – would regard him as simply responding to Allied attacks. The 'V' is sometimes translated into English as 'vengeance', but that is not right as the term in German connotes reprisal. The first of such weapons was their V-1 cruise missile, the 'buzz-bomb' (p.99) and now they had the V-2. It would surely strike terror into the hearts of those who challenged German supremacy.

Aspects of the design were refined and developed by teams in companies including Zeppelin Luftschiffbau and Heinkel, and the final production version of the V-2 was a brilliantly successful rocket. Over 5,000 would be produced by the Germans. The production model stood 46ft (14m) tall, was 5ft 5in (1.65m) in diameter, and weighed over 5 tons of which 70 per cent was fuel. The tanks held 8,300lb (3,760kg) of fuel and just over 11,000lb (5,000kg) of liquid oxygen at take-off. The combustion chamber consumed 275lb (125kg) per second, emitting exhaust gases at a velocity of 6,950ft/s (2,200m/s). The missile was steered by vanes in the exhaust and could land with an accuracy better than 4 per cent, or so claimed the designers. No metal could withstand the intense heat, so these internal fins were constructed from carbon. They ablated in the heat, but could not burn away rapidly due to the lack of free oxygen and lasted long enough for the entire rocket burn. For the time, the V-2 was – and it remains – an extraordinary achievement made in record time.

Dörnberger tried to take full advantage of the success. Ever since the United States had declared war on Germany on 8 December 1941, the balance of power had begun to tip against the Nazis and Dörnberger knew the time was ripe for official endorsement of his teams' progress. Hitler had been to see static tests of rocket motors at Kummersdorf but he had not been greatly impressed by the noise, fire and smoke. These were so exciting to the rocket enthusiasts – it was what rocketry was all about – but Hitler could not imagine how these 'boys' toys' could transmute into agencies of world domination and he was reluctant to give the rocket teams the high priority they sought.

Dörnberger was frustrated by the bureaucracy and the lack of exciting new developments. Some of the pressure had been temporarily relieved from Dörnberger on 8 February 1942 when news reached him that the Minister for Armaments and Munitions, Fritz Todt, had died at the age of 50. Todt was aboard a Junkers Ju-52 aircraft on a routine tour when it crashed and exploded shortly after take-off. Albert Speer was supposed to have been on the same flight, but cancelled at the last minute. Speer was immediately appointed by Hitler to take Todt's place, and he was far more interested in what Dörnberger had to say. Speer was a professional architect and had joined the Nazi party in 1931. He had soon become a member of Hitler's inner circle and had gained the Führer's trust after his appointment as chief architect. Speer clearly felt that Hitler could be reconciled to the idea of the V-2 as progress continued.

As luck would have it, the new committee was put under the charge of General Gerd Degenkolb, who disliked Dörnberger intensely. Von Braun said at the time: 'This committee is a thorn in our flesh.' One can see why. Degenkolb exemplified that other German trait, a talent for bureaucracy and administrative complexity. He had been in a group including Karl-Otto Saur and Fritz Todt, who espoused Hitler's policy of being 'not yet convinced' by the rocket as a major agent in military success. Degenkolb immediately began to establish a separate bureaucratic structure to work alongside Dörnberger's. Details of the design of the V-2 rocket were reconsidered in detail by Degenkolb's new committee, and some of their untried new recommendations were authorized without Dörnberger's knowledge or approval.

Progress remained problematic even following the successful launches. The Director of Production Planning, Detmar Stahlknecht, had set targets for V-2 production which were agreed with Dörnberger – but which were then unilaterally modified by Degenkolb. Stahlknecht had planned to produce 300 of the V-2 rockets per month by January 1944 – but in January 1943 Degenkolb decreed that this total be brought forward to October 1943. Stahlknecht was aiming for a monthly production target of 600 by July 1944; Degenkolb insisted the figure be raised to 900 per month, and the date brought forward to December 1943. The success of the rocket was encouraging the policy makers to raise their game, and their new targets seemed simply unattainable.

THE CAPITALIST DREAM

At this point, Dörnberger was presented with a startling new prospect. He learned of a bizarre idea to capitalize on the sudden enthusiasm for the new rockets. He was told that it was being proposed to designate Peenemünde as a 'land' in its own right. It would be jointly purchased by major German companies like AEG and Siemens who would pay more than 1,000,000 Reichsmarks for the property and then charge the Nazi government for each missile produced. AEG, in particular, were highly impressed by the telemetry developed for the V-2 rocket and recognized that it had far-reaching implications and considerable market potential.

The guidance systems were remarkably advanced. They had been developed by Helmut Gröttrup, working alongside Von Braun, though there was little friendship between the two. Dörnberger fought to have Peenemünde maintained as an army proving ground and production facility, and won the battle only after bitter negotiations. This had been a narrow victory for Dörnberger, and was one that he would have been unlikely to win without the support of Speer.

Three sites were immediately confirmed for the production of the new rockets: Peenemünde, Friedrichshafen and the Raxwerken at Wiener Neustadt. Degenkolb issued orders at once, but he failed to see that the senior staff were not available in sufficient numbers to train and organize production on such a rapidly expanding scale. Degenkolb refused to be challenged and insisted that production begin immediately – and, when the engineers explained the impossibility of the task at such short notice, Degenkolb issued orders that they be imprisoned if his schedule was not met. Clearly, he meant business.

THE V-2

After the success of the V-1 flying bomb, the cheapest and crudest of Nazi secret weapons, the V-2 was a terrifying rocket that was undetectable until after it had struck. Under the direction of rocket pioneer Wernher von Braun, the V-2 was developed at Peenemünde but work had to be moved to Poland when the Allies bombed Peenemünde. The V-2 went into production in 1944 and caused widespread damage across Europe.

Three illustrations depicting early German test rockets: the grey rocket (left) is the A-3; it originally had a bare metal finish but was painted dark grey for trials. The yellow and red rocket is an A-5, and these rockets were painted in a range of colours. The A-4 rocket shown has a cartoon painted near the base, as was often the case with early A-4 test missiles. (Robert Calow © Osprey Publishing)

The V-2 was an intercontinental ballistic missile weighing 28,000lb (12,700kg). It stood 46ft (14m) tall and was 5ft 5in (1.65m) in diameter. With an operational velocity of 3,580mph (5,760km/h) – more than twice the speed of sound – it could travel over a distance of 220 miles (320km) and deliver 2,200lb (980kg) of Amatol high explosive. The design was re-used by the US as the the Redstone rocket after the war. (John Batchelor)

Troops pose on a railway wagon loaded with a captured German V-2 rocket in April 1945, linking hands to convey the size of the missile. (IWM BU 3694)

American photographs of the V-2 in flight. These photographs were taken in 1946 by an automatic camera at the White Sands proving ground in New Mexico, where the rocket was being tested prior to the design being adapted for the US space missions. (Getty Images)

Albert Speer was appointed Minister of Armaments and Munitions upon the death of Fritz Todt. Speer was an enthusiastic proponent of the development of German rockets. (Popperfoto/Getty images)

Although Degenkolb saw Von Braun as a personal rival, and someone he disliked, he recognized that his participation was crucial to the success of the rocket development. Others knew this too. At one stage, Von Braun had even been arrested by the authorities under the suspicion that his covert purpose was not the bombardment of foreign cities for the benefit of the Fatherland, but that he was secretly planning to develop rockets for space exploration at government expense. At first, Von Braun's protests came to nothing and a lengthy bureaucratic enquiry seemed inevitable, until Dörnberger intervened to say that, without Von Braun, there could be no further progress. At this, Von Braun was released and sent back to his work. Dörnberger reported his frustrations with a lack of progress towards full production. Speer understood that the heavy-handed administrative interference of Degenkolb had introduced an unnecessary hold-up (reckoned by Dörnberger to be a delay of 18 months) and promised to remove him if it would help.

In the event, Degenkolb survived because of the influence of Fritz Todt's long-standing friend, Karl-Otto Saur. Saur himself had a remarkable instinct for survival and, after the war, he was used as a key witness for the prosecution on behalf of the American authorities and was subsequently released. The fact that Karl-Otto Saur was designated by Hitler to replace Speer as Minister for Armaments was not a sufficient crime for him to be tried as a war criminal, and he eventually set up a publishing house back in Germany named Saur Verlag. The company survives to this day publishing reference information for librarians – a curious legacy from World War II.

The remaining serious challenger to the V-2 was the Luftwaffe's buzz bomb, the V-1. Its proponents pointed out that it was cheap to fly, economic to fuel, easy to produce in vast numbers and surely a far better candidate for support than the costly and complex V-2. Dörnberger argued strongly in favour of his own project. The V-1 needed a launch ramp, whereas the V-2 could be launched from almost anywhere it could stand. The flying bomb was easy to detect, shoot down or divert off course, whereas a rocket was undetectable until after it had hit. In the end the Nazi authorities were persuaded by both camps and the two weapons were ordered into mass production. Nonetheless, the delays remained an obstacle to progress, and by the summer of 1943 – with Degenkolb's production target of 900 per month looming ever closer – the engineers protested that their highly successful engine was still not ready for manufacture in large amounts by regular engineers.

Once again there were conflicting interests and opposing policies. Adolf Thiel, senior design engineer on the V-2, protested that mass production was not likely to be achieved before the war had come to its natural conclusion. Friends of Thiel reported he was close to a nervous breakdown, and wanted to stop work at Peenemünde and retire to an academic career at university. However, Von Braun remained obdurately convinced that they were close to success and, on balance, Dörnberger sided with that view.

WATCHING FROM LONDON

Meanwhile, British Intelligence was watching. A major breakthrough for the British came on 23 March 1943. A captured German officer, General Wilhelm Ritter von Thoma, provided timely information that the Allies would find of crucial importance. Back on 29 May 1942 the Nazi Lieutenant-General Ludwig Crüwell had flown to inspect German operations in Libya when his pilot mistook British soldiers for Italian troops and he landed the plane alongside them. Crüwell was taken prisoner and on 22 March 1943 he was placed in a room with General Von Thoma. The room was bugged, and their muffled conversation was partly overheard by the eager British agents, listening in the next room. The notes were recorded in the secret *Air Scientific Intelligence Interim Report* written up on 26 June 1943, and now held in the archives at Churchill College, University of Cambridge, England:

> No progress whatsoever can have been made in this rocket business. I saw it once with Field Marshall [Walther von] Brauchitsch. There is a special ground near Kummersdorf. They've got these huge things which they've brought up here... They've always said that they go fifteen kilometres up into the stratosphere and then ... you only aim at an area. If one was to ... every few days ... frightful! The major there was full of hope – he said, 'Wait until next year and the fun will start. There's no limit [to the range]...

Further substantiation came in June 1943, when a resourceful Luxembourger named Schwaben sent a sketch of the Peenemünde establishment to London in a microfilm through a network of agents known as the Famille Martin. This fitted well with the other reports that had been arriving, including eye-witness accounts and notes smuggled out from secret agents about activity at Peenemünde. The intelligence service kept meticulous records of the reports of vapour trails, explosions and occasional sightings that were relayed back to London from those witnesses who were anxious to see an end to Nazi tyranny. Churchill appointed his

Left: Secret reconnaissance flights by the British brought back this remarkable picture of Test Stand VII at Peenemünde. This is a more detailed shot of the site than the image on p.125. Among the important features were the elliptical protective wall and a concrete pit for the exhaust gases from firing the rockets. Most important (marked B near the bottom of this picture) are two V-2 rockets lying in the bright sunshine, neither of which is camouflaged. The British immediately began to plan bombing raids. (Getty Images)

Above: This action photograph shows the Allied view of Operation *Hydra* on the night of 17–18 August 1943. Bombs are exploding among buildings at the northern end of the Karlshagen Housing Estate (middle and lower left) and part of the V-2 rocket production works at Peenemünde South are visible in the lower right corner of the image. (IWM C 3747)

An annotated enlargement of a vertical photographic reconnaissance aerial picture taken over Test Stand VII in the German Army Research Centre, Peenemünde, after the heavy bombing attacks by aircraft of Bomber Command in 1943. As a result of the attacks, Peenemünde became inoperable and V-2 development was moved to Blizna in Poland. (IWM C 4783)

son-in-law, Duncan Sandys MP, to head a committee to look further into the matter and on 12 June 1943 an RAF reconnaissance mission was sent to fly over the site at high altitude and bring back the first images of what could be seen at Peenemünde. The unmistakable sight of rockets casting shadows across the ground could be picked out in the images. Measurements suggested to the British that the rocket was about 38ft (11.5m) long, 6ft (1.8m) in diameter and had tail fins. The intelligence report estimated the mass of each rocket must be between 40 and 80 tons. It was guessed that there might be 5 or 10 tons of explosives aboard.

This was partly right, and partly a gross exaggeration. The V-2 was actually 46ft (14m) long and 5ft 5in (1.65m) in diameter, so the measurements calculated by the British were reasonable estimates. But the weight of the missile was wildly over-estimated – rather than 40 tons or more, it weighed just under 13 tons and carried 2,200lb (980kg) of explosive rather than 'up to 10 tons' of the British estimates. A 'rough outline' drawing of the rocket was prepared for this report and it looks more like a torpedo. Perhaps the missile as drawn lacked its 7.5ft (2.3m) warhead nose cone. In that case, the dimensions were surprisingly accurate – though there is no accounting for the gross over-calculation of the weight.

Although the guesswork about the rocket's weight was wrong, the comments that R. V. Jones added to the secret intelligence report of 26 June 1943 show a remarkably clear analysis of Germany's position at the time.

The evidence shows that … the Germans have for some time been developing a long range rocket at Peenemünde. Provided that the Germans are satisfied with Peenemünde's security, there is no reason to assume the existence of a rival establishment, unless the latter has arisen from inter-departmental jealousy.

Almost every report points to the fact that development can hardly have reached maturity, although it has been proceeding for some time. If, as appears, only three rockets were fired in the last three months of 1942, with two unsuccessful, the Germans just then have been some way from success and production.

At least three sorties over Peenemünde have now shown one and only one rocket visible in the entire establishment and one sortie has perhaps shown two. Supposing that the rockets have been accidentally left out in the open or because the inside storage is full, then the chances are that the rocket population is less than, say, twenty. If it were much greater, then it would be an extraordinary chance that this number should always be one greater than storage capacity. Therefore the number of rockets at Peenemünde is small, and since this is the main seat of development, the number of rockets in the Reich is also likely to be relatively small…

Since the long range rocket can hardly have reached maturity, German technicians would probably prefer to wait until their designs were more complete. If, as seems very possible, the genius of the Führer prevails over the judgement of the technicians, then despite everything the rocket will shortly be brought into use in its premature form.

Jones drew this conclusion: 'The present population of rockets is probably small, so that the rate of bombardment [of London] would not be high. The only immediate counter measure readily apparent is to bomb the establishment at Peenemünde.'

Jones was right, and plans for a massive bombing raid began at once. Three days later, on 29 June 1943, a meeting was convened at the Cabinet War Room at which Duncan Sandys revealed the contents of the photographs. He had short-circuited R. V. Jones's connections with the photo labs and insisted that they all be sent first to him. One of those attending the meeting was Professor Frederick Lindemann, Viscount Cherwell, who immediately poured scorn on the idea of a rocket base. Lindemann was a German-born physicist and Churchill's chief scientific adviser. He said at the meeting that a rocket weighing up to 80 tons was absurd. The rockets, he insisted, were an elaborate sham; the Germans had mocked them up to frighten the British and lead them on a false trail. It was nothing but an elaborate cover plan. After his analysis, which left the officials in the room sensing that a dreadful mistake was being made, Churchill turned to R. V. Jones and said that they would now hear the truth of the matter. Jones was crisp and to the point. Whatever might be the remaining questions over the details of these missiles, said Jones, it was clear to him that the rockets were real – and they posed a threat to Britain. The site must be destroyed. The idea of sending further reconnaissance flights was quickly dismissed, for it could alert the Germans to the fact that the Allies had discovered the site.

Peenemünde was too far away to be in contact by radio, and out of range of the fighters; so the Allied bombers would be completely unprotected. German fighters would soon be on the scene, and heavy Allied losses were likely. The conclusion was that the heaviest bombing would be arranged, and it would take place on the first night that meteorological conditions were suitable. The attack was code named Operation *Hydra*.

OPERATION *HYDRA*

On 8 July 1943 Hitler was shown an Agfacolor film of the launch of a V-2 and was finally convinced that the monster rocket could win him back the advantage. Having been sceptical, Hitler was now an enthusiastic supporter. He immediately decided that new launch bases would be needed across the northern coast of continental Europe in order to maximize the range of the rockets and the number of launches that Germany could make against Britain. He also ordered that the production of the V-2 was now to be made a top priority. Hitler believed that with these rockets he could turn the tide of war against the Allies. The Germans were busy working to comply with orders to construct a production line at the Peenemünde Army Research base just as the Royal Air Force was instructed to launch Operation *Hydra* to destroy the establishment.

The planning of Operation *Hydra* was meticulous. Bombing would be carried out from 9,000ft (about 3,000m; normally bombing raids were from twice as high), and practice runs over suitable stretches of British coastline were quickly arranged. The accuracy improved greatly during the practice sessions, an error of up to about 1,000 yards (900m) improving to 300 yards (270m). None of the aircrew were told the true nature of their target; they were informed that the installation was a new radar establishment that had to be destroyed urgently. By way of encouragement to be thorough on the first raid, they were also told that repeat attacks would be made, regardless of the losses, if they did not succeed first time. Meanwhile, a decoy raid was arranged, code named Operation *Whitebait*. Mosquito aircraft were to be sent to bomb Berlin prior to the raid on Peenemünde in the hope of attracting German fighters to the area. Further squadrons were meanwhile sent to attack nearby Luftwaffe airfields to prevent German fighters taking to the air over Peenemünde. As the attack began, a master bomber, Group Captain J. H. Searby, would circle around the target to call in successive waves of bombers.

On the night of 17 August 1943 there was a full moon, and the skies were clear. At midnight the raid began, and within half an hour the first wave was heading for home. Over the target, however, there was some light cloud and the accuracy of the first bombs was poor. Guns from the ground were returning fire, and a ship off-shore brought flak to bear on the bombers, but no fighters were seen. The second wave of Lancasters was directed at the factory workshops and then at 12.48am the third and final wave attacked the experimental workshops. This group of Lancaster and Halifax bombers overshot the target and most dropped their bombs half a minute late, so their bombs landed in the camp where conscripted workers were imprisoned. By this time German fighter aircraft were arriving, but they were late and losses to the British bombers were less than 7 per cent.

However, the laboratories and test rigs were damaged – and the Germans now knew, with dramatic suddenness, that their elaborate plans were known to the Allies. On the brink of realization, the plans to manufacture the V-2 at Peenemünde had to be abandoned. The Germans decided to fool the Allies into thinking that they had caused irreparable damage, so they immediately dug dummy 'bomb craters' all over the site, and painted black and grey lines across the roofs to look like fire-blackened beams. Their intention was to fool any reconnaissance flights into believing the damage was much worse than it was, thus convincing the British that further raids

A German V-2 rocket in Cuxhaven, Lower Saxony, in preparation for launch. Careful examination of this photo reveals the men who are installing the rocket and they give scale to the size of this mighty weapon of war. (Getty Images)

were unnecessary. The British still had one further element of retaliation, however; a number of the bombs were fitted with time delay fuses and exploded randomly for several days after the raid. They did not cause much material damage, but the continued detonations delayed the Germans from setting out to move equipment from the site.

THE MOVE TO POLAND

As the Germans sought to recover what they could from Peenemünde, the top-secret development work on the V-2 was immediately transferred to the SS training base near Blizna, deep inside Poland, where it would be undetected by the British and less easily reached by air. Meanwhile, a launch site at Watten, near the coast of northern France, had already been selected as a V-2 base. Work had started in April 1943 and was duly reported to the British by agents of the French resistance. Dörnberger had long recognized that a V-2 could be launched from a small site – it would be a case of 'shoot and run'. But after the raid on Peenemünde, Hitler decided that further major new launch and storage sites were the prime requirement. At d'Helfaut Wizernes, a site inland from Calais in northern France, they constructed a huge reinforced concrete dome, La Coupole, within a limestone quarry. The idea was to store the rockets within reinforced bomb-proof concrete chambers and bring them out for firing in quick succession. In May 1943 reconnaissance photographs disclosed details of the work, and by the end of the month bombing raids had been sent to the site. The timing of the bombing was set to coincide with freshly laid cement, so that the ruins would harden into a chaotic jumble that would be difficult for the Germans to repair. Repeated bombing by the Allies led to the idea being abandoned. The V-2 bombardment was then carried out from small scattered sites, as Dörnberger had always envisaged. The vast German bunkers were never fully operational, and they stand to this day as a World War II museum.

After the raid on Peenemünde, the main manufacture of the V-2 rockets was transferred to the Mittelwerk in Kohnstein. The rockets were manufactured by prisoners from Mittelbau-Dora, a concentration camp where an estimated 20,000 people died during World War II. A total of 9,000 of these were reported to have died from exhaustion, 350 were executed – including 200 accused of sabotage – and most of the rest were eventually shot, died from disease, or starved. By the war's end, they had constructed a total of 5,200 V-2 rockets. On 29 August 1944 Hitler ordered V-2 attacks to commence with immediate effect. The offensive started on 8 September 1944 when a rocket was aimed at Paris. It exploded in the city, causing damage at the Porte d'Italie. Another rocket was launched the same day from The Hague, Netherlands, and hit London at 6.43pm. It exploded in Staveley Road, Chiswick, killing Sapper Bernard Browning who was on leave from the Royal Engineers. A resident, 63-year-old Mrs Ada Harrison, and three-year-old Rosemary Clarke also perished in the blast. Intermittent launches against London increased in frequency, though the Germans did not officially announce the bombardment until 8 November 1944.

Until then, every time a V-2 exploded in Britain the authorities insisted it was a gas main that had burst; but with the German announcement the truth had to emerge. Two days later, Churchill confessed to the House of Commons that England had been under rocket attack 'for the last few weeks'.

Over several months more than 3,000 V-2s were fired by the Germans. Around 1,610 of them hit Antwerp; 1,358 landed on London, and additional rockets were fired into Liege, Hasselt, Tournai, Mons, Diest, Lille, Paris, Tourcoing, Remagen, Maastricht, Arras and Cambrai on continental Europe. In Britain, Norwich and Ipswich also suffered occasional V-2 attacks. The accuracy of the rockets increased steadily, and some of them impacted within a few yards of the intended target. The fatalities were sometimes alarming. On 25 November 1944 a V-2 impacted at a Woolworths store in New Cross, London, where it killed 160 civilians and seriously injured 108 more. Another attack on a cinema in Antwerp killed 567 people. This was the worst loss of life in a single V-2 attack.

THE V-2 FALLS INTO ALLIED HANDS

The Allies were receiving regular intelligence reports about the rockets, but knew little of the precise design details until a V-2 was retrieved from Sweden and examined in detail. On 13 June 1944, a V-2 on a test flight from Peenemünde exploded several thousand feet above the Swedish town of Bäckebo. The wreckage was collected by the Swedes and offered to the

British military artist Anthony Gross captured this scene of an unfinished launch platform for the V-2 rocket near Cherbourg in 1944 during the liberation of France. (IWM ART 4477)

British for reconstruction. Officially neutral, Sweden was also secretly supplying the German weapons factories with up to 10,000,000 tons of iron ore per year. To maintain their ostensibly neutral stance, the Swedes asked for some British Supermarine Spitfire fighter aircraft in exchange. In August 1944 reconstruction of the rocket was begun, and the resulting insight into the construction of the missile was highly revealing to the Allies. As it happens, this particular rocket was fitted with a guidance system that was never installed on the rockets raining down on Britain, and so the British were more impressed with the technology than they might otherwise have been. Yet the fact remained: although the design of the V-2 was now thoroughly understood, it was abundantly clear there was no defence against them. These weapons arrived at supersonic speeds, so there could be no advance warning and it seemed as though there was nothing that could be done to resist the onslaught.

Or was there? The resourceful officers at British Intelligence had a simple response. Because the area of damage was small, they began releasing fictitious reports that the rockets were over-shooting their targets by between 10 and 20 miles (16 to 32km). As soon as these covert messages were intercepted by the Germans, the launch teams recalibrated the launch trajectory to make good the discrepancy ... and from then on, the rockets fell some 20 miles short of their target, most of them landing in Kent instead of central London. The final two rockets exploded on 27 March 1945 and one of these was the last to kill a British civilian. She was Mrs Ivy Millichamp, aged 34, who was blown apart by the V-2 at her home in Kynaston Road, Orpington in the county of Kent, just 20 miles from the centre of London.

As the V-2 was proving the reliability of the ballistic missile, larger rockets were soon on the drawing-board. The A-9 was envisaged as a rocket with a range of up to 500 miles (800km) and an A-10 was planned to act as a first-stage booster that could extend the range to reach the United States. The original development work had been undertaken in 1940, with a first flight date set for 1946, but the project – as so often happened – was summarily stopped. When the so-called Projekt *Amerika* re-emerged in 1944, work was resumed, and the A-11 was planned as a huge first stage that would carry the A-9 and A-10. The plans (which were released in 1946 by the United States Army) were for a rocket that could even place a payload of some 660lb (300kg) into orbit. The proposed A-12 fourth stage would have a launch weight of 3,500 tons and could place 10 tons into orbit. In the event, all these plans were to fall into Allied hands as the European war drew to a close. During the spring of 1945 the Allies advanced from the west, and the Russians closed in from the east. When news reached Peenemünde that the Soviet Army was only about 100 miles (160km) away, Von Braun assembled planning staff and broke the news. It was time to decide by which army they would be captured. All knew that the world would regard them as war criminals, and the decisions were not easy.

The dreadful destruction and the mass killings reported early in the campaign make the V-2 seem like a terrifyingly successful rocket, but was it really valuable as a weapon of war?

Let us look at the figures. It has been estimated that 2,754 civilians were killed in Britain by the 1,402 V-2 attacks. A further people 6,523 were injured. These simple facts reveal that the V-2, as a weapon of war, was a costly failure. Each of these incredibly expensive and complex missiles killed about two people, and injured roughly six more, indeed it has been calculated that more casualties were caused by the manufacture of the V-2 than resulted from its use in war. The reality was that they were inefficient in terms of killing the enemy – but they had proved how successful they were as rockets. Von Braun had always wanted to build rockets, and had held in his heart the ultimate ambition of building a space rocket. The Nazis held onto the propaganda value of their successful launch series, even though remarkably few people were being killed by the V-2 attacks. The Nazis had been used by Von Braun to fund his private ambitions; Hitler's doubts about the V-2 as an agent of warfare were right after all.

One of the first initiatives after the Allies invaded Peenemünde was to test the V-2 rockets before any were moved to other countries. In October 1945, the British Operation *Backfire* fired several V-2 rockets from northern Germany. There were many reports of what became

Following a V-2 rocket attack on Farringdon Market in London, rescue workers including ambulance driver Jean Grover (right) and her unnamed nurse (left), are quickly on the scene to help the wounded. (Getty Images)

Operation *Backfire* was a British venture designed to evaluate the V-2 rocket system. Following the fall of Nazi Germany, flight tests were undertaken at a gun testing range at Cuxhaven, part of the British zone of occupation. (SSPL/Getty Images)

known as 'ghost rockets', unaccountable sightings of missile trails in the skies above Scandinavia. These were from Operation *Backfire*: not only did the Nazis fire their monster rockets from Germany, so too did the British.

THE SOVIET OPTION

It has been widely reported that the Germans unanimously decided to surrender to the Western Allies. This is not the case. Some of the scientists were more impressed by the Soviet system than they were by American capitalism, and Helmut Gröttrup was the most conspicuous of these. Gröttrup was an electronics engineer who no longer wished to 'understudy' Von Braun as he had done in the development of the V-2 rocket. Gröttrup decided to approach the Soviets and was offered a senior position in Russian rocket development. Between 9 September 1945 and 22 October 1946 Gröttrup with his loyal team of researchers worked for the USSR in the Soviet Occupied Zone of Germany (later to become the German Democratic Republic). His director of research was Sergei Korolev, Russia's leading rocket scientist. In the autumn of 1946, the entire team was moved to Russia. Gröttrup had cooperated with Russia in bringing 20 of the V-2 rockets to the newly established rocket research institute at Kapustin Yar, between Volgograd and the deserts of Astrakhan. The base is known today as Znamensk and it had opened on 13 May 1946 specifically to offer facilities to German experts. In charge was General Vasily Voznyuk and on 18 October 1947 they launched the first of the V-2 rockets brought in from Germany.

Gröttrup worked under Korolev to develop the Russian R-1 project; these were in reality V-2 rockets built using Russian manufacturing and materials with the German designs. The People's Commissar of Armaments, Dmitry Ustinov, requested that Gröttrup and his team of technicians design new missile systems, culminating in the projected R-14 rocket which was similar to the design of long-range missiles that Von Braun was developing during the war. The site at Znamensk developed into a top-secret cosmodrome and the small town itself was expanded to provide a pleasurable and civilized lifestyle for the families of the research teams working on the rockets. It was no longer included on Russian maps, and there were strict rules against disclosure of what was going on.

The value of the German expertise to the Russians proved to be limited and, in due course, the authorities allowed the research workers to return to their homes in Germany. The design of rocket motors in Russia by Aleksei Mikhailovich Isaev was already superior to the German concepts used in the V-2 rockets, and their lightweight copper motors gave rise to the first intercontinental ballistic missile, the R-7. It was this design advantage that gave the Russians technical superiority in rocketry and led to their launching the world's first satellite Sputnik 1, and subsequently to the launch of Yuri Gagarin as the first man into space.

The same technology gave the Russians the capacity to launch the first lunar probe, and later the spacecraft sent out towards the planets. Indeed, this design of rocket is still in use today. Once it was recognized that there was little point in keeping the German rocket specialists in Russia, on 22 November 1955 Gröttrup was given leave to return to his native Germany. In cooperation with Jürgen Dethloff he went on to design and patent the chip card which was to become so important in modern banking systems, and so his post-war genius is with us today.

MOVING TO AMERICA

Most of Von Braun's team opted to surrender to the Western Allies, rather than the Russians. With the position of Germany deteriorating rapidly, conflicting orders began to arrive. The rocket technicians were ordered to move *en masse* to Mittelwerk; then they received orders to join the Army and stay to fight the invading Allies. Von Braun opted to hide in the mountains, out of harm's way and nearer to the advancing American and British forces. Several thousand employees and their families left their homes, voyaging south in ships and barges, by rail and road. They had to dodge Allied bombing raids and deal with Nazi officials at checkpoints. Von Braun was fearful that the defeated SS might try to destroy the results of their work, so he had blueprints of all their designs hidden in an abandoned mineshaft in the Harz mountains where he could later retrieve them.

In March 1945, his driver fell asleep at the wheel and Von Braun was left with a compound fracture of his left arm. Insisting on being mobile, he had the fracture roughly set in a cast. It was unsatisfactory, and so in the following month he had to return to hospital where the bone was broken again and re-aligned correctly. He was still in plaster as the Allied troops advanced.

Suddenly the team was ordered to move to Oberammergau in the Bavarian Alps. They were placed under guard by the SS who had orders to shoot everyone if they were about to fall into Allied hands. Von Braun got wind of this, and persuaded the SS officer in charge that keeping them together made them a sitting target for Allied bombing raids. Since they were important personnel, Von Braun argued, it would surely be safer to distribute the members of the team among the nearby villages. In one of these villages, on 2 May 1945, Von Braun's brother Magnus – also a rocket engineer – suddenly encountered an American private of the 44th Infantry Division named Fred Schneiker. Magnus von Braun rode up on his bicycle, and announced: 'My name is Magnus von Braun. My brother invented the V-2. Please, we want to surrender.' Von Braun was immediately locked up, and so were thousands of the others, as war criminals - the large photo on page 120 shows a handful of eminent figures upon their arrest by the US Army. The factories were quickly overrun and between 22 and 31 May 1945 a total of 341 railway trucks were used to move as many V-2 rockets as possible and the manufacturing equipment to Antwerp, from where 16 Liberty ships transported them to the port of New Orleans. From there the rockets and equipment were transferred to the New Mexican desert under conditions of extreme secrecy.

Схема — общий вид I этап

То-же — II этап

То-же — III этап

Пусков. средства д/пуска подуг.
а) Сфера — сфрое испол
б) Устройство д/впуск. сфрр

Схема пассаж. ракеты

OPERATION *PAPERCLIP*

The German rocket engineers themselves were also taken to the United States covertly, as part of Operation *Paperclip*. This secret scheme was set up by the United States Office of Strategic Services (OSS), which in turn gave rise to today's Central Intelligence Agency (CIA). It had been assumed that the personnel involved in creating the weapons of mass destruction would be put on trial for war crimes, but during the closing stages of the war it was decided instead to see if the United States could secretly harness their knowledge. Agents within the United States resolved to bring these people to America and use the benefits of their research, at the same time denying the benefits to their allies, the Soviet Union and the British.

Although relatively unknown, there was a similar scheme operating for the British. This was code named Operation *Surgeon* and it was intended to bring promising research engineers to Britain and to deny them to the Soviet Union. The official policy was not to involve suspected war criminals, but to capture some 1,500 research personnel and to remove them forcibly. The document setting this out was entitled *Employment of German Scientists and Technicians: Denial Policy*, and it survives to this day at the National Archives, Kew, United Kingdom. It was explicit about the need to obtain personnel, and said they would be removed 'whether they liked it or not'. Many of the individuals on the lists offered their services to other Commonwealth countries, with some opting to go to South American countries (including Brazil) and others going to Scandinavia and Switzerland. The scheme was the first to come into operation, and ran from the time the British forces overran the German research establishments until all the scientists and engineers had been accounted for.

Not until September 1945 was Operation *Paperclip* authorized by President Harry S. Truman. The President's orders stated that nobody should be included who had 'been a member of the Nazi Party, and more than a nominal participant in its activities, or an active supporter of Nazi militarism'. Included under that clause as Nazi sympathizers were many of the senior figures like Von Braun who was stated, at the time, to be 'a menace to the security of the Allied Forces'.

As a result, the aims of Operation *Paperclip* were clearly unlawful and what is more OSS agents acted in direct defiance of the President's orders. In order to make the most desirable personnel seem acceptable, the representatives of the OSS constructed false employment and faked political biographies for the chosen scientists. All references to Nazi party membership, and any political activity in Nazi Germany, were removed from the record, and new résumés were concocted by the American secret service. At the end of each exercise, a German specialist – often with enduring Nazi sympathies – had been provided with a fictitious political history and an imaginary personal life. The documents were typed up, carefully countersigned,

Opposite: Insights into a powerful engineering mind. This page from Sergei Korolev's notebook shows designs and notes by the Soviet Union's leading rocket scientist. (RIA Novosti/Science Photo Library)

President Truman announces the end of the war in August 1945. In September, the President authorized Operation *Paperclip*, but with limits. He did not want it to include anyone who had had more than nominal involvement with Nazism. (Keystone-France/Gamma-Keystone/Getty Images)

German rocket pioneer and inventor Wernher von Braun (left) smiles with his brother Magnus, having surrendered to US 7th Army troops. (Time & Life Pictures/Getty Images)

and attached to their birth certificates with paperclips – which gave the operation its name. In the meantime, Von Braun had disappeared. He found himself secretly jailed at a top-secret military intelligence unit at Fort Hunt, Virginia, in the United States. It had no name, and was referred to only by its postal code 'PO Box 1142'. This was a top-secret confinement facility undeclared to the Red Cross and was thus in breach of the Geneva Convention.

Another of the senior scientists who was taken to America by the Allies was Adolf Thiel. Before he had joined Von Braun at the Peenemünde research laboratories, Thiel had been Associate Professor of Engineering at the Darmstadt Institute of Technology. After the war, as part of Operation *Paperclip*, Thiel was taken with Von Braun to Fort Bliss, Texas, and later to the White Sands Missile Range in New Mexico and on to Huntsville, Alabama. His prime responsibility in America was the refinement of the V-2 design into the Redstone missile, and he later adapted it to become the Thor ballistic missile, which was the first stage rocket for the Explorer spacecraft. Thiel was made a Fellow of the American Astronautical Society in 1968 and died in Los Angeles in 2001 aged 86. So he lived into the new millennium, and saw the realization of the dream of space exploration.

Dörnberger was also brought to America and went on to work for the United States Air Force developing guided missiles. Later he was a key figure in developing the X-20 Dyna-Soar which was, in many ways, the ancestor of the space shuttle; he also worked

Von Braun and colleagues outside the research facility at Fort Bliss, Texas. Von Braun was one of many German scientists who were secretly relocated to the USA as part of Operation *Paperclip* at the end of World War II. (TWM HU 33894)

on the Rascal, an air-to-surface nuclear missile used by the Strategic Air Command. He later retired to Germany and died in 1980 at home in Baden-Württemberg. On 8 July 1944 he had received a handwritten note from Hitler: 'I have had to apologize only to two men in my whole life,' the Führer had written. 'The first was Field Marshal von Brauchitsch. I did not listen to him when he told me again and again how important your research was. The second man is yourself. I never believed that your work would be successful.'

AMERICA CONQUERS SPACE

Von Braun was soon working for the United States as their senior rocket designer. Within two years, the United States had test-launched her first spacecraft – a two-stage rocket code named Bumper.

Shortly afterwards, they proudly announced the inauguration of their successful Redstone rockets. The Redstone was described to the world as the first American ballistic missile and it was in service with the United States Army in Germany between June 1958 and June 1964 as part of the Cold War deterrence policy of NATO. The Redstone was also involved in the first United States nuclear missile tests in the Pacific and in 1960–61 a Redstone was used for the pioneering Project *Mercury* manned space flights. Its predictability earned the Redstone nicknames including the 'Army's Workhorse' and 'Old Reliable'. This rocket had its final flight when it launched Australia's first earth satellite in 1967.

Although Bumper and Redstone are claimed as pioneering names in American rocketry, both were actually V-2 rockets. The Bumper, heralded as the first two-stage rocket when it was initially tested on 13 May 1948, was a German V-2 fitted with a little United States Wac Corporal solid-fuel rocket as a second stage. The Redstones were also V-2 rockets, some with

World War II rocket scientist Wernher von Braun, photographed around 1955 with a model of a long-range rocket based on the V-2 design. (Getty images)

A Redstone rocket during the Inaugural Day parade. Under Operation *Paperclip*, Adolf Thiel used the V-2 design to create the Redstone missile for the USA. (Time & Life Pictures/Getty Images)

The start of Cape Canaveral as a rocket base began with this launch of a US Bumper rocket – the first stage being an unaltered V-2 – on 24 July 1950. (Author's collection)

later modifications, but all based on the Nazi-funded research during World War II. When John Glenn rose into space, it was on top of a modified V-2. And when the Australians launched their WRESAT satellite into orbit on 29 November 1967 from Woomera, it was one of those modified V-2 rockets that provided the launch.

Ten years after entering the United States, Von Braun became a naturalized US citizen. He went on to work on the US Army intermediate range ballistic missile programme until this project was absorbed by NASA. Von Braun was appointed Director of the new Marshall Space Flight Center and was the chief designer of the Saturn V launch vehicle which was the rocket that launched the Apollo spacecraft. NASA said he was the greatest rocket scientist in history and his crowning achievement was the Saturn V rocket that led to men on the moon in July 1969. In 1975 Von Braun was awarded the National Medal of Science.

On 16 June 1977, Wernher von Braun died of pancreatic cancer in Alexandria, Virginia, at the age of 65. He had, after trials and tribulations, realized his dream. His experience and training in Nazi Germany had put an American on the moon, and his wartime adventures in designing weapons to aim at the Allies had given the American nation their lead in space.

This striking image shows the Saturn V moon rocket. Designed under the direction of Von Braun and a direct descendant of the V-2, Saturn V carried aloft all Apollo lunar missions including Apollo 11 which first put a man on the moon. (Frank Whitney/AFP/Getty Images)

DOCTORS
AT WAR

MEDICINE BECAME A FOCUS for secret science during World War II. Research workers were instructed to do all they could to find ways of improving the lot of the military, and to find innovative ways of saving lives. New treatments, super-drugs and extraordinary new surgical procedures and many other ways of saving lives and returning trained wounded soldiers to the front as quickly as possible were all developed during the war years. Yet the same specialities were also harnessed to produce new, lethal secret weapons of terrifying potential. Modern medicine owes much to the rapid research of World War II; yet many of the worst excesses were perpetrated by doctors.

CHEMICALS IN WAR

Medical science had already shown that many chemicals have a burning, blistering or destructive capacity against human victims, and experiments to use them against soldiers during wartime date from World War I. Gas shells had been used by the British, the Germans and the French, among others. The choice of poison gases was wide, and they ranged from irritants that incapacitated and temporarily blinded the enemy, to gases that burned the body, destroyed the lungs and liquefied the tissues. First to be used in World War I was a tear gas, xylyl bromide. Most accounts state that this was first used in that war by the Germans in 1915, but it had been used by the French against German troops in August 1914 as the Germans were advancing through Belgium towards northern France. Within a year the Germans retaliated. They launched a well-planned attack by releasing their latest secret weapon, chlorine from gas cylinders, up-wind from the Allied positions at Ypres in April 1915. The Allies immediately condemned Germany for breaching the Hague Convention, with the British a leading voice of protest (though in fact it was the British who by then had the largest stockpiles of poison gas, ready for use in war). The Germans retorted that the Convention spoke only of projectiles – and they had simply unleashed the gas from containers. They added that the French had already used gas against their troops, without similar censure.

In any event, the secret was out and gas war had been officially declared. Within weeks, thousands of the chlorine gas cylinders had been installed by the British on the front line inland from Calais at Loos. But no mention was to be made of the word 'gas'. The cylinders were called 'accessories', and the use of the 'g-word' was a punishable breach of the rules. The attacks were easy to launch – taps on the cylinders were simply opened and the gas rolled along with the breeze. Once launched, they were less easy to control, however; on the day in question the breeze shifted direction and most of the casualties of the first attack were British soldiers, rather than German. It was an historic example of what we now call, with bitter irony, 'friendly fire'. The experience taught a crucial lesson: the gas could not simply be released by an army without compromising its own troops. After this episode, the gases were packed in artillery shells and the Hague Convention was conveniently ignored.

The Germans fired the gas in shells against the Russians in 1915 under the code name T-Stoff. These attacks failed, because the temperatures were low and the liquid did not vaporize as expected. It either lay on the ground, or was wafted back towards the German lines. Other tear gas agents were later used. They were a range of dangerous chemicals including ethyl bromoacetate, bromoacetone (known as BA), bromobenzyl cyanide (Camite), bromomethyl ethyl ketone (Bn-Stoff) and chloroacetone (Tonite). The Germans used them either singly or in combination under the general name *Weisskreuz* (White Cross). The name came from the identifying symbol that was stencilled on each shell.

Chlorine was brought into use as it acts as a disabling tear gas when used in small amounts, but kills painfully by destroying the lung tissues if inhaled in significant quantities. It is a heavy gas and rolls across the countryside, filling holes and trenches where the enemy might be in hiding. It forms a greenish-yellow fog with a penetrating, acrid smell and was also known as Bertholite. Chlorine reacts with the water in the body to produce hydrochloric acid which burns the lungs from within. Germany was the first to use this in World War I at Ypres; there are reports that it was last used in Iraq against coalition forces in 2007.

Phosgene followed, after being first used by the French in 1915. It was a similarly suffocating gas but did not produce coughing, like chlorine; as a result, more of it was inhaled by the victims. The effects also took longer to appear, and often more than a day passed before soldiers started to collapse. It was eventually used by both sides in World War I and was blended with chlorine to produce a mixture called White Star. The gas produced devastating effects by damaging the eyes, burning into the skin – even slight lesions are like frostbite – and causing the lungs to burn and fill with fluid. Sufferers from an attack drowned from within. This was used in many weapons during World War I; it was later used against the Chinese by the Japanese during the Second Sino-Japanese War in 1938. Huge amounts of phosgene were stockpiled, ready for use in World War II, but in the event it was never employed. Hitler was the victim of a gas attack in World War I and resolved never to use it in war. He was well aware of the devastating consequences of retaliation by an enemy using phosgene and knew it would be a dangerous tactic to adopt, in case the Allies hit back with it.

The Germans did plan the manufacture of poison gas in the 1920s, in defiance of the international treaties, and negotiated with the Soviet authorities for the construction of a large chemical weapons factory on the river Volga at Trotsk. Britain similarly produced large amounts of poison gases for stockpiling during World War II. Had there been attacks by an enemy using chemical weapons during the war then the British stockpiles would have been speedily cleared for use. And since that war? Today there is phosgene everywhere, and in huge amounts, for it is an important product of modern-day industry. Phosgene is an intermediate compound in the manufacture of pesticides and plastics, and it is abundantly available in industrial cities throughout the world.

DURING AN AIR RAID

WHAT TO DO IF THE HOUSE IS DAMAGED

At once put on your respirator. If you have to go out of your refuge-room, seek refuge in another room or in another building. If you have to go out of doors keep on your respirator, and wear a mackintosh and goloshes or gum boots if you have them. Avoid all damp splashes on the ground that might be gas. If anyone is injured, a message should be sent to the warden's post, or the nearest first aid party or post. Until help comes act according to the instructions in Section 5, at the end of the book.

HOW TO AVOID INJURY FROM MUSTARD GAS

Mustard gas, whether in the form of liquid or of the vapour which the liquid gives off, will injure any part of the body with which it comes in contact. It also " contaminates " clothing, or other objects exposed to it, making them dangerous to have near you or to touch until they have been " decontaminated." If you have come in contact with the liquid or vapour of mustard change all your clothing as soon as possible, put it right outside the house, and wash yourself thoroughly with soap and water. Your shoes should be taken off before entering the house and left outside. Any outer garment which has actually touched liquid gas should be taken off *immediately*.

To be of use, the washing and changing must be done within twenty minutes at the outside. Take these precautions yourself if you can take them quickly ; if not, go to the nearest first aid post.

If liquid gas has been in contact with your skin, wash that part of yourself *immediately* with soap and water, then change and wash as described above. If you cannot take these measures *at once*, go to the nearest first aid post straight away.

If you have been actually splashed with liquid gas or have passed through an area which has been splashed with it, go to a first aid post for further treatment after taking the precautions described above.

Page 25

The Home Office in London produced series of information leaflets in the lead-up to World War II, this example giving advice on how to avoid injury from mustard gas. (His Majesty's Stationery Office, 1938)

This photo from 1941 shows the equipment that was assembled to decontaminate gas casualties at a cleansing centre in London. Efforts on the Home Front helped ensure that England's civilian population would be well-placed to cope with poison gas attacks. (IWM D 3925)

Mustard gas, or mustard yellow, produces burning blisters over the body. It does not cause an immediate effect, and the symptoms of poisoning often take hours to become apparent. The blisters are large and filled with yellowish plasma; they take a prolonged time to heal, cause great pain, and cannot be touched or treated. It was first used by the Germans at their campaign at Ypres in France during World War I (and was afterwards known as Yperite) and was then employed against the Russian Army by the British in 1919. Indeed, up to half the shells produced by both sides would have contained poison gases had World War I not ended when it did. Since that time mustard gas has been used by Spain and France against rebels in Morocco during the 1920s, by the Italians against Libya in 1930 and Ethiopia from 1935, by the Russians during their incursions in China during the 1930s, and by Japan against the Chinese prior to, and during, World War II. Early in the war years, the United States Chemical Warfare Service carried out mustard gas experiments on some 4,000 American troops. Many of them were volunteers who had conscientious objections to going to war, and

John Singer Sargent's vivid depiction of the aftermath of a mustard gas attack on the Western Front in August 1918 powerfully evokes the helplessness of the victims. The artist was a witness to the scene. (IWM ART 1460)

they were offered the chance to take part in poison gas tests as an alternative to conscription. The tests went on until the end of the war, though the United States did not indulge in gas warfare during World War II. Germany carried out hundreds of experiments in which prisoners were deliberately disabled by the use of poison gases, including mustard gas and Lewisite, at the Natzweiler and Sachsenhausen concentration camps. Various experimental treatments were tried on the disabled and dying patients in the hope of finding ways of treating their wounds.

British-made mustard gas was once used by the Poles against the Germans during the invasion of 1939, though the only further release of mustard gas was accidental and a casualty of war. In December 1943, a squadron of Junkers Ju-88 bombers bombed the southern Italian port of Bari. The attack was later described as the 'Little Pearl Harbor' and several United States warships were sunk, including the SS *John Harvey*, which was moored in the port, ready to be unloaded. This vessel was carrying a large secret consignment of mustard gas shells to be available for possible use in the Allied action against Italy. The bombers struck the ship amidships and blew apart the poison-gas weapons, releasing a vast cloud of mustard gas. So top-secret was this kind of weapon that no mention of it had been made outside the security services. As a result, the doctors had no knowledge of what caused the terrifying symptoms and none of the victims were given suitable treatment. About 70 American servicemen died of the gas; large numbers of civilians ashore were also affected, though no attempt was made to collect figures and the security about the nature of the agent was maintained until long after the war had ended.

The Allies maintained huge stockpiles in case gas weapons were used by the Axis forces against the Allied troops. Australia secretly and illegally imported a total of one million chemical weapons from the British throughout the war, and at the end of hostilities there were large stockpiles of poison gas around the world. Mustard gas weapons were later used against Yemen by Egypt in the 1960s and by Iraq in their war with Iran as recently as the mid-1980s.

Lewisite is a similar blistering gas that was first developed from an idea found in a research chemistry thesis at The Catholic University of America in Washington, DC. It was developed further as a top-secret weapon by the United States military and experiments were carried out in the 1920s, when it was known as the Dew of Death. A total of 20,000 tons of Lewisite were produced by the Americans but by the end of World War II it was obsolete and, in any event, a British discovery, dimercaprol, was an effective agent to counteract its effects and became known as British Anti-Lewisite. During the 1950s, most of the United States' stockpiles of the weapon were neutralized and dumped into the Gulf of Mexico though some were kept as a more modest reserve. Indeed, Lewisite from World War II has recently turned up in the United States capital, Washington, DC, as I am writing these words in 2011. The Army Corps of Engineers, while digging out a site near the American University, have found glass storage vessels filled with Lewisite dating back to the 1940s. More are awaiting discovery. The problem of poison gas, it seems, is still with us today.

But the most dangerous secret chemical weapons of all were the nerve-gas agents developed in Germany. The first was tabun, discovered in 1937, and sarin, first synthesized in 1939. Both were discovered by Dr Gerhard Schrader, a research chemist at the IG Farben Company in Frankfurt am Main. These deadly agents were followed by soman, invented in Heidelberg by a Nobel Prize laureate, Dr Richard Kuhn, at the Kaiser Wilhelm Institute for Medical Research early in 1944. These light liquid agents were the making of terrifying secret weapons with appalling effects on victims. Nothing may be observed after exposure for up to half an hour. Early effects include a runny nose followed by intense pain in the eyeball and blurred vision. The chest becomes tight and breathing difficult; the victim starts to perspire profusely and vomit. Twitching and convulsions occur in the muscles, the victim hallucinates and a sense of fear becomes overwhelming. These gases act by interfering with the transmission of impulses along the nerve pathways of the whole body, and so breathing become impossible and the patients die in unimaginable distress.

During the 1950s, NATO recognized sarin as a useful weapon of war and large amounts were stockpiled by the Soviet Union and the United States. Experiments in chemical warfare also secretly continued in Britain at Porton Down, Wiltshire. In 1953 a young volunteer, who had been asked to participate in tests to 'cure the common cold', was killed by being exposed to British-made sarin. Both Chile and Iraq have subsequently been reported to use sarin. The regime of Saddam Hussein used this gas in attacks against Iraqi Kurds in 1988. It was manufactured from raw materials supplied by the United States.

These agents arose from German research into insecticides during the 1930s. We know that Germany was, for many decades, the world's leader in chemical innovation. During the post-war years, further research at Imperial Chemical Industries (ICI) in Britain led to the discovery of other potent agents. They were too toxic to be released for general use as insecticides, but the toxicity was of immediate interest to the secret weapons scientists at the Porton Down research facility. The result was a new, even stronger class of nerve poisons, the VX agents. Within a few years, the British officially renounced chemical and biological weapons and their research on the VX weapons was passed to the United States under a technology exchange scheme. Throughout the 1960s, large amounts of the VX agents were manufactured in the United States and stockpiled.

THE HORROR OF HUMAN EXPERIMENTS

Many of the warmongers during World War II looked on their subjects as inferiors, as persons who hardly warranted the category of fellow human being. We know that they were conscripted to become slave workers; but many were also used for terrible medical experiments. Some were used for vivisection and for experiments of obscene brutality, and all because the aggressor had constructed a culture of invincible and inhuman superiority. Although the name of Dr Josef Mengele comes immediately to mind, the dawn of medical experimentation lies not with Germany, but with Japan.

JAPANESE HUMAN EXPERIMENTS

In the years leading up to the outbreak of World War II, the Japanese occupied Manchukuo in north-eastern China. There are stories told to this day of disease-infected fleas and of bombs of bacteria that were used by the Japanese against their Chinese foes during these invasions of Chinese territory. As many as 50,000 Chinese are believed to have died as a result of these biological attacks, and it is said that some areas are still regarded as dangerous, lest there be a further outbreak caused by germs lying hidden in the ground.

In the Pingfang district of Harbin the Japanese organized scientific research through a body code named Unit 731. It was embraced by the Kwantung Army, and was officially known as the Epidemic Prevention and Water Purification Department. The authorities of the Empire of Japan set up this Unit under the Kempeitai military police with the covert purpose of developing weapons that could be used against the Chinese, Koreans and other peoples whose territory they wished to invade. Although it was officially designated as an institute focusing on the health of the population, it was really devoted to the development of top-secret chemical and biological weapons.

The institute was the brainchild of Dr Shiro Ishii of Kyoto University, and he was given unlimited resources to build his research laboratories, such as Unit 731. The design of the building was of the highest specifications, with the very best of materials and the latest equipment. Harbin was chosen for its remoteness from the rest of China, and the local workers who were erecting the buildings were told that it was to be a timber mill. The best local craftsmen were used, and the highest quality materials brought in, regardless of expense.

Shiro Ishii (left) founded Unit 731 in Harbin and was an advocate of germ weapons. After the war he was secretly taken to the US to work for America and continued his research in Maryland. (Getty Images)

For decades, little emerged about the work, though it was widely believed that thousands of people died as a result of these grotesque medical experiments. Not until 2002 was a formal academic meeting held that examined the surviving documents in detail. Their revelations were deeply disturbing: over half a million people died as a result of Japan's medical experimentation in camps like Unit 731. The clue to the importance of this research, exactly as in the case of the Treaty of Versailles, lay in international legislation enacted specifically to prevent it. Historian Daniel Barenblatt has put his finger on the dawn of this practice in Japan, when Ishii read a report on the Geneva Convention, published in 1925, which stated:

Protocol for the Prohibition of the Use in War of Bacteriological Methods of Warfare.
The use in war of asphyxiating, poisonous, or other gases ... has been justly condemned by the general opinion of the civilized world ... and [we] agree to extend this prohibition to the use of bacteriological methods of warfare.

Ishii had long tried to convince the Japanese authorities of the value of bacteriological weapons in war, and they had never taken him seriously. Here was the evidence he needed – if bacteriological warfare was regarded as such a threat as to warrant an entire section of the Geneva Convention, then that proved how valuable it could be to Japan. By prohibiting germ warfare, the Convention had clearly documented its potential importance.

To Ishii, the enemy were different – he saw them, as increasing numbers of Japanese were to do, as inferior beings, subservient to Japan, and there only to be used at the will of the conquering Japanese Empire. Unit 731 was the first and main establishment, and others soon followed, including Unit 100 (Changchun), Unit 200 (Manchuria), Unit 516 (Qiqihar), Unit 543 (Hailar), Unit 773 (Songo unit), Unit Ei 1644 (Nanjing), Unit 1855 (Beijing), Unit 8604 (Guangzhou) and Unit 9420 (Singapore).

The experimental subjects were treated worse than livestock. They were brought in from areas occupied by the Japanese in China and Korea, and were held in enclosures. Some were criminals and bandits, others were military prisoners, more still were women – some pregnant – and children, together with the old. One of the stories circulated to explain the new institutes was that one was a lumber mill. It gave rise to the Japanese nickname for the inmates of 'logs '. As military historian Sheldon H. Harris has said, 'they were regarded as logs – you could cut them or burn them with impunity'. In consequence, these hapless prisoners were frequently subjected to vivisection, having limbs or organs removed to study the effects. Men had their extremities frozen until they became gangrenous, so the course of the agonizing fatal infection could be studied. Women were cut open so that their foetuses could be studied; others had limbs cut off so that death through blood loss could be observed. People had air let into veins, to study how they died; some were hung upside down to see how long they survived, others were treated in high-pressure chambers, were spun until dead on giant centrifuges or injected with urine and seawater. Prisoners were also tied to posts and subjected to weapons testing and used for target practice. Others were blown apart by grenades, burned alive with flame throwers and doused with caustic chemicals. The records were written up in meticulous detail, so that Japanese troops – when injured by blast, chemicals or intense cold – could be treated with a better insight into how their wounds would progress. Other victims were injected with disease agents including syphilis or infected with disease vectors like fleas, to see how the diseases were transmitted. Cholera, plague and anthrax were deliberately spread among civilian populations to facilitate ethnic cleansing and to investigate the potential of these diseases as biological weapons.

Secret biowarfare agents resulted. Planes flew low over Chinese cities to spray infected fleas in huge amounts. There were epidemics of bubonic plague spread by this means. Infected food was dropped for starving villagers, epidemics of dysentery, typhoid and even cholera were caused deliberately. Doctors and technicians in protective suits would move among the populations to observe how they died. The International Symposium on the Crimes of Bacteriological Warfare concluded in 2002 that the number of people killed by the Imperial Japanese Army in their medical experiments was around 580,000.

As the war entered its closing phase, Soviet troops invaded Manchukuo in August 1945 and the medical experimentation staff returned to Japan. All were issued with cyanide pills to take in an emergency, and Ishii instructed everyone that they should never speak of what had happened. A few staff remained on site with instructions to blow up the buildings as the enemy troops approached. In the event, the buildings had been constructed too strongly to be so easily demolished, and most were unaffected by the explosives. Today some are museums.

When the Empire of Japan surrendered to the Allies in 1945, the Supreme Commander of the Allied Forces, General Douglas MacArthur, was given the responsibility or restoring peace to Japan. The work at the secret camps had all been well documented, and the research scientists and doctors were all known to the Allies as being among the most sadistic and inhuman individuals of the entire war. They were all immediately categorized as culpable war criminals. Those who had been apprehended by the Soviets were prosecuted at the Khabarovsk

War Crime Trials. Twelve of the top researchers and commanders were prosecuted for their crimes. One was the Commander-in-Chief of the Kwantung Army that occupied Manchuria. He was General Otozo Yamada, in charge of the biological warfare research. He was sentenced to 25 years in a Siberian work camp but was released to return to Japan in 1956. Meanwhile, the Soviets went on to establish a biological research institute in Sverdlovsk that was founded on the findings from Unit 731.

The researchers who were captured by the Western Allies, or surrendered to American forces, were treated very differently. Ishii had lengthy discussions with the Americans and was treated well during his confinement. In May 1947, General MacArthur entered a plea bargain with the Japanese. He informed Washington that, if the perpetrators were guaranteed immunity from prosecution, the United States could benefit from all their findings. The results would not be made available to any other nation. The deal was agreed and, when the Tokyo War Crimes Tribunal convened to try Japanese war criminals, only one case of human experimentation was brought before the courts. This was the alleged use of poisonous serum against Chinese civilians, and the case was dismissed due to insufficient evidence. Large

On board the USS *Missouri*, General Yoshijiro Umezu signs the surrender document as Japan formally accepts defeat at the of end World War II. (Popperfoto/Getty Images)

numbers of those Japanese workers who had carried out the inhuman research were offered freedom in exchange for their findings, and went on to hold positions of importance in academia, politics and business. Many of them practised medicine after the war. One became the head of the leading Japanese pharmaceutical company; another became president of a prestigious American medical school.

And the infamous Dr Shiro Ishii? It is believed that he went to live in Maryland, where he continued his work on bio-weapons for the American military, and died in Japan of throat cancer aged 67. Some of the chemicals agents used in the experiments were carcinogenic. It might have been poetic justice.

GERMAN HUMAN EXPERIMENTS

Germany began experimenting on human subjects from the outset of the war. Top-secret medical experimentation was under way in 1939 at Sachsenhausen, and many other concentration camps were to follow. The buildings remain, and I have found these sites to be a disturbing reminder of state-sanctioned cruelty. The first experiments included tests of poison gas against human subjects. Mustard gas and Lewisite were applied to the bodies, causing severe blistering and burning. The subjects' wounds could be treated in different ways, in order to ascertain which approach gave the best results.

From 1942 onwards, the range of secret medical experiments diversified and greatly increased in number. At the Dachau concentration camp, inmates were deliberately infected with malaria. Once the disease had developed, the victims were used as experimental subjects and given a range of possible treatments in the hope of finding a cure. Half the subjects died. Dachau was also the focus of freezing experiments, in which prisoners were fitted with various designs of protective clothing (designed for pilots) and immersed up to the neck in iced water for prolonged periods of time. Experiments were also carried out in which prisoners were chained in the open air and left naked in sub-zero temperatures for hours on end. The results were noted down, partly to determine how rapidly people succumbed to the cold, and also to attempt different approaches to revival so that the results could be used to treat German military personnel – pilots who had been shot down in Arctic waters, for example. Auschwitz also took part in a similar series of trials in which victims were frozen, sometimes to death. This research increased with the prospect of war on the Eastern Front, and among the victims were Russian soldiers. The Nazis speculated that the severe Russian winters would give the Soviet soldiers a great genetic predisposition to survival in Arctic conditions, and the experiments were run in parallel to see if this was true. The results were communicated directly to Heinrich Himmler and specialist conferences were held, including one in 1942 entitled 'Medical Problems Arising from Sea and Winter' at which the results were presented in the manner of a scientific symposium.

From 1942, inmates of the Dachau concentration camp were tested for the effects of decompression. The Luftwaffe were keen to know what would happen to pilots whose aircraft were destroyed at altitude, and at what height they would parachute to earth. It was known that severe decompression sickness caused many to be incapacitated or killed, and so a hypobaric chamber was constructed that could have the air partially sucked out to simulate the air pressure at high altitudes (up to 60,000ft, about 20,000m). Bubbles of gas appeared in the blood at such low pressures, and most of the victims died in the chambers. They were then dissected so that the effects could be seen. Many were incapacitated, not

Above left: Scenes of immense relief as Dachau concentration camp is liberated. Appalling examples of human medical experiments took place here, including freezing and deliberate infection. (Getty Images)

Above right: Permanently scarred, but lucky to survive, former prisoners of Auschwitz concentration camp show the numbers that were tattooed on their arms during their imprisonment by the Nazis. (Getty Images)

Below: Prisoners of the Dachau camp show their feelings as they are liberated by the US Army. (Getty Images)

killed, and they were subject to vivisection so that their bodies could be studied as the fatal lesions took their toll.

Later experiments at Dachau involved methods of using seawater as an emergency drink. Roma people were chosen for these trials and groups were given no fresh water to drink and were allowed access only to seawater. They became desperately ill as a result, and some were seen licking water from freshly mopped floors. The Roma people were selected for experiments as the Nazis felt they were an inferior race and might have a more robust response to abuse.

At Buchenwald, another of the extant concentration camps that I have visited in the course of research, the effects of poisons were the focus of human experimentation. Toxic compounds were mixed with the inmates' food and some were shot with bullets containing poisons and were later dissected to ascertain the damage that had been done. There have been episodes since the war in which this idea has resurfaced. The most famous of these is the murder of the Bulgarian dissident writer Georgi Markov in 1978. He had a tiny hollow metal pellet shot into his leg by the Bulgarian Secret Service from a modified umbrella as he walked across Waterloo Bridge in central London. The tiny bullet contained ricin, a toxin extracted from seeds of the castor oil plant. Ricin had been patented by the US Secretary of the Army in 1952 for possible use as a weapon, and the patent description concluded that 'the product might be used as a toxic weapon'. At first, Markov's death was put down to food poisoning, and it was only the diligent investigations ordered by Scotland Yard that eventually led to the discovery of the tiny hollow bullet, $1/20$in (less than 2mm) in diameter, inside which the ricin had been concealed. Doubtless the assassins believed such a tiny projectile would never be found, and it is a remarkable story of detection. The use of a chemical poison hidden inside a small bullet stemmed from the ideas that originated in Nazi Germany, and it may still be used again.

Tests at Buchenwald were also done with phosphorus burns to the body. White phosphorus is a particularly inhumane weapon as it sticks to the skin and burns deep into the body. At Buchenwald concentration camp, inmates were covered with white phosphorus of the kind used in incendiary weapons and the effects were meticulously recorded.

The Nazis flourished in the era of eugenics, when the genetic nature of a race was considered an important indicator of what might be called 'social rank'. They felt that weak genetics predisposed races to a subservient role in the global community. It was a highly fashionable belief, but was never based on sound scientific grounds. The remarkable lack of connection between the achievements of parents and children is well observed – we all know bright and highly successful individuals who come from an inauspicious background, and uninspiring people whose parents were overwhelmingly intelligent and gifted in many ways. The roots of our adult selves do not lie in such a simple understanding of genetics.

Nonetheless, to the Nazis, there was a special appeal in studies of identical twins. The main organizer of experiments with twin children was Dr Josef Mengele, who became known as the Angel of Death. He was obsessed with the idea that the physiognomy of an individual

– the surface features of the face – could be correlated with their intellectual abilities. The idea had first surfaced in the pseudoscience of phrenology, in which the exterior of the head was measured, and was taken to indicate the most propitious zones of the brain that lay within. In Victorian times this was a popular topic, but it had been repeatedly disproved until it was abandoned by science. The last official application of the notion was in the 1930s, when the Belgian authorities tried to use phrenology in Rwanda to document the assumed superiority of the Tutsi tribes over the Hutus. It is still practised in some quarters; indeed the state of Michigan announced a new tax on the practitioners of phrenology as recently as 2007.

During his early years as a doctor, Josef Mengele had perceived a strong resonance between Nazism and his private beliefs on genetic superiority, and he published his doctoral thesis for the University of Munich on the subject of 'Racial Morphological Research on the Lower Jaw Section of Four Racial Groups'. It was not an anti-Semitic thesis, but paralleled the Nazis' enthusiasm for the correlation of racial disparity with innate 'worth'. He went on to carry out surgical experiments, including stitching pairs of twins together in an attempt to create conjoined twins, and injecting them to see if the hue of their eyes could be permanently changed. He carried out experiments on about 1,500 sets of whom only 100 individuals were known to have survived.

Some of the trials involved tests of the drug sulfanilamide, a potent anti-bacterial treatment that derived from the research at the giant German drug manufacturer Bayer. Children were deliberately infected with tuberculosis and they were then submitted to surgery for the removal of lymph nodes, both with and without drug treatment, to observe the progress of the disease or the possible success or failure of treatment. The experiments were taking place at the Neuengamme concentration camp, near Frankfurt, and as the Allied forces approached in the closing months of the war, all the surviving children were murdered – along with their carers – in an effort to keep the nature of the experiments secret.

The experiments on human victims gave results that were (and still are) used to understand the dangers facing high-altitude pilots and troops in extreme conditions. There was a wanton disregard for the human rights of the subjects in all all those medical trials – not simply because the doctors were intent on cruelty, but as part of the nationalist culture. Hitler's creed was based on the inherent superiority of the Aryan race. There are many repercussions of these German medical experiments in the modern world. White phosphorus has been widely used in recent conflicts, including the attacks on Fallujah, Iraq, by United States troops from 2004, and again in Afghanistan in 2009. It caused widespread injuries to civilians. In their attacks in south Lebanon and in Gaza, Israeli troops have fired shells of white phosphorus causing terrifying injuries to the civilian population, and Saudi aircraft have been reported to have used phosphorus shells in attacks against Houthi fighters in northern Yemen in 2009. The position is interesting in international law, since the United Nations Convention on Certain Conventional Weapons, which came into force in 1978,

'Angel of Death' Dr Josef Mengele, clad in his SS uniform during World War II. Mengele's notoriety for extreme human experimentation lives on to this day. (Getty Images)

After he was released by US officials in 1945, Mengele started a new life in South America. The front page of the *Correo de la Tarde* made readers aware that Mengele was to be in Buenos Aires. (© TopFoto)

included a protocol banning the use of all incendiary attacks against civilians. The Israelis have never signed this agreement, and in any event the United States sanctions the use of white phosphorus as a means of illuminating a war zone at night. They state that there is no prohibition of this deployment of 'flare' (as phosphorus is known by the American military) and the burning of civilians is thus taken as an incidental side effect, and not the prime purpose.

We now have an extensive understanding of the effect of hypothermia on the human body which is widely published and universally consulted – and all of it stems directly from the medical experiments in Nazi Germany. The United States also has the detailed results from the Japanese medical experiments, but has kept them classified so they remain truly secret weapons to the present day. The legal position remains unclear; when the 23 German medical staff were prosecuted in the so-called 'Doctors' Trial' in 1946–47 they argued that there was no international convention covering medical experimentation.

The prosecution by the Allies of the German experimenters offers a revealing comparison to the way the Japanese were treated by the United States. Whereas Dr Shiro Ishii lived on to die of natural causes, protected through secrecy by the United States, the aim of the Allies with the Nazi perpetrators was to bring them to trial. Some were – those tried at Nuremberg were widely publicized as being the guilty men who were to suffer for their crimes. However, many of the scientists and doctors whose work might prove to be of value to the West were secretly taken to American institutes with their falsified papers and encouraged to continue working for the other side. Josef Mengele responded to the approach of Allied forces by moving to a camp in Lower Silesia and then to the Institute of Hereditary Biology and Racial Hygiene in what is now the Czech Republic. Eventually he was apprehended and arrested by the United States military but they concluded that he had no special knowledge of interest to America, and need not be detained further. In June 1945 he was suddenly released and provided with papers under the name Fritz Hollmann. Under instructions to lie low, he worked as a farmhand until he was able to secure transport to Buenos Aires, Argentina. To this day I have found an acceptance in that fine city of former Nazi officials, many of whom fled there after the war. A number of prominent Nazis also fled to nearby Paraguay, whose leader was of German descent and who involved them in the modernization of the country. Mengele began life in South America as a construction worker but – as more German escapees arrived and befriended him – he quickly rose to the position of co-owner of the Fadro pharmaceutical company. Teams of Israelis went out to find him and capture him to face trial, so he later moved to a bungalow in a suburb of São Paulo, Brazil, for the last years of his life. Shortly before Mengele's death by drowning while on holiday in 1979, he met his son for the first time as an adult and explained that he remained steadfast to his Nazi beliefs, and insisted that he had never harmed anyone in his life. There have since been reports that he continued his medical experimentation in South America for many years.

THE UNITED STATES AND HUMAN EXPERIMENTS

The use of results from human experimentation against prisoners is controversial at best. Yet there had long been examples of top-secret human experimentation of this sort in the United States, albeit on a far more modest scale. During the 1930s experiments were carried out in which people were unwittingly injected with cancer cells and injected with radioactive nucleotides, and in Alabama 400 black workers were experimentally injected with syphilis, while in Iowa 22 orphans were put under such intense psychological distress that they were experimentally turned from being normal children into stuttering, quivering victims. The United States Army infected 400 Chicago prisoners with malaria, without their knowledge or consent.

When the war began, top-secret medical research gained pace. The Chemical Warfare Service carried out tests with poison gases that could be used in secret weapons (Lewisite and mustard gas) on 4,000 unwitting young soldiers. During the development of the atomic bomb under the Manhattan Project, plutonium was injected into soldiers. It is unlikely that they understood the risks, and three became seriously ill. One died.

Late in the war years, the University of Chicago Medical School organized the injection of malaria into mental patients at Illinois State Hospital, and the University of Rochester organized more trials with plutonium being injected into the veins of prisoners. The malaria research continued in Atlanta, with 800 prisoners being infected, and at the Argonne National Laboratories, Illinois, radioactive arsenic was injected in order to study how this element was eliminated from the body.

The most important medical research in the wartime United States was purely beneficial, however. It brought penicillin into widespread use for the treatment of bacterial infections and this launched the present-day era of antibiotic therapy. The antibiotics had been discovered in England, but little had been done by the British to realize their potential as an agent of treatment. It was American enterprise and scientific skill that would bring this from a laboratory curiosity into a therapeutic agent that would save countless millions of lives.

BRITISH DOCTORS AT WAR

The British were among the nations that, when war broke out, had large stockpiles of chemical weapons ready for use. Germany and the Allies both knew how poison gases had been a dominant factor in World War I, and each played a waiting game with the other. Undoubtedly there would have been no reluctance to use these dreadful devices, if the other side had done so first. The only reason gas war did not break out was because of this tactical stalemate; it was not because of principle. From the outbreak of war, the British were all equipped with gas masks and were told to keep them handy. Just as present-day youngsters carry a lunchbox to school, children in wartime Britain ran to school clutching their gas masks in their hands. There were regular drills in how to use them, and practices of mustering in the air-raid shelters hastily constructed in the school yard, every week. The threat of these secret weapons was ever present.

Although British research during World War II was aimed partly at offensive action, through the study of the latest bacteriological and chemical secret weapons, there was also a strong undercurrent of defensive research though the development of new drugs, of which penicillin proved to be the most important. Yet, as we shall see, the existence of penicillin as an off-the-shelf antibiotic was largely due to American enterprise.

The principal research activity into biological and chemical warfare has long been based at Porton Down, near Salisbury, Wiltshire. It was established in 1915 as a laboratory to investigate a response to German chemical weapons, and remains a top-secret facility. Officially known as the Defence Science and Technology Laboratory, it is an agency of the Ministry of Defence. It covers 7,000 acres (2,800 hectares) and also houses the Centre for Emergency Preparedness and Response. Some science-based companies are now also active in the area.

After World War I, a committee had been set up to determine what Britain should do about chemical and biological warfare, and the research at Porton Down was prioritized. Funding was made available, and the establishment began to expand steadily. In 1922, there were 380 servicemen, 23 scientific and technical civil servants and 25 civilian staff acting as secretaries, administrators and clerks. By 1925 these civilians had doubled in number. In 1930, the British ratified the Geneva Protocol with an intriguing and important codicil – in renouncing the use of chemical and biological warfare agents, they reserved the right to use them 'in retaliation'. Research during World War II focused on secret weapons containing mustard gas and phosgene. There was also a continued effort to perfect germ warfare, through biological agents like anthrax and *Clostridium botulinum* toxin.

A successful test of anthrax was carried out on the Scottish island of Gruinard in 1942, which the government purchased from the owners. Eighty sheep were shipped over to Gruinard and the secret weapons – bombs containing a particularly virulent strain of anthrax spores – were exploded nearby. Within days, the sheep began to die. These bacteria grow rapidly in the body and the blood vessels become clogged with a viscous growth that overwhelms the body. The tests were regarded as successful, though the results were pointless – if this were to be used against the German cities, they would be rendered totally uninhabitable, even by the Allies. In my view they would have been better advised to create an anti-anthrax vaccine first. Thus the island was declared officially off-limits and visits were banned, with the exception of masked and gowned bacteriologists from Porton Down who came to check contamination levels from time to time. From 1986 there was a concerted campaign, Operation *Dark Harvest*, designed to have the island cleared for human occupation. Hundreds of tons of formaldehyde were sprayed on the infected regions and the infected top-soil, containing surviving spores, was removed and incinerated. Some sheep were released on the island and carefully observed; all remained healthy. Finally, in 1990, the Junior Defence Minister Mr Michael Neubert went to Gruinard on an inspection tour, and declared it safe to visit. The warning signs were taken down and there have since been no cases of anthrax among the only permanent residents – a flock of sheep.

Later research at Porton Down concentrated on the German nerve gases tabun, sarin and soman which eventually gave rise to the development VX nerve poisons (p.170). This was the research that led to the death from sarin experimentally administered to a young volunteer in 1953. The establishment, which still exists to this day, is now shrouded in secrecy, but it is widely accepted that the main focus of attention at the present time is the prevention and cure of disease and disability caused by possible new secret weapons.

THE MIRACLE DRUG

One of the greatest discoveries of twentieth-century medicine came from an obscure British researcher – yet it languished in obscurity until the urgent demands of World War II suddenly brought attention to bear on ways of treating wounded troops. This was penicillin, the first and most important of all the antibiotics. Although it was discovered by the British, it was the United States that took it from a laboratory curiosity with potential to a major new product for general use. The first famous observation of the anti-bacterial action of this wonder-drug was recorded by a Scottish doctor and Nobel Laureate, Sir Alexander Fleming. In 1928 he showed that the mould *Penicillium notatum* could be grown experimentally in broth, and the result was a liquid that could kill disease-causing bacteria.

Although Fleming was proud to be identified as the discoverer, articles discussing the effects of this blue mould had been published as long ago as 1875, and a bacteriologist in Costa Rica named Clodomiro Twight had investigated the anti-bacterial effects of these fungi during World War I. He was not the first person to investigate *Penicillium notatum*, either; that fungus had been named in 1911 by a Scandinavian scientist who discovered it growing on a pile of decaying hyssop (a medicinal herb). Fleming noticed that the broth in which this *Penicillium* had been grown could kill bacteria, but he did not try to use it to cure disease. A young (and largely forgotten) young doctor named Cecil Paine, who worked in the pathology department of the

Alexander Fleming, the discoverer of penicillin, in his laboratory at St. Mary's Hospital, Paddington. This photo was taken in London by James Jarche in 1943. His laboratory is now a museum. (SSPL/Getty Images)

Royal Infirmary in Sheffield, Yorkshire, read about Fleming's observations and grew the fungus himself. He found it could cure an eye infection in newborn babies, *ophthalmia neonatorum*. During 1930 he treated several patients with eye infections during that year, young and old, wrote up the notes, and – like Fleming – forgot all about it. So Fleming was not the first person to discover the fungus, not the first to describe its effects nor even the first to use it to cure an infection. Why was he regarded as crucially important?

The onset of the war provides the answer. There was now a need to find a super-drug – something that could cure the overwhelming bacterial infections that would take the lives of so many young soldiers, wounded in action and sent home from the front. An Australian scientist, Howard Florey, with a small team including Ernst Chain, Norman Heatley, J. Orr-Ewing and G. Sanders, began work on possible new anti-bacterial drugs at the Sir William Dunn School of Pathology at Oxford University. They had known of the early observations of fungi apparently killing bacteria, and contacted Fleming to ask if, by chance, he still had his original culture of the mould. He had kept it – and thus was able to provide the Oxford group with the source of their much-needed new drug. I knew Florey at Oxford, and found him to be an avuncular and quick-thinking man. He reminded me a little of the comedian Bob Hope in appearance. Another friend, Mrs Monica Dobell, had known Fleming when he was at the prime of his influence. 'I thought he was an unconscionable little man,' she told me. 'Full of himself. He thought he was better than anyone, and said he'd saved the world.'

By 1942 penicillin had been extracted and purified, and this new drug was already being used in clinical trials that proved it to be effective against the common bacterial infections that were claiming young soldiers' lives. Florey, Chain and Heatley discovered how to mass-produce the fungus in milk bottles, but this could never create the drug in large amounts. The use of

A photograph of three British biologists who were involved with penicillin: left to right Sir Howard Florey, Sir Percival Hartley and Sir Alexander Fleming. (Getty Images)

penicillin in treating young wounded soldiers meant that the lives of amputees and others could now be saved, whereas they would almost certainly have been lost before. But it was in the United States, not Britain, that mass-production began. Research at the Northern Regional Research Laboratory at Peoria, showed that a common waste-product, corn-steep liquor, was the ideal growth medium for the fungus. A mouldy melon found in the market at Peoria, Illinois, turned out to provide the most potent source of penicillin yet discovered, and a chemical engineer named Margaret Rousseau showed how to grow it in massive amounts inside large fermentation tanks, something like making beer in a brewery.

By the time of the Allied invasion of Normandy in 1944, the United States had produced over two million doses of pure penicillin. The saving of life because of this spectacular progress was incalculable. Then, as the war drew to a close, Australia became the first nation to mass-produce penicillin for the general public, and Fleming, Florey and Chain were jointly awarded the 1945 Nobel prize in medicine and physiology. Although many bacteria quickly became resistant to the effect of penicillin administration, a number of semi-synthetic penicillins have since been developed, including Flucloxacillin and Amoxycillin.

A British laboratory technician examining flasks of penicillin culture. The Americans showed how the mould could be mass-produced in large vats. (SSPL/Getty Images)

These are based on the original drug, but their molecules have been slightly modified to prevent their being inactivated by resistant bacteria.

We can reflect on the remarkable involvement of medicine and science in World War II. Much cruelty was meted out; unimaginable suffering and terrible torture was a feature of the conflict and is hard, even now, to forgive. But the greatest legacy was the acceleration of top-secret research into a drug whose potential had been widely ignored. Penicillin, and the antibiotics that were subsequently discovered, revolutionized medicine. During the war it was a crucially important means of returning troops to the field of battle in record time, and once the war was over it brought hope to countless seriously ill patients. Its ability to return soldiers to the battle makes it a weapon in itself. This is a major legacy of World War II – and it brings some comfort to know that the lives saved through research on penicillin greatly outnumber those who died in wartime. Norman Heatley, whose work was so crucial to the discovery of penicillin, himself lived through it all; before passing away in 2004.

DANGEROUS
IDEAS

SOME VERY DANGEROUS IDEAS – ranging from the relatively small-scale to those of a world-changing significance – were put into play during World War II. Following her entry into the war, the United States played a role in many of them.

PEARL HARBOR ATTACKED

The attack by Japan on Pearl Harbor in December 1941 was the greatest single blow by a foreign power that the United States had ever experienced. It was also the single stimulus that brought the United States officially into World War II, and led to new and urgent secret weapons research. The Pearl Harbor raid has long been mythologized as an unprovoked and unforeseeable attack by a cruel, silent aggressor against an unsuspecting nation state peacefully going about its business. This is not entirely true. Although Japan had already acted aggressively within the Pacific region and had invaded Manchuria; the United States had repeatedly taken unilateral action against Japan. Worse still, the existence of Pearl Harbor as a probable target was already known to the United States authorities – but was kept a secret from the people of Hawaii. The Japanese aircraft were detected by radar, long before they arrived; but the young operators were told that the weak signals they were detecting were probably nothing important. American aircraft were expected: perhaps that's what they were. In the event, nothing was done and the might of Japan could fall upon the United States.

Ever since the Victorian era, Japan had learnt from the West and had embarked upon rapid industrialization. Japan is unusual in possessing very few natural resources. Britain is also an off-shore nation of similar size (the two have often been compared) yet rests on massive reserves of coal and iron ore, with vast lakes of high-quality natural gas and petrochemicals under her seas. Japan has nothing in comparison, and needs to import to survive. In the decades before World War II, Japan had built up a strong military capability and used it to expand into parts of foreign countries like China and Korea. The Americans, meanwhile, had used their own growing military might to occupy areas in South-East Asia. The Treaty of Paris had given sovereignty of the Philippines and the island of Guam to the United States in 1898 which led to the widely forgotten war of 1899–1902. Americans have been in the area ever since. In many ways the stage was set long before 1941 for a struggle over who was the dominating power in the region.

Matters came to a head when Franklin D. Roosevelt was elected President in 1933. He was a good friend of Britain, and his family had successfully traded with the Chinese for decades, so he looked with increasing distaste at the growing threat of the Nazis, and with even more disapproval at the Japanese invasions of Chinese territories.

When World War II broke out in 1939, Roosevelt's inclinations were to join with Britain and France to defeat Germany – but the people of the United States were opposed to becoming involved in another European war, and the 1940 Presidential elections were looming. The America First movement was growing in strength, spear-headed by such personalities as Charles Lindbergh and supported by anti-Semitic leaders including Henry Ford. But in direct defiance of this movement Roosevelt donated 50 American destroyers to fight for the Allies. This began in September 1940 when the United States government covertly offered Britain 43 destroyers for the Royal Navy; then seven more were given to the Royal Canadian Navy. This was nominally in exchange for 99-year leases for United States bases in places like Newfoundland, Jamaica and British Guiana. American ships were thus fighting for Britain almost from the start. In 1941 President Roosevelt followed this with the innocently named Lend-Lease Bill which led to the steady supply of materiel – weapons, explosives, etc – from 1941 to 1945. At the same time, the United States

Franklin D. Roosevelt, 32nd President of the United States, was in office from 1933 to 1945. When the war began he pledged to keep America out of the conflict. (Popperfoto/Getty Images)

offered the secret use of her ports to Allied shipping. Captain Richard Moss of Cambridge, England, recently told me of the Royal Navy's use of the port of Boston, Massachusetts, for military purposes prior to 1941. The notion that America stayed out of the war is untrue; secretly, she was in from the start.

Germany was also using the help of covertly friendly nations that (like the United States) were ostensibly neutral. Although Sweden made a great show of remaining outside the conflict and loudly proclaimed her neutrality, she supplied much of Germany's iron ore for weapons production through the Norwegian port of Narvik. Without Swedish assistance, Germany could never have produced planes, ships and weapons as she did.

Japan – always needing supplies of energy and raw materials – had signed a commercial treaty with the United States in 1911, and in the years before World War II Japan had adopted an outwardly friendly attitude towards the United States; but the United States unilaterally terminated the treaty in 1939 and then initiated a policy of economic sanction against Japan, designed to curtail aggressive Japanese expansionism into South-East Asia. The Export Controls Act of 1940 restricted the supply to Japan of oil for use as a fuel and lubricant, and was followed by a ban on all exports of scrap iron and steel to Japan.

The Japanese protested, but in vain; and in July 1941, President Roosevelt went on to freeze all Japanese assets in the United States. Britain and the Netherlands did the same. This unilateral action meant that Japan was suddenly unable to purchase oil and the Western action brought further protests, the Japanese emphasizing that they would be obliged to take action against these sanctions.

Japan set out to draw up a plan of war, and proposed to invade Malaya, Burma and the Philippines. These plans were intercepted by Allied intelligence, and the United States knew that her great fleet, based in Hawaii, would be on standby to go to war with Japan once these invasion plans were put into operation. Intelligence agents of the United States continued to monitor messages as Japan planned to take military action.

Japan now stood bereft of essential supplies. They were not so much short of military equipment as of the essentials needed for day-to-day life, including fuel oil. General Tojo Hideki became the Japanese Premier in October 1941, and realized at once that the position of his nation was desperate. He set 29 November as the date on which Japan would take military action against the United States, if no agreement was forthcoming. The United States, meanwhile, was hoping to inveigle Japan into entering the war and knew that the mighty American fleet moored in Pearl Harbor would be more than a match for any attempted invasion of territory by Japan. The intelligence service had heard that one of the targets would be Pearl Harbor; crucially, these revelations were never passed to the military commanders in Hawaii, so no preventive action could be taken. Moreover, Britain had recently perfected a transponder radar system called IFF (Identification, Friend or Foe) which they offered to the United States Army Signal Corps, but they turned it down. According to their leaders, they did not need anything from the British: American systems were best.

The attack, when it came, was unexpectedly from the air and launched with overwhelming force. Military strategists had expected Japan to invade countries to obtain her vital supplies, and the warships in Hawaii were ready to sail out to repel them when they did; nobody had imagined that Japan would instead annihilate the American fleet.

On the morning of 7 December 1941, a radar operator at the Fort Shafter radar station on the island of Oahu saw a large signal appearing on his screen. He asked a private stationed with him to look, and both agreed that there were a large number of aircraft about 130 miles (210km) away and approaching fast. Their superior officer was 1st Lieutenant Kermit A. Tyler, who listened carefully to their reported sighting. And then he reached his fateful decision. A flight of American B-17 bombers was due in that day, and he guessed this must be them. He was wrong: over 180 Japanese fighters, torpedo planes and bombers were heading to Hawaii at top speed. The opportunity to prepare or take cover was lost.

Six Japanese aircraft carriers were within range, and seemingly endless waves of planes had taken off to join forces against Hawaii. Two massive attacks then followed; 3,500 United States personnel were killed or severely wounded and 18 ships of the Pacific Fleet were sunk or badly damaged. More than 350 aircraft were destroyed. Further damage was done by scores of top-secret Japanese midget submarines that penetrated deep inside the port. Every one of the eight United States battleships was sunk; some 1,200 sailors were killed when just the USS *Arizona* was attacked. The United States lost her battleship fleet in the space of 2 hours. The Japanese attack was a complete success and a triumph of top-secret planning.

Much of the technology used in this audacious raid would have a far-reaching influence throughout the course of the war and beyond. Midget submarines were a particularly successful secret weapon. Pearl Harbor saw their first use in World War II but they were also used to great effect by the British and Italians.

The technology developed during World War II for small submarines is still in use to this day, often in unexpected applications. Tourist submarines some 32ft (10m) long are in use around the world, carrying people to see the wonders of life beneath the waves. Recently, secretly constructed submarines (some up to 98ft, 30m, long) have been discovered in Central American waters, where they are used for present-day drug smuggling.

Contrary to what we are so often told, the Pearl Harbor attack was no surprise to the United States government – it was launched after much provocation, and after copious

An artist's impression illustrates Japanese dive-bombers attacking US ships on 7 December 1941. The attack on Pearl Harbor immediately brought America into the war. (Adam Hook © Osprey Publishing)

Listing heavily under attack at Pearl Harbor and burning fiercely, the battleship *Arizona* was destroyed in the Japanese raid. Over 1,000 people died with the destruction of this vessel. (NARA)

warnings; it had even been detected by radar. Whatever else one might argue, it was not an unprovoked attack from an unexpected quarter, though the operation was a triumph of top-secret military planning. Visiting Pearl Habor recently I looked at the sad remains of the American warships, lying in clear water as a homage to those who died. In America, Lieutenant Tyler, the officer who ignored the warnings of the radar operators, carried the memory of that day for the rest of his life. He died in San Diego, California in 2010, just as work was starting on this book.

The United States had their best code-breakers assigned to the difficult task of following the Japanese plans. They were systematically decoding their top-secret messages, and they soon learnt of a plan to lure the remaining American ships into a trap at Midway Island. In June 1942 in the battle of Midway the United States successfully turned the tables by sinking four Japanese aircraft carriers and a heavy cruiser in exchange for the loss of one aircraft carrier and a destroyer. This was the turning-point in the Pacific, and from that time onwards the Japanese headed steadily to defeat.

JAPANESE HYDROGEN WEAPONS

The secret weapons that were developed by the United States against Japan, and vice versa, included some of the most fanciful ever seen in war. The Japanese resolved to launch incendiary attacks against the United States, and manufactured some 9,000 hydrogen balloons to which they fitted small incendiary weapons that could burn for over an hour and 33lb (15kg) of high explosive anti-personnel bombs. The plan was to launch them into the high-altitude jet-stream – which the Japanese had just discovered – so that the weapons were carried across the Pacific to North America. The balloons were made of paper and were assembled by young women, mostly acting students from nearby schools. The *washi* paper for the balloons was made from large sheets stuck together with 'devil's tongue' gel made by boiling the roots of arum lilies. Virtually the entire stocks of the arum root gel disappeared from the stores, partly to feed the balloon industry, but also because it had a pleasant taste and was being consumed by the students in copious quantities. Starting in November 1944, the Special Balloon Regiment established under the Imperial Japanese Army released a continuous stream of these balloons from Ibaraki Prefecture, on the western side of Honshu.

Unlikely as it seems, the ruse worked; most of the balloons burst or deflated, landing in the sea, but over 1,000 of these secret weapons reached North America and a quarter of them caused damage, mostly small forest fires. The first reports of the fireballs descending from the skies were dismissed as farmhand gossip, but towards the end of 1944 the authorities realized what was happening. Some of the balloons landed intact and were examined by the military. The payload contained magnesium as an incendiary device, partly to set fire to the balloons on landing, but also to ensure that the device was consumed in the blaze, so that the Americans would not discover the true nature of these strange balloons.

However, the balloons produced minimal interference with the conduct of the war, and once the nature of the weapons had been discovered, many were shot down by warplanes in mid-flight. A secret agreement was made with newspaper editors, so that reports of successful attacks were never published, and the Japanese could not find out how successful their balloons had been. After five months had passed without any news of damage appearing in the American news media, the Japanese became discouraged and discontinued their attacks. In reality, 285 balloon bomb incidents had been reported and some of the balloons reached as far as Michigan. One was found by a group of holidaymakers in the Oregon woods, all of whom were killed when they tried to move it and the anti-personnel mine exploded.

ANIMALS JOIN THE SECRET WAR

The United States were working on their retaliation with equally bizarre plans. A dentist (and inventor in his spare time) named Lytle S. Adams proposed to send a squadron of B-24 bombers to destroy Osaka, Japan. Each plane would carry 100 incendiary shells – and

Adams had a unique twist to the proposal for a raid: the weapons would contain not bombs but bats. He argued that the bats would home in on the wood and paper buildings that were a feature of that ancient Japanese city. Each bat would carry a small incendiary charge, strapped securely in position. Once they had settled under the eaves or tucked themselves away in the roof spaces of buildings in Osaka, the fuses would light the devices – and the city would be destroyed in a massive conflagration.

The National Defense Research laboratories experimented with lightweight incendiary bombs, and produced a design weighing less than 1oz (28g), including the weight of the small timed fuse that would ignite the package. Adams and his team were meanwhile reported to have visited literally thousands of caves to collect guano bats, which were large enough to carry the little bombs. Some trial flights were made at Muroc Lake in California but they were farcical – the bats were disorientated and flew straight into the ground. A batch of the bats, experimentally fitted with their bombs, later escaped from their shed at an army base in New Mexico and set fire to an aircraft hangar and the military vehicle inside. The United States government response was to take the project away from Adams and his friends, and hand it to the authority of the Marine Corps. They code named it Project *X-ray*, and abandoned the idea soon afterwards.

Conventional incendiary attacks against Japan were soon intensified. The Germans had introduced the concept of fire-bombing civilians with the destruction of Warsaw in 1939. They next burned Rotterdam, even though that city had already capitulated. German forces carried out firebombing raids on an even larger scale with the night-time attacks of London in 1940–41. This led to what is now

Japanese meteorologists were first to discover the high-level airflow we now call the jet-stream, and resolved to use it to carry balloon weapons across the Pacific to America. These were fire balloons (*füsen bakudan*) 32ft 8in (10m) in diameter, made from washi paper produced from mulberry fibre, and fitted with incendiary devices and high explosive. The remains of one are on display at the Historical & Maritime Museum of Coos, Oregon. (John Batchelor)

called 'shock and awe' – the widely televised raids on Baghdad during the Iraq War of 2003–10 are a more recent example of the same tactic. This indiscriminate bombing of heavily populated civilian areas early in World War II seems terrifying to us now, but it was soon to be adopted by the Allies. Hamburg was virtually destroyed by Allied bombing in 1943, and the huge conflagration that the bombs caused led to the death of about 50,000 people, most of them civilians. The destruction of Dresden in 1945 was a later example, by the Royal Air Force and the United States Air Force. Some 1,300 heavy bombers delivered a massive onslaught of almost 4,000 tons of bombs which destroyed 15 square miles (about 40km²) of that historic city. Though there have been many claims that the bridges and industrial complexes were important targets, there is no evidence that these were bombed specifically. Estimates of the number of deaths at the time were as high as 250,000, though it has since been thought that this could be as much as ten times higher than the real figure.

After the attacks on Pearl Harbor, squadrons of B-29 Superfortress bombers were sent to fire-bomb Japanese cities with devastating consequences. In Operation *Meetinghouse*, 100,000 civilians in Tokyo were burned and blasted to their deaths. Altogether, 500,000 Japanese were killed during World War II and 5,000,000 were left homeless. And so – even though the bat bombs of Project *X-ray* were a failure – the Japanese cities were burned after all.

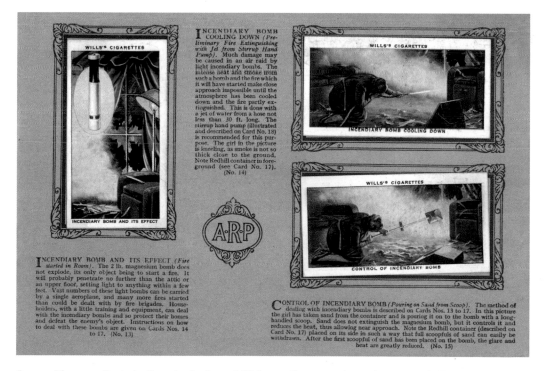

A spread from a collector's album by the Imperial Tobacco Company; these cigarette cards illustrated methods of dealing with incendiary bombs. (Imperial Tobacco Company)

These were not the only experiments to use living creatures as secret weapons. After the attempts to use bats in the war came another project – using pigeons. United States psychologist B. F. Skinner conceived of a scheme to train pigeons to guide missiles against the enemy. His idea was to condition pigeons – by offering them rewards of food – so that they would peck continuously at an image of an enemy warship projected onto a screen inside the tiny cockpit of a Pelican guided missile. As long as the pecking was in the middle of the screen, the missile flew straight towards the target, but if the image was projected to one side, then the pecking of the pigeon would cause the steering system of the missile to correct its trajectory until the picture of the target was once more back on course. The United States National Defense Research Committee was dubious about the idea, but Skinner claimed that, if the missile was released within 2,000ft (about 600m) of the enemy ship, the pigeon on board would guarantee success. Skinner had a high profile as a result of his fashionable ideas, and was considered to be the man of the moment so $25,000 was donated to fund the research. The development came to naught, and in October 1944 the military support was withdrawn – but not for long. In 1948 the United States Navy revived the research under the code name Project *Orcon* and it survived until 1953, by which time electronic guidance was sufficiently reliable and the pigeons were retired.

Anti-tank weapons were always sought by both sides, and an innovation by the Soviets during World War II was the anti-tank dog. These animals were trained to find their food beneath a tank, and were released before a raid. Each of the dogs had a bomb strapped to its back with a sensitive lever fitted to the detonator that would be triggered when the dogs ran underneath a tank to find food.

The animals were left hungry for two days prior to an attack, and were then released against the enemy tank positions. They ran towards the tanks to find food, and immediately burrowed underneath. The lever was touched, and the bomb violently exploded. It is estimated that some 300 German tanks were damaged by these dog-borne bombs during the course of World War II. However, because the dogs were trained with Russian vehicles, they often homed in on Soviet troops rather than the unfamiliar scent of the exhaust from German tanks.

HITLER'S GIANT GUN

Giant guns are a staple in warfare. It was the existence of the supposedly impregnable Maginot Line that marked the eastern boundary of France which had provided the stimulus for the development of Germany's monster guns. The artillery specialist General Carl Becker designed these huge weapons which were manufactured by the Rheinmetall-Borsig Company who named them Karl Gerät 040 after their inventor. The manufacture of these monstrous siege guns started in 1937. They were unmanageable weapons, weighing 124 tons and moving at no more than walking pace. They could be transported by rail as a massive self-contained wagon. Six were manufactured between November 1940 and August 1941. They were designed to fire huge shells of 60 or 54cm (about 2ft) in diameter and produced an enormous recoil when fired. Both wars were known for giant guns, from Big Bertha in World War I, weighing 43 tons, to the Gustav Gun of World War II, which weighed 1,344 tons. They all have a place in military history – though they cannot be classed as 'secret'.

One giant gun can be included in our exploration of the world of secret weapons, however, for it was constructed beneath the ground and the Germans went to great lengths to ensure that nobody would find out about it before the planned attacks began. It was envisaged that the Allies – even when they experienced the effects of bombardment – would never discover where it had originated. The device had several names: *Hochdruckpumpe* (HDP, high-pressure pump); *Fleissiges Lieschen* (Busy Lizzie); *Tausendfüssler* (Centipede, though the literal translation is 'millipede'). It was sometimes even referred to as the V-3 (Vergeltungswaffe-3). Later designs were so novel and potentially far-reaching that it was felt to be in an exclusive class of secret weapons. This multi-charge super-gun was an invention of the Röchling Stahlwerk AG establishment and it took the form of a sectional barrel with paired side-branches like ribs on a fish-bone. In these lateral chambers would be explosive charges, which could be fired automatically in sequence. As the projectile passed each of the branches, the next charge in the sequence would detonate, so building up the pressure until the missile was launched with the formidable velocity of 4,500ft/s (1,370m/s) or 3,000mph (4,800km/h). It was intended to be constructed in subterranean bunkers near the Pas-de-Calais region of northern France and

Big Bertha was a giant long-range gun used during World War I and it featured in Charlie Chaplin's famous movie *The Great Dictator* of 1940. This wooden replica is seen arriving at the Hollywood film studio. (Gamma-Keystone/Getty Images)

used to rain missiles down on London. The first such weapon was designed in 1943 by an engineer named August Cönders of the Röchling Stahlwerk factory. He had designed the Röchling shells, ingenious bombs that could penetrate up to 14ft (4.25m) of reinforced concrete. These shells were regarded by the Germans as a secret weapon in themselves. They were inaccurate, but were impressive enough to be recommended by the Minister of Munitions, Albert Speer. Cönders was instructed to design a prototype Hochdruckpumpe and produced one with just 20mm (about .75in) bore; however, the tests showed that the idea could work. The research was mentioned to Hitler who immediately concluded that 50 of the full-sized weapons should be installed along the coast of northern France to bombard London incessantly.

Cönders began to construct a full-sized test gun at Hillersleben near Magdeburg. It proved impossible to find the best sealing mechanism along the barrel, and so the gun could not be induced to fire reliably. On the few occasions that the device worked, the projectile was shot out too slowly. Hitler would not be dissuaded, and plans were put in place to build a 490ft (150m) gun on the Baltic island of Wolin, near Peenemünde. These Baltic tests proved to be no more successful, and so the Army Ordnance Bureau (Heereswaffenamt) was ordered to take over the development and Cönders was appointed to be a chief engineer. Hitler's driving ambition – to have a super-gun sending a cascade of high-explosive bombs to London – meant that by the middle of 1944 there were four designs for the 150mm finned projectiles, all separately manufactured by Fasterstoff, Bochumer, Witkowitz and Röchling.

Further urgent tests took place in the Baltic. More effective seals were used, which not only held the explosive charge behind the moving projectile, but also prevented premature ignition of the charges further along the barrel. During 1944 the success rates improved, and some of the projectiles landed some 50 miles (80km) from the gun that launched them. In July 1944 eight consecutive rounds were test-fired from the gun on Wolin but then it burst violently and further use was impossible.

Nonetheless, Hitler ordered that sites be found for the installation of the gun in France. One was at a limestone hill 3 miles (5km) from the Hidrequent quarry near Mimoyecques in Pas-de-Calais, a region of northern France near Cap Gris Nez, where V-1 and V-2 rocket sites were already being constructed. The site was 5 miles (8km) from the coast of the English Channel and 100 miles (160km) from London. In September 1943 construction of the railway track began, and work started on digging out the gun shafts. Two identical sites were worked on simultaneously, about 3,300ft (1,000m) apart. They contained provision for up to 50 of these giant guns, an extraordinary amount.

In London, British Intelligence learned something was afoot and orders were given for routine aerial reconnaissance photographs of the work. Within weeks, plans were laid by the Allies and air raids started on 5 November 1943 during Operation *Crossbow*. Some workers were killed in the raids, and the excavations were damaged but work continued. The Germans planned to have the first groups of five guns complete and ready to be commissioned in March 1944. Tests in the Baltic were still a disappointment; the guns had not been proved to work reliably, and so this work was curtailed. Then in July 1944, the War Ministry in London issued orders that the emplacement be attacked with the 12,000lb (5,400kg) Tallboy deep-penetration bombs that had been designed by Barnes Wallis. The weapons were to be dropped by 617 Squadron, still under the command of Guy Gibson, who had proved themselves in the Dambuster raid. The resulting destruction at Mimoyecques was so extensive that all work ground to a halt.

After the war, a joint project between the United States Department of Defense and the Canadian Department of National Defence revived something similar. It was a project to see if a satellite could be launched from a massive gun, and was entitled the High Altitude Research Project (or HARP). It was the idea of a Canadian ballistics engineer named Gerald Bull. Trials were carried out from a test range at Seawell Airport, Barbados. Bull's experimental team eventually fired a test missile weighing 400lb (180kg) at 8,000mph (13,000km/h) to an altitude of 112 miles (180km). It was an extraordinary achievement. Buildings and private

The V-3 was an extended gun with side-chambers that fired in sequence to project a shell over 100 miles (160km). It was fired against London and Luxembourg in 1944 and 1945. (Author's collection)

In close view the side-chambers of Hitler's V-3 weapon can be clearly seen. They were designed to fire in sequence to attain maximum muzzle velocity but difficulties in coordinating the explosive charges proved tough to overcome. (Cody Images)

homes for miles around reported the damage caused by the powerful shock-waves – cracked sinks, split concrete, damaged walls – which the authorities refused to entertain.

Bull remained as fixated as Hitler on the lure of a super-gun, and kept on with his research even after support was withdrawn by the United States and Canadian governments. He sold a giant gun to South Africa and was gaoled in the United States for breaching the trade embargo then in force. After his release, Bull moved to Brussels, Belgium, and negotiated a deal for the development of a satellite launch (code named Project *Babylon*) with Saddam Hussein. In March 1990 Bull was shot dead in his Brussels apartment, reportedly by agents of Mossad, the Israeli secret service. Parts of his super-gun were later impounded by the British customs authorities as an illegal export (as of 2011, parts of an Iraqi super-gun are held at the Imperial War Museum, Duxford, UK). It was a remarkable end to a saga that had its roots in the wild ambitions of Hitler in wartime Nazi Germany.

THE POWER OF THE ATOM

George Johnstone Stoney was the Irish scientist who coined the term 'electron' in 1894, and three years later J. J. Thomson at Cambridge University first recorded the existence of this subatomic unit. A French scientist, Antoine Henri Becquerel, discovered radioactivity accidentally in 1896 when he noticed that uranium fogged a photographic plate, even in the dark. In 1932 Ernest Rutherford, the father of nuclear physics, set up an experiment in Cambridge in which the splitting of the nucleus was observed; also in Cambridge, and during the same year, James Chadwick first observed the neutron. During 1938, Otto Hahn and Fritz Straßman showed that the fragments of the split atoms weighed about half as much as the original uranium nuclei – they had split the atoms in two (for this crucial discovery, Hahn was awarded the Nobel Prize in 1944). Hahn published these results at once, and sent the details to his friend Lise Meitner who was working in Stockholm. With her nephew, Otto Frisch, she soon calculated that colossal amounts of energy would be released in a sustained nuclear reaction. The short paper announcing the work by these two physicists appeared in the journal *Nature* in 1939, and the matter was suddenly out in the open. The next crucial publication came from a French physicist, Frédéric Joliot in Paris; he showed that, when the atomic nuclei were split in two, neutrons were ejected – and they would trigger a chain reaction.

The whole scientific world could now see that an atomic bomb could be manufactured: now it was only a matter of time.

GERMANY AND THE ATOM BOMB

Within weeks, German scientists pooled their ideas and formed the Uranverein (Uranium Club). Word spread, and three émigré Jewish scientists in the United States, Albert Einstein, Leo Szilard and Eugene Wigner, sent a note to President Roosevelt to warn him of the

Nazis' intention of constructing an atomic weapon. Some months later the German Army Ordnance Office began to compile reports on a possible *Uranmaschine* (a nuclear reactor) and on methods of purifying uranium isotopes. The consensus was that a nuclear reaction could clearly liberate huge amounts of energy, but that it would take years to perfect. The war was going well at that time, and so policies turned against the idea and the research was divided up among institutes scattered across Germany – laboratories in Berlin, Cologne, Hamburg, Heidelberg and Leipzig were among the many that were charged with carrying on nuclear research. The brilliant young physicist Carl Friedrich von Weizsäcker (whose brother Richard later became President of the Federal Republic of Germany) was an ardent supporter of Adolf Hitler at the time, sensing the atmosphere of renewal and expansion that was everywhere in Germany, and enthusiastically began work on atomic research. Ten of the German atomic scientists were secretly recorded in discussion at the end of the war in late 1945: Erich Bagge, Kurt Diebner, Walther Gerlach, Otto Hahn, Paul Harteck, Werner Heisenberg, Horst Korsching, Max von Laue, Carl Friedrich von Weizsäcker and Karl Wirtz. The transcripts were not declassified until 1992 and they proved to be inconclusive about the motives and ambitions of these scientists. A public airing was presented as a radio play entitled *Nuclear Reactions*, written by Adam Ganz and transmitted by the BBC on 15 June 2010.

Ever since World War II there have been persistent stories that the Nazis constructed an atomic bomb, and even that they tested a crude device in the closing phases of the war. It is true that an atom laboratory exploded in Leipzig in June 1942, when a nuclear pile went critical, and overheated, but the stories of a Nazi nuclear bomb have no basis in reality. As in other scientific nations, there were people in Germany who knew how an atomic bomb could be made, but some were too isolated to bring the ideas to fruition, and others seemed to have been determined to prevent the Nazis from finding out how to make a nuclear weapon. Dr Horst Willkomm, a leading German physicist, knew many of the principal players well and tells me that Otto Hahn and his research colleagues were determined not to give the Nazis the possibility of an atom bomb, and concentrated on working in theoretical physics and the design of a nuclear pile reactor. When Hahn heard that the Americans had constructed atomic weapons – and had dropped them on densely populated cities – Willkomm tells me that Hahn was 'highly terrified'. No-one can doubt the veracity of that.

ATOMIC SCIENCE IN JAPAN

As the Uranium Club was meeting inconclusively in Germany, American physicists were meeting to discuss how to proceed. In Denmark, the great nuclear scientist Niels Bohr was beginning to formulate plans for an atomic weapon, and he was smuggled to the West by the British Secret Service shortly before the Nazi occupation of his homeland in 1940. One of Bohr's great friends was a Japanese physicist, Yoshio Nishina, who had also known Albert

THE SCIENTISTS

The discovery of the nuclear fission predated World War II, and the revelation was followed up under conditions of top security in several countries – but most successfully by the United States. Among the leading figures were Niels Bohr, Lise Meitner and Otto Frisch.

Top left: Danish physicist Niels Bohr studied under Ernest Rutherford at Cambridge University, UK, and became centrally involved in the Manhattan Project. He was code-named Nicholas Baker for security. (SSPL/Getty Images)

Top Right: Lise Meitner was an Austrian scientist who was hugely significant in the research into nuclear physics, and whose work laid the foundations for nuclear projects and the development of nuclear weapons. (Getty Images)

Left: Along with his aunt, Lise Meitner, Otto Frisch focused on nuclear physics. The pair made the discovery that vast amounts of energy are released during nuclear reactions. (© Science and Society/SuperStock)

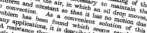
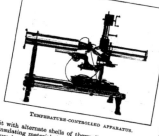

TEMPERATURE-CONTROLLED APPARATUS.

Atomic energy suddenly became a clear candidate for a super-weapon with the discoveries of Lise Meitner and Otto Frisch. Their epoch making paper, describing a 'new type of nuclear reaction', appeared in *Nature* on 11 February 1939. Their publication concludes with mention of nuclear 'fission' – this new term appears in italics and it ushered in a new era of science and warfare. (Author's collection)

Einstein. In the 1930s he had built cyclotrons in Japan, and in 1940 he was sent a report by Lieutenant-Colonel Tatsusaburo Suzuki, a military scientist, which proposed that Japan should embark upon a nuclear weapons project. Nothing was done until April 1941 when the Japanese Prime Minister, Hideki Tojo, reviewed the proposals and issued orders for development work to proceed. By the end of the year, over 100 research scientists were working on an atomic bomb, and mineralogists were sent out across Korea, Burma and China in search of uranium ore.

As we have seen, it is a tradition in many nations that the various arms of the military do not engage with each other, and so the Imperial Japanese Navy instructed their Research Institute to prepare their own study of nuclear weapons with several professors from the Imperial University in Tokyo. The conclusions were that a nuclear bomb was certainly a possibility, and that the Americans and Europeans would be working on the subject themselves; but that it was impossible for a weapon to be in production by the end of the war, and – since this would apply as much to the Allies – there was no need to pursue the matter.

The Imperial Japanese Naval Command also investigated the possibility of manufacturing nuclear weapons. A senior physicist was Hideki Yukawa, who was awarded the Nobel Prize for physics in 1949. (Getty Images)

In 1943 the Imperial Japanese Naval Command returned to the topic with a pilot project under the leadership of Dr Bunsaku Arakatsu, a physicist who had studied under Rutherford at the Cavendish Laboratory, Cambridge, and at Berlin University, under Albert Einstein. One of his team was Hideki Yukawa, who would later become the first physicist from Japan to be awarded the Nobel Prize in 1949.

The Army, meanwhile, embarked upon their own version of the project at Riken, while a separate arm of the Navy, the Fleet Administration Office, began funding research physicists at Kyoto University to design an atomic bomb of their own. The various schemes were surrounded by bureaucracy and little progress took place. Had the teams worked together, the outcome might have been different – but, as matters stood, the research made slow progress and there was never sufficient funding. Not until 1945 were the teams near the production of uranium for an atom bomb, and then the laboratories were attacked by the United States. By the time the Americans were inspecting the ruins of Japan at the end of the war, they discovered that the research laboratories at Riken – which they had expected to be state-of-the-art and advanced – were run down and neglected for lack of finance.

Just as in the case of the Nazis, there have been allegations that the Japanese detonated a test weapon, on 12 August 1945 at Hungnam, Korea, a few days after the atomic bombs had been dropped on Hiroshima and Nagasaki. Here too, there is simply no evidence for the claim.

RUSSIAN QUEST FOR AN ATOM BOMB

The idea of an atom bomb in the Soviet Union led to the People's Commissariat of Internal Affairs (NKVD) setting up an information-gathering project in 1940 and, at a conference on nuclear physics in Moscow, the proposal for research into atomic weapons was formally adopted. When Germany attacked Russia in 1941 all research was curtailed; not until 1942 was Stalin interested in an update on current knowledge. He had been lobbied by several leading nuclear physicists who had received smuggled copies of the British Maud Committee reports which said that an atomic bomb was a possibility (p.208). In spite of the pressures upon the Russian economy, Stalin at last gave the go-ahead. Espionage was stepped up and, because of the fashionable belief in communism that was emerging in Britain, a steady flow of information about the use of plutonium was beginning to reach Moscow from well-connected spies in Britain as well as America. They were also learning of the American plans for a nuclear reactor to be built in Chicago (p.212) and in 1943 an eminent physicist named Klaus Fuchs came to the United States with the British team to continue developmental work.

However, Fuchs was a Russian agent, and began to send the details of the work back to Moscow. He was posted to Los Alamos with Julius Rosenberg, another spy who was later executed with his wife. By the end of the war, all the current information on the bombs that

Klaus Fuchs was a German-born physicist and spy for the Soviets. He was tried in London's Old Bailey on charges of disclosing atomic secrets, gaoled and released after nine years. He moved to East Germany, and is said to have helped the Chinese develop their hydrogen bomb. (Getty Images)

the Americans were to successfully produce had already been sent to Russia, and teams of Soviet and American experts went on to pursue rival claims for supplies of uranium ore as Germany was invaded. For Russia this was of overwhelming importance, as they knew of no sources from which they could mine their own uranium. The Americans retrieved about 1,100 tons, ten times as much as the Soviets.

Work in America had been well planned and perfectly coordinated. It was believed to have been carried out under complete secrecy, and the Americans were convinced that nobody outside the research project could possibly know anything about what was planned. On 16 July 1945 the first bomb was exploded in New Mexico, and at the Potsdam Conference later that month President Truman revealed to Stalin that America had a new super-weapon. The President was taken aback by Stalin's reaction: the Russian leader seemed to be not in the least surprised. In August, the Soviet Union formally declared war against Japan and Stalin ordered that an atomic bomb should be manufactured 'as quickly as possible'. It was by then, of course, too late.

The uranium brought back from the Soviet conquest of Germany was used to build Russia's first nuclear reactor, code named F-1, which was first initiated on 25 December 1946. They later found supplies from East Germany (the German Democratic Republic), and also in Czechoslovakia, Poland, Bulgaria and Romania. The Russians subsequently found large domestic supplies, and their first atomic explosion, code named First Lightning, took place on 29 August 1949. The design was based on the United States' plutonium weapon, nicknamed Fat Man, details of which had been smuggled by spies back to Russia. And so the years of the Cold War began.

Meanwhile, the Russians speedily designed and built the world's first nuclear power station at their 'science city' of Obninsk, about 60 miles (100km) from Moscow. It was an experimental pilot station designed to produce about 30mW of thermal power, sufficient for 2,000 homes. The construction started in 1951 and the plant was connected to the domestic supply in June 1954. It ran successfully until April 2002.

ATOMIC PROJECTS IN FRANCE AND CHINA

The involvement of the French in nuclear research had been assured by Pierre and Marie Curie, who worked with radium. Yet there was no finance available for developing nuclear weapons during World War II and the Fourth Republic proved to be a weak and ineffective government. Members of Marie Curie's team later worked as part of the British group in the Manhattan Project and so helped the United States to build the atomic bomb.

At the end of the war, all her native knowledge had gone and France had to begin afresh. Even so, the French reputation for scientific progress proved well-earned when the first French nuclear reactor went critical in 1948 and during the following year they were producing small quantities of weapons-grade plutonium. France carried out her first atom bomb test, the Gerboise Bleue (Blue Jerboa) on 13 February 1960 in the Sahara desert. In May 1962 an underground test of a bomb four times as powerful as the Hiroshima bomb went drastically wrong. The sealing of the shaft was blown out by the explosion, and many of the personnel were contaminated by the radiation.

China did not develop atomic weapons in World War II either, and indeed did not carry out much research into particle physics until after the war. The first Chinese atomic bomb was tested on 16 October 1964 and yielded 22 kilotons. Within three years, China had tested their ultimate secret weapon of war – a hydrogen bomb.

The People's Republic now has an immense arsenal of nuclear weapons – and one of the main production facilities for the warheads is at Harbin, where the infamous Unit 731 was constructed during World War II (see p.171).

France tested nuclear weapons following the end of World War II. Life-sized dummies were set up to assess the blast damage from the detonation of an A-Bomb code-named Gerboise Rouge, 'Red Jerboa'. France's first atomic bomb test had been named Gerboise Bleue. (Getty Images)

BRITISH WORK TOWARDS AN ATOM BOMB

Before the outbreak of war, two expatriate German nuclear physicists, Otto Frisch and Rudolf Peierls, had come to work on nuclear fission at the University of Birmingham under Professor Marcus Oliphant. It was believed at the time that the world's supply of uranium would be too limited to allow the making of a nuclear bomb within a matter of years, but when they came to reconsider the problem they calculated that just a few pounds (a matter of kilograms) of uranium would be sufficient to produce a bomb of immense power. This finding was classified as top secret, for it had enormous implications for the prospects for nuclear bombs as weapons of war. Oliphant considered this to be a startling revelation, and at once communicated the findings to Sir Henry Tizard, who was chairman of the Committee on the Scientific Survey of Air Defence, and one of the top military experts in Britain. A crucial breakthrough came at the Cavendish Laboratory, Cambridge, with the discovery that plutonium-239 was a by-product of the nuclear reactions of uranium.

The result was the setting up of a committee, code named Maud because that was the name of the governess whom Niels Bohr had employed for his children. By the end of 1940, the team had discovered that the making of a bomb from radioactive uranium was possible – and, as they later concluded, not only possible but inevitable with the eternal pressure for progress. In 1941, Peierls calculated a new 'critical mass' for Uranium-235 (U-235) at 18lb (8kg); the amount that would be necessary to sustain an atomic reaction if surrounded by a suitable reflector to retain stray neutrons could be half as much. The British were well aware that the work on nuclear fission had begun in Germany, and they were concerned that the Nazis might already be rushing ahead at the Kaiser Wilhelm Institute. The committee produced two highly influential top-secret reports. The first was entitled *On the Use of Uranium for a Bomb* and set out in detail how a bomb could be made with 27lb (12kg) of radioactive isotopes that would have the explosive power of 1,800 tons of TNT. They pointed out that radioactive contamination would make the surrounding area unsafe for humans for many years, and calculated that it would cost millions of pounds to produce. The main thrust of the American research at the time was the possibility that atomic power could be used for power generation, or as an energy source for submarines, and the Maud Committee proposed that the United States – who alone had the money for this project – should look instead at making an atomic bomb.

Their second report was *On the Use of Uranium as a Source of Power*. They worked out how to produce an atomic reactor, and even how to moderate the rate of the reaction with graphite rods. They concluded that this system could produce an endless supply of heat and electricity for the future, but (with the demands of a world war) there were no resources available to develop the idea any further in Britain at present. Research went ahead on a shoe-string budget under the code name Tube Alloys in Britain, while the secret reports were sent to the Americans for their response – yet nothing happened. Eventually an emissary was sent to find out what was being decided, only to find that the reports had been sent to Lyman Briggs as Director of the top-secret United States Uranium Committee. He was described by the British as 'inarticulate' and it turned out that he had not understood the scientific reports, so he had just locked them away in the office safe.

When the truth was revealed, it was agreed that the atom bomb would cost $25,000,000 and, although Tube Alloys could see how to make a bomb, the project lacked spare facilities. Even though the British handed over all their knowledge to the United States, the remarkable Calder Hall reactor in Cumbria (near the English Lake District) became the first nuclear power station in the world to deliver commercial quantities of electricity for public consumption in 1956, following the Russian pilot experiment that began in 1954 (p.206). Meanwhile, a British atomic bomb was eventually manufactured and was detonated on 3 October 1952 at the Montebello Islands off the coast of Western Australia.

The English nuclear power station Calder Hall was opened in 1956. Contrary to what is often claimed, this was not the world's first atomic power station; the Russians had opened one in 1954. Calder Hall was, however, the first to deliver large amounts of electricity for public use. (Gamma-Keystone/Getty Images)

CANADIAN NUCLEAR RESEARCH

Although little is said of it now, the Canadians were also in the forefront of following up the revelations about the atom. Their scientists were concerned because crucial observations were being published by expatriate German nuclear scientists; it was feared that German science was secretly pressing ahead, and the Canadians were convinced for a time that there would be a Nazi atom bomb – and that would end the war with Germany as the victor. The early experiments in Ottawa demanded supplies of heavy water. This strange-sounding substance is an isotope of the water with which we are so familiar. Normal water, H_2O, is composed of

The 'heavy water' used in nuclear reactors truly is heavy. The glass on the left contains ice made from heavy water, which sinks to the bottom. The other glass contains frozen tap-water and this ice is visibly less dense. It floats as one would expect. (Charles D. Winters/Science Photo Library)

A PETITION TO THE PRESIDENT OF THE UNITED STATES

Discoveries of which the people of the United States are not aware may affect the welfare of this nation in the near future. The liberation of atomic power which had been achieved places atomic bombs in the hands of the Army. It places in your hands, as Commander-in-Chief, the fateful decision whether or not to sanction the use of such bombs in the present phase of the war against Japan.

We, the undersigned scientists, have been working in the field of atomic power. Until recently, we have had to fear that the United States might be attacked by atomic bombs during this war and that her only defense might lie in a counterattack by the same means. Today, with the defeat of Germany, this danger is averted and we feel impelled to say what follows:

The war has to be brought speedily to a successful conclusion and attacks by atomic bombs may very well be an effective method of warfare. We feel, however, that such attacks on Japan could not be justified, at least not unless the terms which will be imposed after the war on Japan were made public in detail and Japan were given an opportunity to surrender.

If such public announcement gave assurance to the Japanese that they could look forward to a life devoted to peaceful pursuits in their homeland and if Japan still refused to surrender our nation might then, in certain circumstances, find itself forced to resort to the use of atomic bombs. Such a step, however, ought not to be made at any time without seriously considering the moral responsibilities which are involved...

Leo Szilard and 69 co-signers

atoms of oxygen and hydrogen. Normal hydrogen atoms contain a proton as the nucleus and a single electron orbiting round. Heavy hydrogen (deuterium) has an extra neutron in the nucleus – it contains a proton *and* a neutron. The extra neutron is important in regulating nuclear reactions. Heavy water is very like normal water, and indeed is only very slightly more dense. Almost of all the heavy water in existence at the time was 407lb (185kg) that French scientists had obtained from a Norwegian hydroelectric plant. The nuclear physicists in charge of the research, Hans von Halban and Lew Kowarski, escaped to England, bringing this with them – at the time, almost all the heavy water in the world. They planned to use the heavy water to produce plutonium, and early experiments in Cambridge suggested it could work. It was then agreed that the British teams would work in cooperation with a team in Canada, safe from the threat of German bombing.

The nuclear research in Ottawa set out to test whether the heart of a nuclear reactor, an atomic pile, could be constructed. They set to work with a bin measuring 8ft 9in (2.7m) in diameter containing 1,000lb (450kg) of uranium oxide obtained from Eldorado Gold Mines Limited. The British chemical company Imperial Chemical Industries (ICI) gave them a grant of $5,000 and they were able to make substantial progress during 1942 – but this was overtaken when the Chicago reactor became the first in the world to function. From that time on the Canadians devoted themselves to carrying on research to support the American effort.

However, their research left them a useful legacy. By the time the war ended, Canada had the second largest nuclear research establishment in the world, overshadowed only by the United States. Their work on constructing nuclear reactors led to the building of the NRX (National Research eXperimental) reactor at the Chalk River Laboratories near Ottawa. It remained the world's largest nuclear reactor for many years and soon began producing radioisotopes. Those are still used today to diagnose and treat cancer, and Canada has since been the world's largest exporter of radioisotopes. Another reactor ten times as large was soon under construction and this became the NRU (National Research Universal) reactor. When it began work in 1957 it was, like NRX, the most powerful reactor in the world, and remained so for many years.

THE MANHATTAN PROJECT

The United States, however, became the focus of nuclear research and was destined to become the first nation to exploit the power of the atom. In 1939, Albert Einstein wrote a key letter that was delivered personally to the President. In it he stated: 'A single [atom] bomb might well destroy a city and some of the surrounding territory'. President Roosevelt was impressed, and he immediately appointed Lyman Briggs at the National Bureau of Standards to set up the 'Uranium Committee'. Once the recommendations of the Maud Committee had been discussed, and the Americans knew that a bomb could be built with far smaller amounts of fissile materials than anyone had realized, it was decided to press ahead urgently with development. In 1942 this led to the Manhattan Engineer Project which had the express aim of producing an atomic bomb. The project derived its name from the concentration of expertise in Manhattan itself. Within the borough there were some ten research sites, almost all of which stand to the present day. Their original headquarters were in a skyscraper adjacent to City Hall. Little has ever been said about these establishments since; the tourist or investigator will find little to remind today's citizens of what went on. A historian of the period, Dr Robert S. Norris, says that as many as 5,000 staff were coming and going. Each person knew only enough to do their job – few had any sort of overview.

The scientists originally on the committee were from various nations: the United States, Germany, Hungary, Italy, Denmark, Switzerland and Britain. To the British, where the research had made most progress, it seemed timely to shift the work to America where there were more resources, and where – unlike Britain – the industrial and research establishment was not overrun by the need simply to survive the onslaught of Germany. In the United States there was an immediately warm response to the project. Soon, however, the disparate nature of the nationalities involved was seen as problematical. Many of the British team had family in Europe, including some in nations that were now enemies of the Allied cause. The Americans felt that this could compromise security, and soon took over the project.

They envisaged two types of atom bomb, one using uranium, the other plutonium. Work began at once on constructing an atomic pile under the leadership of a brilliant physicist, Enrico Fermi. It was called Chicago Pile-1 (CP-1) and stood on a rackets court under the abandoned west stands of the original Alonzo Stagg Field stadium at the

Enrico Fermi led the US research into uranium and plutonium for potential use in nuclear weapons. In 1942 the US achieved the first sustained nuclear reaction, an important milestone in the development of nuclear power. (Library of Congress)

University of Chicago. In December 1942 the first sustained nuclear reaction was started – and the dream of atomic power was known to be real. America could now produce the isotopes (like U-235) she needed to plan an atomic bomb.

Work on the project now proceeded rapidly and a prototype weapon was successfully tested at Alamogordo, in the deserts of New Mexico, on 16 July 1945. Although the United States now had the atomic bomb, the war against Germany was already at an end, and the conflict with Japan was nearing its close. On 17 July 1945 Leo Szilard and 69 co-signatories from the Manhattan Project in Chicago petitioned the President of the United States with their avowed opposition to any use of such a weapon against civilians in war (see p.211). One of them was a good friend of mine, George Svihla. He said to his dying day that the use of the bomb against Japan was indefensible: the United States could have announced the success of the atom bomb tests, and warned the Japanese that the weapon would assuredly be used if they did not capitulate; but to use it on cities crammed with civilians in the dying days of conflict seemed inhuman and morally wrong. The signatories also foresaw an era when atomic weapons would be used indiscriminately by all sides, with devastating effects. In that sense the petition was wrong – the ever-present threat of annihilation acted as a deterrent against the use of nuclear weapons from that day on, and no nuclear bomb has since been used in warfare.

THE ATOMIC BOMB

The work of the Manhattan Project culminated in the dropping of the atomic bomb Little Boy on Hiroshima on 6 August 1945, followed three days later by the detonation of Fat Man over Nagasaki. The detonation of these atomic bombs marked the end of World War II, and went on to shape the rest of the twentieth-century history.

Left: Colonel Paul Tibbetts stands by the B-29 Superfortress bomber *Enola Gay* which dropped the Little Boy bomb on Hiroshima. The plane was named after Tibbetts's mother. (IWM HU 44878)

Top right: A replica of the Little Boy bomb, which was dropped by the crew of the *Enola Gay* on the city of Hiroshima in the final days of World War II. (SSPL/Getty Images)

Bottom right: A replica of the Fat Man bomb which was detonated by the United States over Nagasaki on 9 August 1945, just three days after the first atomic bomb had been dropped on Hiroshima. (SSPL/Getty Images)

Opposite: The B-29 Superfortress *Bockscar* dropped the Fat Man bomb over Nagasaki and produced this dramatic mushroom cloud. The second nuclear bombing in the space of a few days, it convinced the Japanese that Hiroshima was not an isolated incident, and was followed by their capitulation. (Department Of Defense)

Hiroshima in 1945 following the detonation of the first atomic bomb to be used in warfare. The prominent building is the former Industry Promotional Hall, and it has been left in its ruined state as a memorial to all those who perished as a result of the atomic bomb. To the Japanese it is also a symbol of their indestructible technology. (IWM MH 29427)

World leaders always seem to want to find a war in which they can prove their might, and the newly elected President Truman was convinced that America could make the ultimate grand gesture by using her new bomb, and hasten the end of the war into the bargain. He considered the appeals, but decided to disregard them. On 6 August 1945 a B-29 Superfortress bomber named *Enola Gay* delivered its uranium bomb (code named Little Boy) to Hiroshima. It was 9ft 9in (3m) long and 2ft 4in (71cm) in diameter and weighed 8,900lb (4,000kg). Its design was unbelievably simple: two sub-critical masses of U-235 at each end of the bomb were forced together in an instant by conventional explosive, and exploded straightaway. Of the 131lb (59kg) of the uranium in the bomb, less than a kilogram underwent nuclear fission. The force of the explosion was roughly equivalent to 15,000 tons of TNT and it is believed to have killed 140,000 people outright. Yet the amount of uranium that was directly converted into energy is unbelievably small. It amounted to just 600 milligrams – $^1/_{50}$ oz.

On 9 August a second atomic bomb was dropped. This was a plutonium weapon code named Fat Man and was detonated over Nagasaki. This bomb was 10ft 8in (3.3m) long and 5ft (1.5m) in diameter, weighing 10,200lb (4,600kg). Its explosive was a different man-made isotope, plutonium-239. In this alternative design, a single sphere of plutonium weighing 14lb (6.35kg) was installed in the weapon, and 64 detonators fitted around it fired simultaneously. These compressed the sphere so that it imploded on itself and, with the atoms now more tightly packed, it went critical and detonated. The energy released was equivalent to 21,000 tons of TNT, yet it came from the conversion into energy of less than 1 gram of the plutonium ($^1/_{30}$ oz). It killed about 40,000 people in an instant, and the following day Japan capitulated.

There is a now a new threat, namely that warmongers in unruly states may release nuclear weapons for terrorists to detonate. There is much money floating around in the impenetrable strata of the terrorist world, and the price of a nuclear bomb, purchased illicitly from a state that no longer needs them – or from agents of a state that doesn't know they are being offered for sale – would be affordable by many terrorist groups. So, although the global warfare foreseen by the signatories of the Szilard petition has not come to pass, the threat of an atomic weapon is still the greatest terrorist threat of all. The ramifications of the secret weapons of World War II remain in most of our minds for much of the time.

DOOMED TO FAIL

THERE IS NO LIMIT TO THE CRAZY IDEAS dreamt up by the wartime scientists and inventors. Hitler was the target of plans to change his sex, by secretly dosing his vegetable garden with female hormones, or to blind him with toxic vapours smuggled aboard his train in a vase of flowers. There were schemes to drop bombs containing molasses in front of the advancing German troops, to trap their boots in a sticky mass that prevented them from moving forward, or to smother them in coils of barbed wire dropped from aircraft. From South Africa came the idea of emptying millions of poisonous snakes on the heads of enemy troops. Once Italy joined the war, there was even a proposal to drop huge amounts of bombs into the mouth of Vesuvius, causing it release a flood of molten lava across southern Italy. There was a plan to poison thousands of tons of cabbages, and drop them in enemy fields to wipe out their farm animals, with the idea that starvation would soon bring Germany to its knees. There was also a scheme to light up the whole of southern England with tens of thousands of searchlights, so that enemy bombers could be easily seen at night – heedless of the fact that, in Britain, more than half the days are cloudy. Another abortive idea was to cover the innumerable rivers and lakes in Britain with a coating of oil and coal dust, to prevent reflections from water at night giving the German pilots valuable navigational clues. The first trials failed to dull down the water, and instead covered the technicians with a thick layer of sticky black oil. Proposals were then put forward to equip fighter aircraft with long, sharp blades that could be used to sever the cords of parachutes, causing troops to plunge to their deaths; it was even planned to release a cloud of chloroform or ether from Allied bombers, so that pursuing enemy fighter pilots would become unconscious and crash.

German saboteurs came up with equally bizarre proposals. They designed detonators that fitted inside a pen and pencil set, a shaving brush, a tin of talc, torch batteries and a bar of toilet soap. Bombs were designed to be smuggled inside a can of motor oil, a Thermos flask, lumps of coal, car batteries and the heel of a boot. A bomb disguised as a tin of Smedley's brand English Red Dessert Plums went into production. They even designed a hand grenade the size and shape of a bar of chocolate, and planned that this should be presented to the Royal Family. Another bomb was designed to be smuggled inside a stuffed dog. An MI5 file entitled: 'Camouflages for sabotage equipment used by the German sabotage services' listed many such secret weapons, and was kept top secret for over 50 years after the war (it is now in the National Archives). The SS and the Hitler Youth set up a series guerrilla teams, code named Werewolf Units, who would carry out sabotage operations when Britain was under German occupation. They trained in assassination and how to poison the food and water needed by the civilian population. As many as 6,000 recruits were signed up by early 1945, and German inventors were asked to provide examples of secret weapons with which Germany could overcome her enemies.

The most controversial of all these inventors was probably Viktor Schauberger, who had unconventional views on water and fluid flow ('Water is alive!' he used to say). He became known to Adolf Hitler because the two men were Austrian, and Hitler felt this gave them a sense of connection. Schauberger came up with a variety of ideas for motors to power submarines and even flying saucers. For a time he was imprisoned in a mental institution, and at the end of the war he was secretly confined for nine months by the Americans who interrogated him in the hope of obtaining some crucial information. His most famous design was for the Repulsin weapon, a kind of flying saucer, and rumours have persisted that the Nazis flew his design and that the Americans stole the idea and kept it secret. The United States is the most enterprising and entrepreneurial nation in the world, and it can safely be assumed that – if there was anything in these ideas – they'd be mass-producing the device and marketing it all over the world. The Nazi flying saucer is, I fear, just a legend.

DEATH RAYS

One of the most enduring myths of the saga of secret weapons is the death ray. The story has its roots in the tales from antiquity of mirrors being massed against an enemy fleet, the concentrated sun's rays setting fire to raiders' wooden ships. Indeed, Archimedes was reported to have set fire to the Roman fleet at Syracuse this way in 212 BC. An American inventor

Serbian nuclear pioneer Nikola Tesla, inventor and engineer, photographed in the early years of the twentieth century. Tesla was among those who believed in the possibility of a death ray. (Getty Images)

Antonio Longoria and his 'death machine'. The death ray concept generated much interest, and while some contraptions saw more success than others, it was never developed into a weapon of warfare. (Gamma-Keystone/Getty Images)

named Edwin R. Scott claimed to have perfected a death ray in 1924, and the same year Harry Grindell-Matthews asked for money from the Air Ministry in London to reveal how a death ray worked. Most interesting of all were the claims in the 1930s by the distinguished nuclear pioneer Nikola Tesla who regularly said that he could make a death ray gun; the boasts were echoed by a Spanish physicist, Antonio Longoria, who claimed that he could kill small animals over a long distance.

In military history, tales abound of secret teams of scientists perfecting this ultimate weapon of war – or, if not perfecting it, coming close. There is no doubt that the Imperial Japanese General Headquarters investigated whether *Ku-go* (Death Rays) would be feasible. There had been claims that a German 'electric wave' had been developed during World War I, and later American reports of the 1930s used to speculate on claims that a death ray could bring down aircraft – in large numbers – hundreds of miles away. It is easy to dismiss this as scientific nonsense, but to the non-scientific mind there is always the consciousness that science once suggested that powered flight was impossible, and that motorized transportation

Japanese physicist Sinitiro Tomonaga was among the pioneers of research into microwaves. He is seen taking part in a press conference at his home in Tokyo on 21 October 1965, shortly after being informed that he would be the Nobel Prize Laureate for Physics. (© TopFoto)

faster than a galloping horse would prove to be fatal ... and so the realism of science was quickly countered with a demand to press on with research and achieve the impossible.

An article on death rays from the United States, which was picked up by the Japanese authorities, led to research into methods of producing beams of microwaves. The work began in 1939 at laboratories in Noborito with a group of fewer than 30 scientists. Later Shimada City was a site of scientific research into secret weapons, and in 1943 their research teams had developed a high-powered magnetron that could generate a beam of the radiation. To the scientists, this was a necessary step in studying microwaves and infrared radiation. The Japanese developed heat-seeking technology which is used today in order to have a missile home in on the engines of a plane, and microwaves are widely used in many present-day applications including communication systems, medical treatment, radio astronomy and navigation (so not only to warm your pie). Among the physicists conducting this research was Sinitiro Tomonaga and by the end of World War II he and his team had produced a magnetron 8in (20cm) in diameter with an output rated at 100kW. Could this have been developed into a weapon? We cannot tell for sure, because the research papers were all methodically destroyed before the Allies invaded and occupied Japan, although there are reports of how effective it could have been in theory. The calculations suggest that, if properly focused, the beam available by the end of the war could have killed a rabbit over a distance of 1,000 yards (or metres) – but only if the rabbit stayed perfectly still for at least 5 minutes. Nothing more was heard of the Japanese death ray, though it would be wrong to regard Tomonaga as a forgotten scientist. After the war, Robert Oppenheimer invited him to carry on his research at Princeton University in the United States and Tomonaga was eventually awarded the Nobel Prize for physics – jointly with Richard Feynman.

THE INVISIBLE SHELL

It is August 2009. On BBC television from London is one of those pop-science shows, where the eager presenters are all hyperactive and hypnotically confident, and where any need for the viewer to think scientifically has been surgically excised. The set is rich in bright gadgets of every hue, the teeth dazzling, the smiles fixed. 'Welcome to my world,' says the presenter excitedly, this being the world of the vortex gun. 'My prototype vortex cannon blew a bottle into a bin from twenty feet [about 6m],' he reports. But he wants to go 'a lot, lot further'. With a budget of £7,000 ($10,000) and the help of some technicians, the BBC have constructed a cannon in which acetylene and oxygen exploded to drive a spiralling plug of air, a cross between a smoke-ring and a whirlwind, for many yards across a disused quarry in rural England. First a pile of straw, then a wooden box, and finally a target made by piling bricks upon each other are knocked sideways by the blast of the high-speed vortex. It's an excellent demonstration, and the script emphasizes its uniqueness. This, the viewer is told, has 'never been seen before' in this country.

It is an important codicil, for thousands of vortex guns have been built elsewhere (mostly in the United States). The British viewers had the impression that this was a leap in the dark, unprecedented and unique, and no mention was ever made of the thousands of earlier vortex cannons already in existence for over 100 years. In reality, this was not new at all. There are booklets, kits, magazine articles, demonstrations on YouTube; building a vortex cannon is a well established weekend hobby for enthusiasts, and has been done for decades. Although the show said nothing of the fact, this had an earlier history, as a secret German weapon of World War II.

The vortex cannon was constructed in early 1945 by an engineer named Dr Mario Zimmermayr at Lofer in the Austrian Tyrol. He came up with two designs, the *Wirbelwind Kanone* (Whirlwind Cannon) and the *Turbulenz Kanone* (Vortex Cannon). The design of the Vortex Cannon proved to be most promising. It was essentially that of a large mortar buried in the earth, which fired an explosive into a cloud of fine coal powder. The idea was to create

Top left: Nazi engineers developed vortex guns in the hope of incapacitating overflying aircraft by the pressure of sound waves. Hydrogen and oxygen were detonated inside the angled tube of the cannon and projected a plug of compressed air towards enemy aircraft. This example was commissioned by the Reichsluftfahrtamt (Office of Aeronautics) and was used, without effect, to defend a bridge over the Elbe River in 1945. (Author's collection)

Top right: Nazi scientists believed that sound could be harnessed as a secret weapon. This apparatus was designed by Richard Wallauschek and comprised two large reflectors over 10ft (3m) across. An explosive mixture of oxygen and methane was fed into combustion chambers and the resulting noise was concentrated by reflectors to produce a beam of intense sound energy. Over 160ft (50m) away the sound pressure was more than 1,000 millibars which could prove lethal within half a minute. (Author's collection)

Left: Vortex guns had first been constructed in Italy in 1896 to deflect hailstorms from vineyards. The conical cannons were 6ft 6in (2m) tall and produced a smoke-ring vortex that rose rapidly some 1,000ft (300m) upwards. Here we see them in the French magazine *L'Illustration*, exhibited in Italy in 1902. (Author's collection)

a whirling tornado of air that would bring down enemy aircraft flying overhead. High-speed cine cameras were used to film the experiments, and they showed that a large and energetic vortex of exhaust gases was expelled from the device. It was reckoned that this could have an effective range of just over 300ft (100m) though it was never used in practice against enemy aircraft. There were reports of a similar vortex cannon being used against personnel in Poland although these have never been substantiated.

But the concept was not new, even in World War II. Vortex guns had been built in Italy since the late 1800s, where they were used to fire vortices into the clouds above the Italian vineyards, in the hope of encouraging rain to fall and to break up large hailstones that could decimate a crop. At the beginning of the twentieth century, an Australian government meteorologist named Clement Wragg saw these guns exhibited in Europe. An article from the *Melbourne Argus* newspaper dated 29 January 1902 says: 'Sufficient funds have been collected to purchase a Stiger vortex battery for preventing hailstorms, and tenders are now being called for a battery of six guns.' These vortex cannons were impressive, each with a barrel 10ft (3m) long, and they were installed at Charleville, an agricultural township 470 miles (760km) west of Brisbane. On 26 September 1902 the mayor ordered six of the guns to open fire, and ten shots were fired at the clouds from each barrel. A few drops of rain were felt, and several hours later there was a light shower. Nobody could be sure the vortex cannons had caused it, but the results were encouraging and eventually 13 more were built in Australia. Some have been preserved and stand in Charleville to this day.

A similar concept lay behind the *Windkanone* (Wind Cannon) that was manufactured in Stuttgart during World War II. This was a large angled cannon which could eject a high-speed mass of compressed air that was intended to bring down nearby aircraft. The device used a critical mixture of hydrogen and oxygen in the ratio of 2:1, obtained from electrolysis of water. The sharp explosion produced a bolus of highly compressed air that could cause damage at a distance. When experimentally demonstrated at Hillersleben in Saxony, it could break a wooden board 1in (25mm) thick at a distance up to almost 700ft (200m). It was recognized that it would be hard to aim and control the projectile, and so further tests were carried out using nitrogen dioxide, a brown gas which allowed the engineers to study the path it took. A prototype was installed to protect bridges over the river Elbe, though no hits on aircraft were ever recorded.

Plans were also drawn up to use the pressure of sound waves against personnel, rather than aircraft. The *Schallkanone* (Sound Cannon) was designed by Dr Richard Wallauschek and was first produced in 1944. It comprised two parabolic sound reflectors that projected a beam of intense sound waves against enemy troops. A pulse of intense sound waves was produced by detonating a critical mixture of oxygen and methane that was forced under pressure into the detonation chamber. The chamber was carefully calibrated to produce a resonance of the frequency that increased dramatically in intensity up to a pressure of an atmosphere (15psi or 1 bar) some 175ft (50m) away. This was calculated to be enough to incapacitate a soldier instantly. There were reports that experiments with it worked, for example a dog tethered over 125ft (40m) from the weapon was said to have been killed.

The device has re-emerged in more recent times. This kind of weapon appeared in the adventures of the boy detective Tintin, by the Belgian author Georges Prosper Remi (popularly known as Hergé), entitled *L'Affair Tournesol* which was published in English as *The Calculus Affair*. It has been used in fact, as well as fiction; ships are now being fitted with sound guns based on the same principle. The LRAD device, currently manufactured in the United States, is being fitted to ships around the world and is commonly brought out and primed for action as ships enter dangerous waters, or when they come into port where a raid might occur. The design initiated by the Nazis has found a peacetime application in keeping cruise passengers safe from modern-day pirates.

STRANGE TANKS

During the war there were several designs for modern and state-of-the-art tanks. Super-heavy tanks were soon on the drawing board, and there were also attempts to find a method of transportation that would provide better traction than the standard caterpillar tracks. Few

were as bizarre as the Tsar tank that the Russians had first manufactured in World War I. Instead of having parallel tracks it was fitted with two spoked wheels some 27ft (8m) in diameter. A single trailing wheel at the rear was only 5ft (1.5m) in diameter. The idea was that the large wheels could overcome obstacles on the ground and it was tested before the Army High Commission in August 1915 near Moscow. The rear wheel was liable to sink into the ground, and the front wheels were too narrow, and so they sank into mud; the prototype was marooned where it stood for years, and was eventually broken up for scrap iron by the Bolsheviks in 1923.

An equally bizarre idea for propelling tanks across muddy terrain was the spiral drive which was proposed during World War II. Prototypes were constructed in which the vehicle was driven, not by giant rotating wheels, but by a cylindrical drive

British naval officer Captain Lord Louis Mountbatten in 1942. Geoffrey Pyke's proposed research into spiral-driven tanks was approved when Mountbatten became Chief of Combined Operations in 1941. (Getty Images)

Top left: Vickers produced this amphibious lightweight tank which was crewed by two soldiers. This model was never used by the British Army though it was sold to the Chinese, the Thais and the Dutch troops in South-East Asia. Vickers Amphibious Tanks were sold to the Soviet Union who based their T-37 tank on the British design. (Author's collection)

Top right: Russia introduced the Tsar Tank with the largest drive wheels of any military vehicle in history: 27ft (8m) across. It was a failure. (Author's collection)

Left: Curious versions of army tanks abound; here we see a design by Johannes Rädel. In 2006 British adventurers adapted a Bombardier snow truck and fitted it with screw propulsion. (Author's collection)

featuring spiral ridges like a corkscrew. They were unable to cross flat, level, solid ground but were excellent in mud and also for crossing snow. This idea was originally proposed to the War Office in London by Geoffrey Pyke, a strange combination of journalist and inventor, as a solution to the difficulties in crossing snow during the Allied invasion of Norway. At first it was rejected, but when Louis Mountbatten became Chief of Combined Operations in 1941, the proposal was accepted for development and a version of a screw-driven vehicle was built for testing. It was named the Weasel, though it existed only as a rough prototype. The concept was later considered by the Russians during the war years. They developed the idea still further and produced some more elaborate prototypes, but these strange tanks were not available until after the war.

THE SECRET STORY OF THE ICE AIRFIELD

Geoffrey Pyke, whom we encountered above as the designer of a screw-driven tank, became better known for his ambitious proposals for a kind of floating mid-Atlantic airbase constructed of ice. His idea was first promoted in 1942 as an ice aircraft carrier, and magazines featured pictures of a conventional aircraft carrier of a translucent, glistening appearance looming like a ghost out of the mist. Pyke's idea was rather different – it was for a floating raft to act as a fuel base. The concept was developed starting as Project *Habakkuk*, from the biblical text that includes the words: 'Be utterly amazed, for I am going to do something in your days that you would not believe, even if you were told.' Pyke consistently misspelt it *Habbakuk*, and that is how it is usually recorded. The idea was for the construction of a vast floating air base made with a mixture of wood pulp and ice. The compound substance was slower to melt and more bullet-resistant than ice alone, and was named Pykrete. But in fact, although his name is forever associated with this grand design, neither the concept nor the substance were really Pyke's. The first proposal for an ice airbase actually came from a German engineer, Dr Gerk, and was reported in 1932.

Gerk's proposals from that time look very like the later magazine illustrations that Geoffrey Pyke promoted. What is more, Pyke was not even the inventor of what became known as Pykrete. The secret story behind this curious idea began when Pyke was shown a paper written, many years earlier, by Professor Herman Mark in Austria. Mark was a former professor of physical chemistry at the University of Vienna and an expert on the structure of plastic materials. For many years he studied X-ray diffraction, a technique in which the effect of a material on a beam of X-rays can be used to work out the molecular structure that lay hidden within the material. In 1926 he joined the chemical company IG Farben and worked on the development plastics that we now take for granted – PVC, polystyrene, polyvinyl alcohol and synthetic rubber.

Mark laid plans to leave Germany as Hitler was preparing for war. He had a huge store of platinum wire that he wished to take with him because it is a catalyst that is crucially important for his research. He knew the authorities would not permit him to remove such an important element from Germany, so Mark conceived a way of smuggling the wire with him.

ICE-ISLAND in *Mid-Atlantic* Proposed

Drawing shows ice island, frozen by liquid air, proposed by German scientist as a floating harbor and landing field.

SEADROMES for ocean landing fields are not a new idea, a steel 'drome designed by Edward Armstrong, recently described in these pages, being well on the road to practical acceptance. But the proposal to build seadromes of ice, recently advanced from Germany, seems fantastic until one realizes that the idea has already passed the experimental stage with flying colors.

The German scientist Dr. Gerke of Waldenburg two years ago erected an ice island in Lake Zurich by artificial means, which endured six days after the refrigerating machinery was switched off. His proposal for a mid-Atlantic way station of ice involves the construction of a framework of hollow tubing which, when filled with liquid air manufactured in a refrigerating plant, freezes the water surrounding it into a solid mass.

Design of the island would call for a section on which a landing field and buildings for offices and refrigerating plants could be built.

This article, published in October 1932 in *Modern Mechanics* magazine, claims that Dr Gerk of Waldenburg, Germany, had constructed a trial version of an ice airfield which survived for six days after the refrigeration machine on board was turned off. The idea was revived during World War II. (Author's collection)

He bent the platinum wire into the shape of coat hangers, and his wife knitted neat covers for them all. When his suitcases were checked for contraband, the coat hangers did not even attract a second glance. The Canadian International Pulp and Paper Company in Dresden had asked Mark to come and organize research at their research headquarters in Canada, but the Gestapo arrested him, confiscated his passport, and gave him an official order not to contact any Jews. By bribing an official with a payment equal to his annual salary he secretly retrieved his passport, and – with the help of the paper company – he managed to obtain a visa to enter Canada. In April 1938 he mounted a Nazi pennant on the front of the family car, tied their skis to the roof of the vehicle, and drove across the frontier to Zurich, Switzerland, with the clothes (on their coat hangers) safely concealed in suitcases. From here they set off to reach London, England, where Mark boarded a transatlantic vessel to sail to Montreal.

He ended up carrying out research on paper pulp not in Canada, but in the United States at the Brooklyn Polytechnic where he set up the first course in the world for students of polymers and plastics. Mark was convinced that there was an important future for composite materials made from fibres held together in a mass by a plastic bonding agent. He was right, of course; the new Boeing Dreamliner is largely constructed from just such composite plastic materials. One of Mark's early trials was an investigation of a wood pulp composite that was bonded, not with plastic, but with ice. The resulting material had properties rather like present-day fibreglass and was very strong.

A model of Boeing's 7E7 Dreamliner, on display in November 2004. The Dreamliner is constructed of composite materials, an idea originally thought of by Austrian Professor Herman Mark during World War II. (Mike Clarke/AFP/Getty Images)

In 1942, Mark sent a paper on his research to one of his former students, Mark Perutz, who had escaped from Germany to England. Perutz is the scientist who coined the term 'molecular biology'. I knew him later at Cambridge. When Perutz passed the papers to Geoffrey Pyke, it was Mark's research on which Pyke set out to base his proposals for a floating mid-Atlantic airfield. His plan was for a top-secret 'aircraft carrier' made of ice and pulp that floated in the middle of the Atlantic; it would allow planes to stop and refuel, thus bringing Europe within easy flying distance of the United States. But would it work? Several practical trials were carried out in the summer of 1943, and a small prototype was constructed at Patricia Lake, Alberta, Canada. It measured 60ft (18m) by 30ft (9m) and was thought to weigh 1,000 tons. A 1hp (0.75kW) engine drove the freezer unit to keep the ice solid. Pyke himself was not permitted to join these trials, as he had already caused problems when the Weasel idea was being investigated in America, but he remained a persistent advocate of the concept.

Pykrete proved to be a solid material; buoyant, slow to melt, low in density and floating high in the water. In recent years television documentary producers have recreated Pykrete and there is no doubt that it works. But Pyke was not easy to work with, the scaling-up of the project would have cost prodigious amounts of money, and the sheer size of the project meant it was never tried on a larger scale. As a result, Pyke's private experiments continued and he is, to this day, firmly associated with the strange saga of the aircraft carrier to be made of ice; but both the concept, and the material, had already been published years before. The secret origin of Pykrete was nothing to do with Pyke, and Professor Mark surely deserves his own place in the history of World War II.

AMPHIBIOUS VEHICLES

Just as the Russians had contrived methods of propelling tanks though mud and snow, the British worked in secret on designs that would allow conventional vehicles to operate in difficult conditions. The Bedford Giraffe was a modified van intended for beach landings. The important items – cab, instruments, engine, etc – were raised on a frame for working in water. The engine was 7ft (2.13m) and the driver's seat 10ft (3.05m) above the water's surface. Tests proved satisfactory and the first orders were placed but, at the last minute, it was discovered that the vehicle was not reliably waterproof in choppy seas and the problems could not be solved. The project was abandoned.

The Vickers Company produced an amphibious tank during the 1930s. It was not put into production by the British during World War II, though a later model, designated the Vickers-Carden-Loyd M1931 Light Amphibious Tank, was sold in some quantity to the Chinese Nationalist Forces in the years leading up to the war.

At the other end of the scale came the gigantic *Maus* (Mouse) tank. A mock-up made from wood was shown to Hitler in May 1943. The final version of the tank would weigh a colossal 190 tons. The Führer immediately ordered that 150 be manufactured and by

November 1943 the first prototype was ready for demonstration. Despite being powered by a modified aircraft engine by Daimler-Benz the tank's vast weight made it difficult to move. Even when that was overcome, and the tank could crawl along at a maximum velocity of 8mph (13km/h), it was soon realized that it could not cross any existing bridge in Germany without bringing it down. The Maus was therefore fitted with a snorkel system so that it could pass underwater through rivers up to 26ft (8m) deep. It thus became the largest amphibious vehicle in history. But it remained over-engineered, too heavy and too slow. Hitler, once more, changed his personal preferences and so the entire order was dropped.

More successful was the *Landwasserschlepper* (Land-Water-Tractor) that was commissioned by the Heereswaffenamt in 1935. It was intended for use as a light tug that could also travel on land. The vehicle was designed by the Rheinmetall-Borsig Company in Düsseldorf and looked like a boat mounted on tracks. Its original function was to work on rivers where the bridges had been destroyed, but with the plans advancing for the German invasion of Britain under Operation *Sealion*, it was envisaged as hauling assault barges onto the shore. It entered service after considerable testing and modification in 1942 and saw service in North Africa and on the Russian Front. Towards the end of the war, a new design was introduced which featured a protected cockpit for the driver and was manufactured on a Panzer Mark IV tank chassis. Even though it was beset with problems, this bizarre Landwasserschlepper was still in operation at the end of the war.

Amphibious tanks meet with varying degrees of success. Here, the Americans test out their sea-going tanks on the beaches of the Solomon Islands. (Getty Images)

PANJANDRUM FOLLY

Britain's greatest mistake was one of the most spectacular follies of the entire war. It was a secret weapon that was doomed to fail from the start – the giant Panjandrum. This was to be a large explosive wheel that could roll up the beaches and destroy German fortifications on the coast of Normandy, France. The unlikely name came from the theatrical writings in London of Samuel Foote in 1754: 'The grand Panjandrum himself ... playing the game of catch-as-catch-can till the gunpowder ran out at the heels of their boots.'

In construction it was to be a pair of large wheels, each some 10ft (3m) in diameter and with a tread around the periphery about 1ft (30cm) in width. In the middle, at the hub, there was to be a substantial explosive charge fitted with a fuse that would detonate on impact. Around the rim of the two wheels would be cordite rocket charges that would spin the whole device up the beaches of northern France during the Allied invasion. In use, it would look like a pair of Catherine wheel fireworks.

The original idea was approved by the British Royal Navy's Directorate of Miscellaneous Weapon Development based on rough sketches prepared by a Combined Operations group-captain. In August 1943, at Leytonstone in East London, construction of a prototype began. Within a month it was ready for testing. Let us step back and examine the idea in principle. At once a serious defect in the design becomes apparent. If the wheels were propelled forwards by rockets that burned only when facing to the rear, it would be driven along at increasing speed like any other reaction-propelled vehicle. This dramatic concept of the rocket-propelled weapon was no doubt what immediately appealed to the designers. But think about it: the Panjandrum was not a reaction-propelled vehicle at all. The rockets burning around the periphery were going to exert their effects in turning the wheel – in creating torque, as an engineer would say – and it was the torque, rather than the backward thrusting rockets, which was going to drive the device forward.

There are clear differences between a reaction-propelled rocket vehicle and one driven by torque. For instance, if the number or power of the rockets on a reaction-driven trolley (where all the rockets point backwards) is increased, then the contrivance will go correspondingly faster. This is not, however, the case with the Panjandrum. In this case, more rockets, or an increase in their power, could well lead to an increase in torque but that might just as well manifest itself as wheel-spin, rather than forward movement. Half the rockets are pointing backwards, true; but half are directing their thrust forwards, against the direction of movement. This is what the experimenters were to find. If the number of the rockets was too low, the device would not be able to overcome the rolling resistance of the sandy beach. However, if the number and power of the rockets were substantially increased, then wheel-spin could set in. There was no means, as it were, of slipping the clutch as the giant wheels slowly gained forward velocity.

There was an added problem: the device was not a carriage fitted with wheels – rather, it was a large pair of wheels. It would have only to run over a relatively small object (like a rock) to tilt sideways and substantially change course. One or two such perturbations could cause it to change direction several times, with possibly drastic results.

The mathematics of all this is involved, though not obscure; and even common sense would show that the Panjandrum was unlikely to succeed. A wheeled mine, driven by rear-mounted rockets, might well have been practicable. It would have no problems of torque, and would tend to maintain its straight course, as any four-wheeled vehicle would tend to do. Furthermore the manufacturing technology, being more conventional, would have posed fewer problems. I can see several alternatives. One would be the trolley, as I have already said. If the wheels were really necessary, then it might have been feasible to mount the rockets near the hub, on gimbals fitted with weights that caused them always to point to

In the final stages of the war, the British tried to find a way to breach the Nazi defences in northern France and came up with this bizarre contraption to carry a ton of high explosive up the beaches. Tests in Devon showed that it was unstable and could not maintain speed; the project was eventually cancelled. (John Batchelor)

the rear. Another design that could have worked would be to have had the rockets mounted around the edge of smaller wheels that were geared to drive the larger, outer wheels. That way, the drive wheels would be spinning round at speed, and reduction gears would have transmitted their energy to the main wheels, turning more slowly as they gathered momentum.

But to the minds of the Directorate, the uncomplicated image of a vast, rotating, fiery wheel spewing its way up towards the enemy fortifications was romantic, bizarre, frightening even; the practical problems did not commend themselves to anyone on the team. The prototype was constructed under conditions of the greatest secrecy. When it was finished, it was transported under the closest security to the West Country with a police guard, moving only under cover of complete darkness. Once it arrived safely at the seaside town of Westward Ho! in Devon the security measures were forgotten about and the Panjandrum was unveiled, ready for the tests. Local residents, even people on holiday, crowded round the device with bemused interest.

On its first run it was clearly underpowered. Had anyone calculated thrust values (assuming that the complication of torque did not exist) they would have seen that the rolling resistance of such a vast, heavy object against sand was going to be considerable. But they did not take this into account, and the first test run came to an ignominious end as the 'secret weapon' trundled down a ramp with its rockets feebly firing and rolled steadily to a dead stop.

The plans had been for the Panjandrum to storm across the beach at up to 60mph (almost 100km/h) and the depressing exhibition the device gave of itself must have been profoundly disappointing. So the number of rockets was increased; and they were clamped to the inside edges of the wheels, as well as the outside. The next firing was a failure because of the excessive torque. Not only that, but one of the wheels sank into the sand which threw the vehicle off course, and several of the rockets broke free and zoomed crazily across the beach. The spectators looked on in astonishment and not a little fear.

To correct the instability was the next priority. But how could this be achieved? It was decided to try fitting a third, central wheel. It is fairly obvious that, on even slightly rough terrain, this would add to the instability rather than correcting it. The test that followed proved the point. The huge contraption ran a little way up the beach, powered by a total of 70 rockets instead of the original 18. It lurched to one side, then turned back on itself, ran back into the sea and fell on its side, the rockets boiling the water around. Other rockets became detached and flew off low across the sands. Clearly, the middle third wheel was not an improvement. It was found to have been bent and buckled after this test run, and was abandoned.

Engineers and military officials gather around a prototype Panjandrum at Westward Ho! in Devon. The first tests were attempted on 7 September 1943. Although the whole project was top secret and the manufacture in London had been carried out under conditions of high security, this changed dramatically when the Panjandrum was rolled out on a beach crowded with holidaymakers. Thousands of civilians watched as the tests failed; at one stage a dog took to chasing the device along the sand. (Author's collection)

During the month of October 1943 further trials were arranged in which heavy cables were attached to each end of the hub and secured to two winches which could, it was hoped, steer the contraption safely up the beach. Of course, when the test was run the clouds of smoke and flame from the combustion of the rocket fuel obscured the direction of travel from the controllers manning the winches, and the increased drag from the cables was itself an added disadvantage. There was yet another practical problem in the design that began to emerge. The breaking-up of the rocket units was clearly very dangerous, yet it was obvious that the rockets might disintegrate. They were designed, as rockets always are, to produce a steady backwards thrust and by being fixed to the periphery of the Panjandrum wheels they were being submitted to centrifugal forces for which they were never intended. These acted laterally against the casings and the force would become considerable when we consider the dimensions involved. A 20lb (9kg) rocket whirling on the edge of a large wheel moving at speed is clearly subject to lateral forces of considerable magnitude and the break-up of some of the rockets was clearly probable. Yet this hazard was also ignored, and was omitted from the design calculations.

A further test took place over an uneven surface. The wet sand was specially cratered for this trial run. After a distance of only 140 yards (about 130m) the wheels of the Panjandrum buckled, the winches seized and the cables became entangled; its trajectory this time had been a wild zigzag pathway across the sand, ending up with the giant device lying pitifully on its side, spent rockets still smoking. If any further evidence of the impracticality of this absurd contraption were needed, this surely was it. But no – development work continued, in spite of all the accumulated evidence. Two new prototype Panjandrums were constructed. They were ready early in the New Year and an official demonstration was arranged in January 1944. A number of senior government officials came to witness this latest test run and several senior members of the Armed Forces were also in attendance. It was to be an auspicious occasion.

The rockets on the first Panjandrum were successfully ignited and the monster began to roll forward. But within a short distance, the first rocket exploded violently and disintegrated, soon to be followed by others. The great wheel, as it gathered speed, began to weave dangerously from side to side and then erratically to change direction. It was completely out of control, and began to head straight towards a group of terrified photographers. The VIPs leapt behind a sand-dune and fell into a tangle of barbed wire. The roaring device turned again, headed down the beach back towards the sea, then in a cloud of smoke and a series of explosions it crashed heavily on its side. Rockets broke away and screamed across the beach in all directions, at least one being vainly pursued by a holidaymaker's dog. All that remained of the secret weapon was a scorched and twisted hunk of metal beneath a lingering cloud of black smoke.

So, at last, the project was terminated. All the scientific and engineering data should have shown that it could not work. Even a cursory examination of the elementary physics involved would have shown that it was doomed from the start. The cost of the project is unknown, but was clearly considerable, and the wastage of time was immense. At the time, a financial saving, or the

HOW YOUR SALVAGE HELPS TO
MAKE A RESCUE LAUNCH

① SCRAP METAL
SCRAP IRON NEEDED FOR STEEL HULL. STEEL NEEDED FOR MAKING ENGINE AND MACHINE-GUNS. BRASS MAKES CARTRIDGE CASES. 3-PINT TIN KETTLE MAKES 40 MACHINE-GUN BULLETS. PHOSPHOR BRONZE NEEDED FOR PROPELLOR. COPPER FOR RADIO COMPONENTS

② ROPE, STRING, TWINE
MAKE NEW SHIP'S ROPE

③ WASTE PAPER
ONE ENVELOPE MAKES 50 WADS FOR MACHINE-GUN CARTRIDGES. TWELVE OLD LETTERS MAKE A CARTRIDGE BOX. WASTE PAPER ALSO MAKES GASKET WASHERS FOR ENGINE AND PROVIDES INSULATION FOR RADIO

④ SCRAP RUBBER
MAKES ELECTRICAL AND RADIO INSULATORS AND COMPONENTS

⑤ BONES
GIVE GLYCERINE—A COMPONENT IN CORDITE CHARGES FOR MACHINE-GUN CARTRIDGES

⑥ RAGS
COTTON RAGS MAKE SPECIAL GRADES OF PAPER FOR CHARTS ALSO ENGINE WIPERS

release of a few thousand man-hours, would have been of the greatest value to the war effort. Householders were giving up their kitchen saucepans in order to supply light alloy to the aircraft industry and railings were being torn up and melted down to make steel sheet for weapons manufacture. To have these resources diverted to the Panjandrum project was unjustifiable.

This was not the last we heard of the wasteful Panjandrum fiasco, however. It has re-emerged in more recent times. A lightweight reconstruction featured in the BBC's wartime comedy series *Dad's Army*, first broadcast on 22 December 1972. This episode featured the many problems that befell the device, and paralleled the original trials in some ways. The only time a Panjandrum ran successfully was in 2009 when a 6ft (1.8m) diameter replica was constructed to mark the 65th anniversary of D-Day. Like their wartime predecessors, these designers also envisaged that it would speed along the beach, heedless of the problems caused by the question of torque and the backward pointing rockets. It was ignited in a ceremony for the Appledore Book Festival in Devon, and ran down a small ramp. Although it worked to a fashion, the model trundled for several yards, mostly moving at walking pace, before it slowed to a halt and its rockets burned out.

Opposite: During World War II, graphic artists were commissioned to design posters that would encourage civilians to contribute to the war effort. This poster, published by the London and North Eastern Railway (LNER), encouraged people to recycle. (SSPL/Getty Images)

Below: Under cover of a smokescreen, soldiers of the US 9th Army use Alligator amphibious vehicles to cross the Rhine. The Americans researched options to design an exploding version of these vehicles that could break through German defences. However, this project was neither economically viable nor, in the end, necessary and so it was cancelled. (Getty Images)

And so attention turned to designing an explosive landing craft. It was planned that this could deliver a load of explosives to breach a protective Atlantic Wall of concrete and allow the Allied troops through to the plains of France. It was being argued privately, that – even if the Panjandrum had delivered its load of explosives – they would not have exerted the desired effect. To give full benefit, an explosive charge would have to be clamped firmly against the wall. The blast would otherwise be dispersed and dissipated as it produced a huge crater in the sand. The proposed landing craft were designed with hydraulic rams which would provide the desired result – they would extend to force the explosive charge firmly against a concrete wall, maximizing its effect.

The vehicles chosen were Alligator landing craft made in the United States. They were based on the amphibious DUKWs vehicles but had caterpillar tracks instead of conventional wheels. Attached to the tracks were spoon-shaped paddles which propelled the craft through the choppy seas until it came to land, when it would rise from the water and proceed up the beach like a conventional tracked vehicle. The Directorate planned to fit each craft with a 1-ton bank of high explosive mounted on a mattress base; this – on contact with the concrete wall – would be firmly clamped in position by the hydraulic rams and automatically detonated.

The Alligator itself was a formidable device. Each was 26ft (10m) long overall and more than 10ft (3m) wide, weighing about 11 tons. But once in the water they were cumbersome and slow, and under sea trials they ran into repeated problems of instability that are reminiscent of the Panjandrum tests. On one occasion the hydraulic ram mechanism was actuated while the craft was still at sea. Its 1-ton mattress of explosive, ballasted with sand, tilted the whole contraption upwards at a crazy angle and a serious accident was narrowly averted. The Alligator took with it more casualties than its fiery predecessor had done as it spiralled up the beach.

As with the Panjandrum, eventually someone realized that they were unlikely so succeed with this project and the Alligator too was cancelled. It was just as well. Both devices were being specifically designed to blast through an impenetrable wall of concrete behind which the Germans would be hiding. But, as intelligence showed (and as the Allied landings would confirm), the concrete wall simply did not exist. The Germans had never thought to construct an impregnable wall, and the Allied strategists had been developing weapons against a target that had never even been built.

There was one final attempt to use rockets as a secret device for the Normandy landings that would aid the Allies, and intimidate the Germans. This was a novel idea: to drop containers of vehicles and equipment from low-flying bombers, using retro-rockets to slow the descent and cushion their landing on the beaches of Normandy. The Army proposed this novel idea to the Admiralty's Directorate of Miscellaneous Weapon Development, who had been working on parachuting equipment during the invasion. Using parachutes to drop heavy equipment was no problem, but the relatively heavy impact was causing damage. Surely a retro-rocket assembly could cushion the landing. The preliminary designs seemed perfectly satisfactory, and the device was code named Hajile.

The idea was to set off a battery of rockets when the container was a few yards from the ground. Solid-fuel rockets could not be relied upon to ignite at exactly the same time, and early tests showed – when the smoke had cleared – that the container was often left crunched into the ground. It was decided that it would be safer to carry out some tests over the open sea, and the site chosen for the observers was the holiday pier at Weston-super-Mare, which was designated HMS *Birnbeck* during the war. It was decided to drop a large container, fitted with its retro-rockets, from a Lancaster bomber but the pilot's aim was not accurate and the horrified technicians realized that it was heading straight towards the buildings. They ran back along the pier, just in time to avoid the container as it crashed through the roof and demolished the workshops.

There were plenty of other tests. One of them involved dropping containers from a tall crane. On the second attempt, the container hit the ground just as the rockets fired with a massive roar – this propelled the container back up into the air, where it smashed into the jib and demolished the crane that had dropped it. Several of these containers were built for the D-Day landings, but the device was never formally commissioned and remains a peculiar sideline to the war effort. The only remaining secret was the strange name given to the device: Hajile. Unlike Panjandrum, it seems to have no meaning at all, but its roots lie in the Old Testament. Elijah is said to have ascended unto heaven in a pillar of fire, remember?

Suddenly, all is clear: Hajile in simply Elijah in reverse.

ELECTRONIC
SECRETS

DETECTING THE ENEMY at a distance has long been an aim of any warring nation. The first distant detection system relied upon the sound of the enemy, and methods of picking up and amplifying faint noise are more than a century old. In 1880, the pages of *Scientific American* featured the topophone, invented by Professor A. M. Mayer, which was intended to amplify a distant noise and make it possible for the user to detect the direction from where it originated. The use of sound reflectors to concentrate distant engine noise from enemy aircraft dates from World War I when Professor F. C. Mather dug a parabolic reflector into the cliff near Maidstone, Kent. This was in 1916 and the reflector was used to detect incoming aircraft or Zeppelin airships. An observer would be stationed at the focal point of the acoustic reflector, listening for distant sounds. The experiments worked well, and a similar reflector was then dug out in Baharic-Cahaq on the Mediterranean island state of Malta. Further examples were planned for Aden, Gibraltar, Hong Kong and Singapore.

A British parabolic concrete sound collector 20ft (6m) in diameter was erected near Dungeness, Kent, in 1928. A larger reflector 30ft (9m) across was built two years later, together with a large concave concrete reflector 200ft (60m) from end to end. During the 1930s, portable and steerable reflectors were designed. They could detect faint sounds over large distances, and the position of the sound source could be confirmed by the direction in which the reflectors were pointed to collect the loudest sound. By the beginning of World War II, as an alternative to the fixed parabolic reflectors, conical sound collectors had been built in Britain and were being successfully tested. Some were in the form of directional funnels that could be moved from place to place and could indicate the position of incoming planes. This was, though, a doomed technology. Detecting the sounds of aircraft engines was relegated to the sidelines when radar began to emerge.

RADAR ARRIVES ON THE SCENE

It is hard to imagine contemporary transportation without radar. All the airliners in the world are tracked by operators using real-time images of where they are in the sky. Every liner and container ship is watched intently from the shore; and they see each other with an unblinking eye. Even little yachts can carry a radar device to survey the surrounding seas, and they have a radar reflector at the masthead to ensure they are seen by the rest of the community. Radar is taken for granted, and – were it to vanish overnight – global transportation would be finished. It is clear that the modern world relies on radar to a great degree, but this important technological development has a long and interesting history.

ORIGINS OF RADAR

Many of the resonances between the secret weapons of World War II and today's high-tech world will have come as a surprise. Radar, by contrast, is something with which we all feel

A Victorian woodcut shows the topophone, invented and patented by Professor A. M. Mayer in 1879 and featured in *Scientific American* in 1880. The instrument was designed to amplify noises and help the listener determine their exact direction. (© Bettmann/Corbis)

The first military aircraft detectors were built near Dungeness, Kent, by the British authorities after World War I. Constructed of concrete, they focused distant sound rays onto a microphone mounted in the middle. (Author's collection)

British physicist Robert Watson-Watt (1892–1973) carries out an experiment at Sunnymeads in Berkshire. Watson-Watt was pivotal in the development of radar. (Fox Photos/Getty Images)

Experiments with sound receivers developed after World War I. As electronic amplifiers were yet to be perfected, acoustic horns were used instead. These detectors were used to detect distant aircraft. (Library of Congress)

more comfortable. It is widely believed that it was the urgency of World War II which led to the invention of radar, and that is was the brainchild of Robert Watson-Watt, the brilliant British electronics engineer and visionary. It may come as a surprise to many, then, to hear that radar was in existence prior even to World War I.

It arose from the grief of a radio engineer named Christian Hülsmeyer from Düsseldorf, Germany. One of his closest friends lost his mother at sea when two ships collided in fog. Hülsmeyer was greatly saddened by the death of someone so close, and began to speculate on a means of trying to prevent a recurrence. He had been studying radio waves, which had been examined since 1887 by Heinrich Hertz, who is now commemorated by the use of the term 'Hertz' to describe the frequency of a radio beam. Hertz made many observations that were of interest to science – and one of them was that radio waves could be reflected from a metallic object. This caught Hülsmeyer's attention and he began to carry out experiments to see whether the metallic object might be a ship at sea, and whether the nature of the reflection could tell you where it was. In the 1890s Hülsmeyer was a school teacher and devoted his spare time to these experiments; he later joined the Siemens Company. In 1902 he met a successful businessman from Cologne who agreed to speculate on the invention and advanced funds for the work. They called it the *Telemobiloscope* and together they launched a company called Telemobiloscop-Gesellschaft Hülsmeyer und Mannheim. A public exhibition took place on 18 May 1904 in Cologne. Hülsmeyer set up his apparatus on the Hohenzollern Bridge, and as soon as a ship sailed into the forward-facing beam a warning bell sounded loudly. Then, as the ship sailed away from the beam, the ringing stopped. Hülsmeyer had demonstrated the remote detection of a ship – it could have saved the life of his friend's mother. There were rounds of applause from the spectators, and positive reports in the press.

They took out patents on this remarkable new device, and in June 1904 the detector was demonstrated at a shipping conference in Rotterdam. The Telemobiloscope used a spark transmitter operating on a wavelength of 15.7–19.7in (40–50cm). The spark gap was submerged in oil to prevent it from burning away and the radio beam was emitted from a reflector shaped like a cone. To prevent a stray signal from some other transmitter

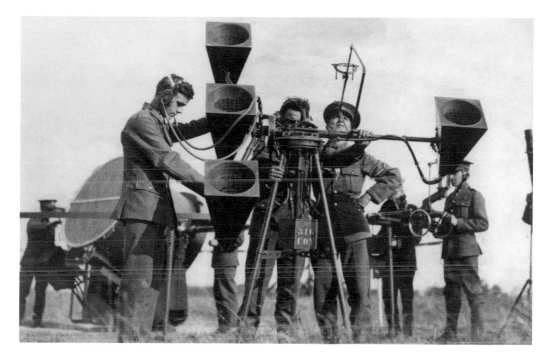

An early radar system in operation in the south of England, around 1930. The importance of this technology was recognized, and it became increasingly significant and advanced during World War II until it became vital to the modern world. (Getty Images)

Christian Hülsmeyer demonstrated that remote detection of objects was possible. He is here seen with his patent for the Telemobiloscope dating from 1904. (akg-images/ullstein bild)

Manuscript by German physicist Heinrich Hertz, who studied radio waves from 1887. Hertz is now the internationally recognized term to describe the frequency of a radiating beam. (SSPL/Getty Images)

from triggering the alarm bell, there was a time delay built into the circuitry so that the bell did not ring when the first signal was detected, but only when a second pulse was registered. This reduced the likelihood of a false alarm. Using this device, ships could be detected by simply aiming the beam in a given direction. Although there was no timing device to detect the delay between sending and receiving the signal (which would have given an immediate indication of the range) Hülsmeyer managed to show how to obtain a rough idea of the distance of the ship. The beam could be moved up and down, and – once you knew the height of the transmitter above the surface of the water – it was easy to work out the range.

Hülsmeyer and Mannheim were delighted with their success and felt that their time had come. Details of the invention were sent to the Naval office and also to commercial shipping companies, but nobody seemed interested. Their hopes were dashed, and the Telemobiloscope remained a mere curiosity. A similar device, which detected radio beams bounced back from the surface of the ground, was invented by R. C. Newhouse at the Bell Laboratories in the United States. This was patented in 1920, and it later gave rise to an altimeter worked by radio (rather than air pressure). The first British patent for what was called radio location was taken out by L. S. Alder for His Majesty's Signal School in 1928, and the Italian wireless pioneer Guglielmo Marconi – who knew that one could use radio to detect a moving object – demonstrated a device that could detect distant objects in 1933.

This was the year when Hitler swept to power over Germany, and the emergent German Navy began to investigate harnessing the power of radio detection or *Funkmesstechnik*. In the following year, research started in Russia and successfully detected aircraft up to 55 miles (88km) distant. Nothing further happened at the time, though a French vessel in 1935 demonstrated a radio beam as a method of avoiding collisions, and this *Barrage Electronique* system was used early in World War II.

SEEING THE INVISIBLE

And so, by the mid-1930s, there had been a range of different developments that allowed observers to penetrate fog or to detect ships in the darkness of night. Italian, German, British and American research had all played their part in harnessing the effects first observed by Hertz in the Victorian era. Even before World War I it had been possible to detect an otherwise invisible ship, using marine radar, even though few were interested in the idea. And since the time of World War I the directional use of sound detection had been used to give warning of distant aircraft. A combination of the two – detection funding from a transmitted pulse of sound – gave rise to sonar, which was developed by separate Canadian, British and American researchers starting in 1912.

As war began to loom, increasing efforts were directed to defending Britain from attack. Robert Watson-Watt was a meteorologist who had studied the detection of lightning through the radio interference that was caused by the discharge, and he was approached about stories that were beginning to filter out from Germany. The Nazis, it was said, had a death ray. They could beam a radio transmission and wipe out populations at a considerable distance. Britain needed one too, it was agreed, and Watson-Watt must be the person to approach. It did not take him long to calculate that it was impossible, and he wrote a report to defuse the concern felt in official circuits. At the end, he added a note on a different problem that was 'less unpromising' than a death ray. This was the detection of objects by reflected radio waves. A report on that, he said, will be 'submitted when required'.

AIRCRAFT AND RADAR

Watson-Watt did not invent the idea of detecting objects by reflected radio signals. This had long been established as a way of detecting shipping, where the metallic mass reflected the beam, but what about using this approach on aeroplanes? They were not heavy steel objects, and were often made of cloth and wood, but could they still reflect a radio beam? In February 1935 Watson-Watt wrote a top secret memorandum for the Air Ministry in London. He entitled it *Detection and Location of Aircraft by Radio Methods.* This was a radical new departure, and the Air Ministry asked for a demonstration. Within weeks, an experiment was set up at Litchborough, near the BBC shortwave transmitters at Daventry. Two transmitters were set up so that their signals cancelled each other out. Anything that interfered with the signal would deflect a spot on an oscilloscope screen. Only three people were involved: Watson-Watt and his assistant Arnold Wilkins, with a representative of the Ministry, A. P. Rowe. A Handey Page Heyford bomber was chosen as the first target. The Heyford was a biplane built in 1930, and was the last heavy biplane to be used by the Royal Air Force. Its wing-span was also exactly one-quarter that of the wavelength of the radio beam, which

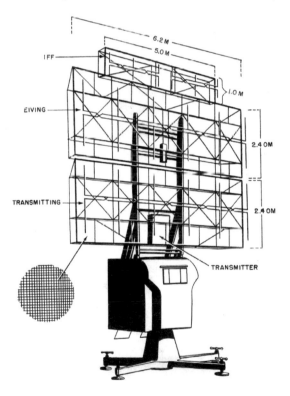

'Freya' was the codename given to the German early warning radar system. This is a diagram of the Freya radar, the discovery of which helped the British find the radar at Würzburg, the target of the Bruneval Raid. (US War Department)

would maximize the chances of generating a positive echo in the signal. Flight-Lieutenant R. S. Blucke was the pilot that day, and he took off from the airfield at Farnborough and climbed slowly to 6,000ft (1,830m).

When he reached Daventry, the team on the ground saw the oscilloscope signal suddenly begin to flicker. The three men watched until the signal returned to normal when the aircraft was 8 miles (13km) distant. The principle was proved – not only heavy steel ships, but even lightweight aircraft, could be detected by the reflections of a radio beam. Within four short years, the system was refined until planes could be detected at a distance of 100 miles (160km) and work began on erecting a series of detector stations. This became the Chain Home network, known as CH for short, and it was fully operational in 1937, long before World War II broke out. This was the first radar system detecting aircraft in the world. When the war began in 1939, many nations were harnessing the same effect: France, Germany, Hungary, Italy, Japan, Netherlands, Russia, Switzerland and the United States were all investigating radar systems of their own.

The true value of radar was recognized during the Battle of Britain in 1940–41, when the system gave advance warning of attacks, and knowing the direction of incoming German aircraft enabled fighters to be dispatched in good time. Reports of planes being detected by the CH stations scattered across the south of England and the Isle of Wight, were sent by telephone to 'filter rooms' which brought all the results together. Orders were then issued to

AMES Type 1 Chain Home East Coast radar installation on England's south coast. On the left are three (originally four) transmitter towers, with the heavily protected transmitter building in front. Four receiver towers can be seen on the right of the photograph. Chain Home was the world's first radar system to detect aircraft. (IWM CH 15173)

An artist's depiction of the Bruneval Raid. The plan was for British troops to disassemble and remove the Wurzburg radar aerial. This allowed the scientists in England to understand the German radar system, and develop counter-measures. (Howard Gerrard © Osprey Publishing)

the airfields to coordinate a response by British fighters. The Germans failed to grasp the way the CH system worked, and did not investigate how to jam the transmissions.

Radar was not always a success. We have already seen (p.190) that good radar reflections from incoming Japanese warplanes were detected prior to the attack on Pearl Harbor – but radar was relatively new, as were the observers, and so the all-important advance warning was fatally disregarded. Radar detectors were subsequently erected by the Germans on the coast of northern Europe, facing England. In February 1942, one of their Würzburg radar stations was detected by British reconnaissance near Bruneval in Normandy and close-up photographs were taken in a daring daylight raid. The British realized that the obvious answer would be to raid the radar establishment and bring the important components back to England. The idea was quickly approved, and R. V. Jones was the first to volunteer to go along and act as the technical specialist – but the authorities decided against sending anyone with specialist knowledge. If captured, they would be aware of details that the Germans could perhaps extract.

The plan was for this audacious raid to be carried out by 'C' Company of the 2nd Battalion, 1st Parachute Brigade commanded by Major John Frost. Their specialist would be radar operator Flight-Sergeant C. W. H. Cox. None of the men was told anything about the raid until the last minute, and training went on with scale models of the enemy terrain and with trials on the beaches of southern England.

On the night of 27 February 1942 the teams were dropped by parachute from Whitley aircraft flying at just 600ft (180m). The beach was secured, and teams rushed to the villa where they found a single German soldier guarding the equipment. German troops from a nearby pillbox were firing into the site as the British troops disassembled the Würzburg radar aerial, removing the important components which were all packed and taken quickly to the beach. There were problems making radio contact with the Navy, who were supposed to be ready to collect the men and their spoils, but had encountered a German warship and had to take evasive action. The German pillbox had been silenced and red flares were shot into the sky – at which point the Navy appeared in rough seas to retrieve the teams. Under enemy fire six landing craft arrived to collect their precious cargo. The ship was escorted back to Portsmouth Harbour by Royal Navy destroyers with RAF Spitfires flying overhead; the patriotic song *Rule Britannia* was played at high volume from loudspeakers. The raid was entirely successful. The airborne troops suffered only a few casualties, and the pieces of the radar they brought back, along with a German radar technician, allowed British scientists to understand German advances in radar and to create counter-measures to neutralize those advances.

Brave members of the French resistance continued to supply information to Britain and it was soon discovered that all German radar stations operated on a small number of frequencies, and they could easily be jammed. When a huge and devastating Allied bombing raid on Hamburg was planned for July 1943, fragments of metallic strips were dropped – once again, exactly one-quarter as long as the wavelength of the German radar beams, to maximize reflections – and the signals from the radar stations were completely obliterated. This chaff was known as 'window' by the Royal Air Force and had been independently discovered in Germany, where it was known as Düppel. It is a sign of the confused strategic planning by the Nazis that, having pioneered the use of reflecting chaff, the Germans did nothing to prepare themselves for its use by the Allies.

AMERICAN RADAR

The Germans lacked the ability and knowledge to manufacture radar systems in which the radio beams could be tuned to a desired frequency, and this capability gave the British superiority in this vital area of defensive warfare. The early radar trials in Britain used a frequency of about 10MHz and the Chain Home stations began at 20MHz and later extended their range up to 70MHz – but the tracking radars operated at 200–800MHz. In 1940 the Americans began to use a cavity magnetron transmitter which went from the megahertz range up to gigahertz frequencies. It was small enough to fit into aircraft, and the

H2S radar which was used by United States Air Force bombers had a frequency of 3GHz. It could show the details of the ground beneath the aircraft with unprecedented accuracy – but it was decided never to use it over Germany. Allied intelligence had reported that the Germans believed 800MHz was the highest frequency that radar could use, and it was feared that – if an American plane was shot down, and the secret of its radar was discovered by the Germans – the balance of power could radically change.

In the event, this proved to be a groundless fear. In the spring of 1943 an American bomber was brought down near Rotterdam, Netherlands, and the onboard H2S radar and the intact magnetron fell into German hands. They set out at once to reconstruct their own version, code named Rotterdamgerät, but the first examples were manufactured only when the war was nearing its end.

Installations of British radar detectors on Royal Navy ships allowed them easily to detect German submarines on the surface of the sea, and so the Germans worked on methods of preventing their U-boats from generating an echo, so they could thus escape detection. They soon found that a mixture of rubber and carbon painted onto a submarine's superstructure greatly diminished the strength of its radar signature, and they tested it in a dry dock until they had perfected the ideal recipe. Surprisingly, the British warships continued to detect the submarines as though nothing had happened. The reason was simple – when wet with seawater, the protective layer no longer worked and radar detection could function as normal.

A map of Oslo used to plot the positions of German shipping revealed by H2S radar. This radar system had the power to show the details with unprecedented accuracy but it was decided not to use it in flights over Germany as there was a risk of revealing the secret to the Nazis if an aircraft was shot down. (© TopFoto)

We must not dismiss the German idea out of hand, however: this was the origin of what we now know as 'stealth technology'. Once again, a development from World War II underpins a crucial aspect of present-day warfare.

THE IMPORTANCE OF RADAR

Radar in Britain had a decisive effect on the conduct and duration of the war. Following enemy aircraft and ships that were otherwise invisible was of crucial importance. The Chain Home network was even shown to be able to detect V-2 rockets long before they reached the British coast and, although nothing could be done to prevent their arrival, this is historically significant as the first ballistic missile radar detection system in the world. These systems are now everywhere. It is also important to note that Hungarian scientists used their own radar to bounce signals off the moon in 1944. This was the first time it was ever achieved, and they accurately measured the distance of the moon from the earth for the first time in history.

Radar was firmly established and had become refined by the end of World War II. During the Vietnam War of 1955–75, anti-radiation missiles were developed which would home onto the beam emitted by a radar transmitter and destroy the installation, thus using the radar against itself. As devices became increasingly compact, radar speed detectors entered service with the police force. And so we can look back at the stimulus that World War II gave to the development of radar – and can bear in mind that the same principle had been used to detect shipping before World War I began. Radar has enjoyed a lengthy history. It can now entrap you on a highway, it is an integral part of global transportation, and it promises to have an illustrious future.

RADIO GUIDANCE FOR AIRCRAFT

Harnessing reflections of radio waves bounced back from aircraft and ships was the principle behind radar – but great effort also went into using radio beams themselves as an aid to navigation. This was born in 1932 as an aircraft landing system developed by the German company Lorentz AG, and was the brainchild of Dr E. Kramar. Like all good ideas, it was rooted in simplicity and was a brilliant innovation. It worked by having three radio masts that were transmitting 38MHz signals towards an approaching plane from the end of the runway. The antenna in the middle sent a single, continuous signal; the others (to the left and right) turned on and off alternately. The antenna to the left sent dashes each lasting $1/8$th second, whereas the right antenna sent alternate dashes each $7/8$th second long. The pilot of an approaching aircraft that was exactly on the correct, central flight path would tune to the radio signal and hear a continuous tone. If the plane was too far to the left, dashes would be heard; if it was over to the right then the short dots would be received. It was the first successful remote landing system and within two years it had been installed by Lufthansa on their aircraft, and was widely sold around the world. It was ahead of its time, and worked reliably over a distance up to about 30 miles (50km). As the Luftwaffe expanded, they experimented with a range of alternative solutions to the same problem. The British, meanwhile, trained their pilots in celestial navigation to aid flying at night; the Luftwaffe ignored something so old-fashioned, concentrating on wireless systems instead.

The Lorentz system was widely installed in airfields across Germany and its use soon became a standard procedure. During the early war years, the German Air Ministry introduced a long-range alternative code named Sonne. Some of the receivers and documentation were captured by agents of the British, who adopted it for the RAF. The British renamed the system Consol.

As the transmitters became more powerful with each new generation, the range was extended and the Lorentz transmitters were used to guide bombers out across the North Sea to London. Here they encountered a problem, for the signals could guarantee that a bomber was flying along the correct straight course, but gave no information as to how far the bomber had flown. Headwinds could have the pilot far from the target, even though pointing in the right direction. For this reason, the Germans decided on a modification: they would set up two beams from Lorentz aerials that were widely separated. The beams would intersect over the target. The pilot's task was near foolproof: he would fly along one beam, monitoring the signal

JAMMING ENEMY RADAR

The British worked hard to discover the German secrets and to block or jam their radar, as Robert Cockburn, a scientist with the Royal Aircraft Establishment, explains:

My job was to find out how to jam – or if you like, bend – the German beam. These beams were such an obvious device for the Germans to use but it took no account of the possibility of countermeasures. It was a fairly straightforward job. They used a dot dash Lorentz beam and all I had to do was radiate additional dots. Initially, we did it in synchronism – in other words we received the dots down at Worth Matravers and transmitted them by telephone line to Beacon Hill near Salisbury where we had a jammer. But I very soon realised that it didn't matter a damn whether they were synchronised or not. They just had to be at the same time because when the German pilot got on to the signal beam, he would still hear those extra dots coming through which would make him go off to one side. We were being too meticulous for the rough and tumble of war.

Robert Cockburn, Imperial War Museum Sound 10685

in order to keep on course, until the second signal was suddenly encountered. At this point the crew knew they were on target, and the bombs were dropped. The Germans code named the system Knickebein – the crooked leg.

Knickebein transmitters were first tried in 1939, with one transmitter set up in Stollberg, northern Germany, another at Kleve in the far west of the country near the frontier with the Netherlands, and a third at Lörrach in south-western Germany. Once France had capitulated in June 1940 the Germans constructed more aerials along the French coast with more in the Netherlands and even in Norway. The German code name Knickebein was a very appropriate allusion to the L-shaped beams and they were extremely effective as a world-beating navigational aid. This may explain the British code name for the system: they called it the Headache.

The first evidence that the British had of how the system worked was when a German bomber was shot down and the radio receivers on board were examined. R. V. Jones, the brilliant physicist at the Air Ministry in London, was convinced that the system was far too sophisticated and sensitive to be a mere landing aid. At the same time, code-breakers at Bletchley Park (p.264) had heard mention of 'bombing beams' being used by pilots. Jones's beliefs were not widely shared, and the government's Chief Scientific Adviser, Frederick Lindemann, dismissed the idea out of hand. His reasoning was that the radio beams could not be used, due to the earth's curvature. R. V. Jones persisted, pointing out how high the bombers were, and managed to persuade Churchill to instruct the RAF to send an aircraft with a suitable detector, to search for the beams. The only receiver they could find which could pick up the required frequencies was obtained from an amateur radio shop in London and it was installed in a twin-engined Avro Anson aircraft. Jones's rivals tried to cancel the flight at the last minute, but he reminded them that it had been ordered by Churchill himself – and so it went ahead.

The crew were briefed to search for navigational signals and to note the frequency and the bearing. They managed to find the beam from the transmitters at Kleve, and later encountered the transmissions from the direction of Stollberg. Flying along until both were received, the pilots found they were over the Midlands city of Derby. The place where the beams intersected was directly above the Rolls-Royce factory, where the Merlin engine was manufactured for the fighters of the RAF.

The British effort during World War II was always aimed at finding a simple and effective answer to the German initiatives. As a result, they installed aerials to pick up the navigational signals and then ingeniously rebroadcast them in a different direction. The effect was initially to confuse the German bomber pilots, but as the British became more experienced they were able to fine-tune their transmissions so that the enemy bombers could be induced to drop their payload anywhere the British wanted. Through this simple but effective means, they had found an answer to Headache ... the British code named the new system Aspirin, of course.

A daring low-level reconnaissance photograph of the German 'Freya' radar installations discovered by the Allies at Auderville in northern France. (IWM C 5477)

The Channel Islands were the only part of Britain occupied by Germany. This control tower and observation post was built on Jersey. The tower also contained a radar station – the aerial is visible on the roof. (© TopFoto)

Engineers in Germany moved as quickly as they could to devise an answer to the British jamming. They code named it X-Gerät – or X-device – and it used a complex series of beams operating at a higher frequency. The signals picked up by the pilot were used to time the distance the aircraft was to fly before dropping its bombs. Reception of the first signal was the cue for the pilot to set a specially designed clock ticking in his cockpit. The moment the second signal was received, the hand of the clock would stop and a separate hand would start to move ... when both were aligned the target was directly beneath and the bombs were dropped. The British knew that the Germans were using radio beams to guide their bombers, and Jones had worked out where the beams were probably operating, but they could not detect the X-Gerät signals which were at a much higher frequency. Attempts to jam the transmissions failed. Successful raids against Birmingham, Wolverhampton and Coventry were all conducted by the Germans using this guidance system and without any advance warning being available to the British.

Matters changed on 6 November 1940, when a Heinkel He-111 was shot down off the Dorset coast and sank in shallow water. It was equipped with the new X-Gerät equipment and – once the receivers had been dried out and tested – it was clear that the navigation beams were at 2MHz, much higher than the 1,500Hz which the British had used. Work proceeded at a furious rate, and new jamming transmitters were hurriedly assembled. They were not ready in time to prevent the devastating raid on Coventry on 14 November 1940, but they were in place just five days later, disrupting a massive bombing raid on the city of Birmingham.

Later raids were diverted as the British realized they could send their second beam to trigger the pilot's clock at the wrong time. This caused the bombs to be dropped early. The Germans soon responded by switching on their second beam for a much shorter period of time, making interference increasingly difficult for the British.

As the cat-and-mouse competition continued, the British managed to maintain equilibrium for most of the time, and R. V. Jones was not surprised when messages were picked up about the next generation of navigational aids. This was the Y-Gerät system – code named Wotan. Jones had recognized how perfectly descriptive the code name Knickebein had been, and knew at once that there would be a hidden meaning within the new code name. The Germans were making a fundamental mistake – in choosing witty allusions in their code names, they were giving away the nature of the weapon. When Jones was at Bletchley Park, looking at the incoming messages as they were translated, he took the opportunity to discuss the hidden meaning of Wotan with a German specialist. He was told that Wotan was one of the ancient gods – a god with one eye. At once Jones knew what it meant: the new system would involve a single navigational beam. It could be modulated in some way, and not used in conjunction with a second signal. It would be much harder to fake, and the British knew they would face a new problem in diverting the bombing raids away from English cities. Jones also recalled that something similar had been mentioned in the Oslo Report (p.125).

The new way in which the Y-Gerät worked was to transmit a single beam directed over the target. The planes would be fitted with transponders that would transmit the beam back towards the originating transmitter station. The returned signal was measured automatically and compared with the timing of the original signal; so this gave the exact position of the aircraft along the narrow beam. If any correction was needed, the radio operators could send coded instructions to the pilot, making outside interference difficult. At least, that is how the Germans saw it. It was viewed very differently by the British. The new Wotan signals were soon detected in England, and it was discovered that they were transmitted on a frequency band of 45MHz. This was a standard radio frequency, and was exactly the same as the BBC television transmitter at Alexandra Palace in North London. Alexandra Palace (known as Ally-Pally) had broadcast a regular television service from 1936 but had been closed down by order of the government when war broke out. Jones simply ordered that the signal be turned back on, but operated at very low power. This was calculated to interfere with the timing of the Wotan navigational transmissions – but too weak for the Germans to detect. Jones was a warm and amusing character, and an inveterate practical joker and as time went by he instructed the crew at Ally-Pally gradually to increase the strength of the signal. Communications were picked up, in which the German bomber pilots accused their control room of incompetence; later the Germans believed that the Wotan equipment was at fault. The British counter-measures remained undetected, and the new guidance system could not be made to work.

And so radio became a central theme of aircraft guidance. For a long time the

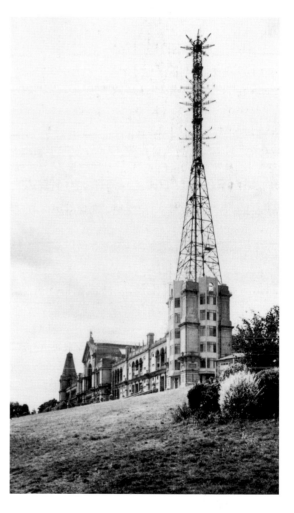

The BBC television transmitter at Alexandra Palace, photographed in the 1960s. With the outbreak of war in 1939 the British television service had been curtailed, but the signal was switched back on to interfere with German transmissions to their pilots. (SSPL/Getty Images)

The front cover of the Coventry regional newspaper dated 15 November 1940 reported the devastation and aftermath of the Luftwaffe bombings. (© Mirrorpix)

Germans held supremacy in their ability to create sophisticated transmitters and receivers which could achieve the impossible. But the British, for their part, realized that here lay the path to successful interference with the whole navigational system – and they used inexpensive and cunning means to subvert, and eventually defeat, the ingenuity of their foes.

The steering and guidance of torpedoes was a different matter. The most revolutionary proposal was for a system that would allow signals to be sent on radio waves that continuously changed their frequency (making them almost impossible to intercept). Surprisingly, the idea was jointly designed by a film star, 'the most beautiful woman in the world', the Hollywood actress Hedy Lamarr and her neighbour, the *avant garde* musician George Antheil. Anthiel had experimented with the automatic synchronisation of pianolas and composed a suite entitled *Ballet Mécanique* in which mechanical pianos played in a synchronous sequence. Under her married name of Hedy Kiesler Markey, Hedy Lamarr designed a system that would use a piano roll to change the frequencies of radio transmissions to guided torpedoes, making them almost impossible to jam. She took out a patent in August 1942, and always wished to join the United States National Inventors Council. She was discouraged because the United States authorities insisted that she could better help the war effort by fund-raising – indeed she is reported to have raised $7,000,000 at a single concert.

The American military did not show interest until 1962 when her idea was first used during the blockade of Cuba. Lamarr's contribution was finally recognized 1997, when she was presented with an award by the Electronic Frontier Foundation. At about this time, the boxes of CorelDRAW software featured a dramatic picture of Hedy Lamarr on the cover, in recognition of her importance as an inventor. Far from being flattered, she sued them for infringement of her image and the matter was settled out of court with a sizeable sum paid in damages. And today? Many of our wi-fi networks use 'network hopping' that is derived directly from Hedy Lamarr's secret inspiration in World War II.

ENIGMA – FICTIONS AND FACTS

The extraordinary story of the German Enigma cryptographic machine has become much better known to the American audience since the movie entitled *U-571* was released in 2000. Directed by Jonathan Mostow, it starred Matthew McConaughey, Bill Paxton, Harvey Keitel and Jon Bon Jovi, among others. The film related how brave American submariners captured the German submarine U-571 and seized their mysterious on-board Enigma machine. As a result, the Allies were able for the first time to decipher crucial German dispatches.

The story is a fake. The submarine U-571 was never captured by anyone, but was sunk by a torpedo dropped from a Short Sunderland flying boat from 461 Squadron of the Royal Australian Air Force in January 1944 off the coast of Ireland. No Americans ever captured a naval Enigma machine.

The British audience knows a different version. They are aware that it was actually the crew of HMS *Bulldog* who captured an Enigma machine from a German submarine, the U-110. The capture took place in the North Atlantic in May 1941, when the United States had not even officially entered the war, and the enterprising British sailors were responsible for seizing the German machine and the documentation aboard.

This allowed their intelligence officers to come face to face with an Enigma machine for the first time, thus finding out how this remarkable machine could operate. That is not true either. Although the dates (and the vessels) are correct, the belief that this was the first encounter with Enigma is a myth.

Long before World War II began, the Enigma machine was already well known to the British, and to many other nations as well. It was not invented for the war, and had begun life as a commercial encryption device that was available for several years by mail order. A German engineer named Arthur Scherbius designed the original machine. It used the now-famous system of rotors and in February 1918 Scherbius patented his device – this was during World War I! In collaboration with a funding partner, E. Richard Ritter, the Scherbius & Ritter Company was established. They immediately approached the German authorities, believing that their machine would be of value for international top-secret communications. The Foreign Office considered the design, and reported back that it held no interest for them. The German Navy were then approached, but they said they were not interested either. Somewhat disillusioned by the response of officialdom, Scherbius and Ritter eventually joined with others to form the Chiffriermaschinen Aktien-Gesellschaft (Cypher Machines Stock Company) in 1923, and began commercial production of the first Enigma machines.

The ingenious device was publicly exhibited for the first time in that same year and mail-order sales began immediately. The main disadvantage of the first machines was their large size. They were was equipped with encryption gears and a full typewriter mechanism, and weighed some 110lb (50kg). The keyboard, rather than being in the standard European QWERTY layout, had the keys set alphabetically. An improved version, the Model B, was somewhat less bulky, and in 1926 the Enigma C machine was released. Instead of the heavy typewriter mechanism, it was fitted with small lamps that the operator had to read, and in consequence was nicknamed the Enigma Glowlamp. During the following year it was replaced with the Enigma D, and this was sold to hundreds of customers during 1927–28. The Enigma was now famous, and was sold across Britain, Italy, Japan, the Netherlands, Poland, Spain, Sweden, Switzerland and the United States.

This Enigma machine was a masterpiece of design. In use, a key pressed by the operator would connect one of 26 letter circuits, passing a current to one of 26 contacts in the encoding unit. Electrical current was then passed through three rotors, each of them wired so that the letter was changed. The turning of the rotors to make a new set of contacts each time a key was pressed meant that each letter was transposed to a different character every time. The problem is that, to decrypt the message, the receiving machine would have to feed power from the keys to mirror the original action exactly. The Enigma designers solved the problem by adding a reflector system that connected each contact to another and routed the circuit back through the three rotors. The original text could then be recovered by the receiver – but not by anyone who attempted to intercept the message en route.

ENIGMA'S FIRST USE

The first nation to adopt the Enigma for military use was Italy, who code named her Enigma machine Navy Cypher D. The same technology was used by the Fascist government of General Franco during the Spanish Civil War, and the Swiss called their Enigma D machine the Swiss K. An Enigma model T was manufactured for use by the Japanese. The codes for many of these were broken by Britain, France, Poland and the United States. But the Germans were becoming interested in how Enigma could be used to encode all their transmissions, and the British were anxious because they lacked the insight into what was going on, and were eager to keep up to date. Already the Enigma machines were being adapted from having three rotors to four, which made breaking the codes far more challenging.

The Germans now had the latest encryption, and they were confident that they could rely upon complete secrecy while sending orders and complex messages from central government to the armed services. The decoding problem was broken in 1928 by the Poles. Their German-language Biuro Szyfrów (Cypher Bureau) BS4, was suddenly informed that a large parcel had been sent by the German government to their legation in Warsaw. Ordinarily, it would not attract attention, but the Germans had dispatched it by unsecured freight mail and, as soon as the error was noticed, they contacted the Polish authorities urgently to check that it was being safely handled. The enquiry was passed to the Polish Customs Authority, who immediately tipped off the intelligence service that there was something crucially important in the box. As a result, the code-breakers at BS4 had a full weekend to work day and night analysing the machine and all its code protocols, before meticulously repacking it for the Monday morning. The Germans were meanwhile assured that yes, the parcel was intact, and it would be ready – perfectly packed – for collection as soon as the office opened for business. The Polish bureau now knew all they needed to know, while the Germans believed their secret was secure.

ENIGMA IN GERMANY

Once the Enigma machines had received official endorsement by the German government, the German Army finally conceded that Enigma was what they required, and in 1932 they ordered the three-rotor Enigma G machines. Within two years it had been improved and was designated the Enigma I and this soon became known as the Wehrmacht (Services) Enigma. It was used throughout World War II. This new version had the addition of a plug-board which allowed the operator to exchange letters in pairs, which added greatly to the security of the codes. The machine was much smaller by this time, weighing as little as 26lb (12kg). Eventually, in 1934 the German Navy brought into use their own version, the Funkschlüssel-M or M3, and in August 1935 the Air Force adopted the Wehrmacht Enigma for their coded messages.

What they did not realize was that the Polish intelligence service was already ahead of them. One of their leading code-breakers, Marian Rejewski, had designed a top-secret machine that could be used to decode the German messages. It recreated the settings of the Enigma machine that had originally encoded the text, and allowed the operator to read the message. Rejewski called it his *Bomba Kryptologiczna* – the 'cryptological bomb'.

Each operator of the Enigma machines was given a three-letter code that was regularly changed. This was sent first, to indicate to the receiver which rotor setting was to be used that day. The three letter code was repeated, so it might be PINPIN. Of course, the message was encrypted by the Enigma machine, so it came out at the other end as random characters – MXZLPD, for instance. This gave Rejewski the vital clue. The techniques to work out the way the three letters were coded were already well established, and the fact that the three letters were repeated was vital. The way the letters had changed when they were repeated let Rejewski work out exactly how the rotors had been installed.

The design of the Enigma machine was being regularly upgraded, in order to add further levels of complexity, and the number of possible combinations that the cryptographer had to try was becoming impossible to manage. A better system was needed. So, in the autumn of 1938, Rejewski designed his first decoding system; it became known to the Allies as the Bombe. In principle, it had the power of six Enigma machines working simultaneously, and allowed one cryptographer to do the work of 100 working alone. Within a year there were six Bombes working at the code-breaking station in Warsaw. It meant that one room contained decoding machines that could do the work of 600 highly trained staff.

By the time the Germans invaded the Sudetenland of Czechoslovakia on 1 October 1938, the Polish cryptographers had been decoding the German Enigma messages for over six years with complete success, and the Bombe had made the process steadily faster and more reliable. The Germans were meanwhile making the machines increasingly complex, and fitted extra rotors, along with a complex plug-board, so the task of decoding became far more complex. Nonetheless, the Poles were able to decode the messages that revealed the Germans' next intention – to cross the strip of Polish territory that separated Germany from the Baltic enclave of Danzig. This would amount to an invasion, and war now seemed inevitable. When it became clear from the decrypted messages that the Germans were ready to invade Poland, all the decryption codes and the Enigma equipment was delivered by the Polish authorities to British Military Intelligence.

January 1939 had marked an important intelligence conference in Paris that brought together officials from the British, Polish and French intelligence services. The Poles revealed

Above left: German soldiers encoding a secret message in the field, using a German Enigma machine during World War II. (Time & Life Pictures/Getty Images)

Above right: A German Enigma machine ready and waiting for use by General Heinz Guderian and his men in a command vehicle in northern France. The machine is visible on the left. (IWM MH 29100)

Below left: Enigma was used for communicating instructions regarding operational matters to and from the German front-line units. The coding system used by this machine had been broken by Polish experts and British intelligence kept pace with the progressive sophistication of the machines. (EN Archive)

Below left: Two wheels from the four-rotor German Enigma cypher machine, displayed to show the electrical contacts between adjacent wheels. Increasing the number of rotors from three to four was one way in which the Enigma machine was adapted for military use, as it further raised the level of encryption. (SSPL/Getty Images)

the extent of their remarkable success in routinely decoding German messages. To the British there was only one possible response – they would expand the Government Code and Cypher School (GC&CS) to take up the task of decoding of the Enigma messages. In August 1939, still before war had been declared, the Government Code and Cypher School moved into its new and expanded premises. This was in the beautiful old house of Bletchley Park, near Milton Keynes in rural Bedfordshire. The building was equipped with a top-secret telephone exchange and a teleprinter room, with a kitchen and dining room alongside. The upper floor was occupied exclusively by the Secret Service MI6. A nearby boarding school was requisitioned to house the Commercial and Diplomatic Section, and a range of wooden huts was speedily erected in the grounds to use as the establishment increased in size. There was a water tower alongside, to supply the historic house, and a monitoring radio station code named Station X was set up at the top, so that its aerials had an unimpeded view across the open landscape. As the lengthy wires of the radio aerials might attract unwanted attention, the radio station was soon moved to nearby Whaddon.

Britain's most brilliant cryptographer was a young mathematician named Alan Turing. He had read mathematics at King's College, Cambridge, and then studied for his PhD at Princeton in the United States. At the age of 24 he published a brilliant paper on 'computable numbers' that was far ahead of its time, and he is widely regarded as one of the founding-fathers of modern computing science.

When the Polish consignment arrived in Britain, it was Turing who had the task of deciding what to do next. He constructed a design for an upgraded version of the Bombe with 108 different places where the decoding drums could be fitted. Each rotor could be set to one of 17,576 theoretical positions and the machines that Turing designed could try them all in 20 minutes. Manufacture of these Bombes was entrusted to the British Tabulating Machine Company at Letchworth, near London, where Harold Keen had led a research project to introduce punched-card technology, introduced from the United States, to calculating machines. The British Bombe machines were, as one commentator said, 'the size of a large book-case' and measured 7ft (2m) wide, 6ft 6in (1.9m) tall and 2ft (0.6m) deep. Each weighed about 1 ton.

In March 1940 the first was completed and installed at Bletchley Park under the code name Victory. A second one followed in August. This had a more advanced diagonal plug-board and was named Agnus Dei (the Lamb of God) but became known as Agnes, or Aggie, for short. Victory was soon upgraded to match Aggie's specifications. Work at the British Tabulating Machine Company was redoubled, and five separate decoding stations were set up around North London, in case the facility at Bletchley Park was destroyed by a German raid. From that time on, the British were capable of overhearing the German military communications. Everything was carried out under conditions of top security and total secrecy, and the staff at Bletchley Park remained famously reticent about their work for

Bletchley Park in the 1930s. It was here that top-secret code-breaking was based throughout World War II. This work played a crucial role in helping the Allies to victory. (Time & Life Pictures/Getty Images)

Bombe code-breaking equipment at Bletchley Park – while the cryptographers did much important original work, they did so with the aid of the Bombe, a machine based on the work of Polish code-breaker Marian Rejewski. (SSPL/Getty Images)

The machine room in Hut 6 at Bletchley Park, showing cryptographers hard at work. Those involved in this top-secret wartime work were true to their word and kept quiet about their experiences at Bletchley for many decades after the war. Some still refuse to discuss their work. (SSPL/Getty Images)

decades following the war. London did not always appreciate the importance of their delicate, private approach; once the building was operational, a group of distinguished officials from London came down to inspect the progress. They arrived in a column of official cars with motorcycle outriders, flags waving, and everyone in full uniform; 'So much for the secrecy,' said one of the scientists.

In July 1942 the drawings and wiring diagrams were passed to the United States Navy, and in September 1942 funding of $2 million was requested for the construction of Bombe machines in America; the project was approved within 24 hours. This new version was built by the National Cash Register Corporation (NCR) in Dayton, Ohio, with full collaboration between the Americans and the Bletchley Park team and had a greatly increased capacity. An order for more than 300 of the American machines was placed.

Alan Turing was seconded to Washington DC to advise in December 1942 and went straight to NCR. He quickly calculated how the machines could be linked together, and determined that a smaller number would be sufficient – so the order was reduced to just 96 machines. The American machines were larger than the British Bombes, weighing 2.5 tons, and could run more than 30 times as rapidly. The first came on stream in May 1943 and in June two American Bombes named Adam and Eve broke a particularly difficult message which many believed it was impossible to decode.

A different design was chosen by the US Army and their contract was given to Bell Laboratories in September 1942. It was fitted with telephone relays instead of combinations of mechanical drums, so rotor changes could be done by pressing buttons rather than physically exchanging the rotors. It was intended only for three-rotor decryption, not the four-rotor traffic that the Navy Bombes could handle, but its refined design greatly reduced the time it took to decode messages.

CHURCHILL'S GOLDEN GOOSE

Ultra was the code name for the British decryption project and it was at Bletchley Park that the Ultra project was based. The teams monitored, and successfully decoded, the messages sent from Germany to the U-boats during the battle of the Atlantic. The Bletchley teams also decoded all the orders sent out in the North Africa campaign in 1941, and General Auchinleck later confessed that 'Rommel would have certainly got through to Cairo' without the Allies having advance knowledge of all the German plans. During the planning of the Allied invasion of Normandy, Bletchley Park gave the Allied commanders full details of all but two of the 58 Nazi divisions situated on the Western Front. The United States were kept fully involved, and Americans had been invited to become part of the Bletchley Park teams from the start; but Churchill did not trust the Soviet authorities and they never knew of Bletchley Park for the duration of the war. Eventually, the term 'Ultra' was adopted by all the Western Allies to signify the decoding of German messages.

BLETCHLEY MEMORIES

When we arrived at Bletchley station we were met by a leading Wren and marched up to a perimeter fence with sentries standing guard. We were then taken to an office in a grand Victorian mansion where we were told that the work we were going to be doing was of the utmost secrecy and vital to the war effort, and we were required to sign the official secrets act. One was left with the distinct impression that contravening it would mean a spell in the Tower at the very least. Next we were escorted across the large grounds to a concrete hut, and had to press a bell and wait to be admitted. When we went inside I was immediately aware of the large back machines making a terrible din and smelling of hot oil. These were the bombes, which were essential to the breaking of the German Enigma codes…

Work in the bombe hut went on 24 hours a day and we worked 8 hour watches with one meal break. The first week was from 8 am to 4 pm, the second 4pm to midnight and the third midnight to 8 am, with one day off each week. On the fourth week we worked everybody else's days off and then had 4 days leave. There were two Wrens to each machine and our job was to change the wheel orders, which has a different colour for each number, in accordance with the list given by the code-breakers in Huts 6 and 8. They also dictated how the alphabetised sockets on the back of the machine should be connected to each other. The piece of paper given to us for this purpose was called, interestingly, a menu - the same word we have for starting points on our computers today. Once all this had been done the machine was started up and it clanked and whirred and eventually it would stop. We noticed the wheel order running at that time and the position at which it had stopped and phoned it through to Hut 6 and 8. This could go for hours or even days, with several machines working on the same job, but eventually the cry would be heard: 'Job up', which meant they had a match. Occasionally the job didn't come up and was abandoned because the next day's settings would now be in operation.

It was quite physical work, plugging and unplugging the menu, working as fast as we could to change the wheel orders and, most importantly, checking the drums when we took them off the machine. The underside of each drum had four circular rows of small wire brushes which had to be kept in a state of perfection. A stray wire could cause a short and distort all the information gathered by the machine, so we had to straighten them with wire tweezers. I don't think all that close work did our eyesight much good and the noise in Hut 11 properly affected our hearing, too.

Anne Chetwynd-Stapylton, courtesy of Bletchley Park.

There was just one major scare, when three bombs were dropped by a German aircraft in November 1940, just as the base was coming fully on stream. It turned out to be an error for the bombs had actually been intended for the nearby rail station at Bletchley. The only effect was that one of the bombs blasted Hut 4, housing the Royal Navy Intelligence Unit, off its brick-built base. Workers simply jacked it up, back into position, and work went on as though nothing had happened. Those who worked at Bletchley Park took their task seriously, and never spoke of it afterwards. Even by the 1990s little had ever been disclosed. Churchill noted the unimpeachable level of personal security when, at the end of the war, he described Bletchley Park as 'The Golden Goose that never cackled'.

By the end of the war, with the code-breaking at its absolute height, there were over 9,000 people employed at Bletchley Park. Of those, 80 per cent were women and most of the men were postal delivery workers, specialists in high-speed Morse code or linguists who could translate German rapidly. The code-breakers were selected at interview if they were, for example, champions at playing chess or finishing crossword puzzles; some were multilingual, others were top mathematicians. At one time, a test involved the ability to solve the *Daily Telegraph* crossword in less than 12 minutes. The winner of the competition was F. H. W. Hawes of Dagenham, East London, who finished the entire puzzle in 7 minutes.

Ultra was certainly vital to the winning of the war. Although the Enigma machines were their best-known target, they also successfully decoded messages from other encryption machines, including the Lorenz SZ series (*Schlüsselzusatz*, 'cipher attachment') and various systems adopted by the Japanese. Churchill is said to have told King George VI, 'It was thanks to Ultra that we won the war.' Western Supreme Allied Commander, Dwight D. Eisenhower, insisted that Ultra was 'decisive' in securing the Allied victory. It has often been said that Ultra advanced the winning of the war by two years; others have emphasized that, without it, the war might not have been won by the Allies at all.

Though there is clearly truth in all this, there are others whose work is equally deserving of commemoration. What of the heroic Poles, whose brilliance gave us the Bombe machines without which the battle of the codes could easily have been lost? The role of the American teams and their Bombe machines is often overlooked – yet, by the end of the war, well over 100 high-specification Bombes had been manufactured in the United States and their teams worked tirelessly to decode the incessant German military messages. The Americans were hugely successful in this vital field.

Alan Turing was crucial to this effort, yet he was to end his days in misery. As a gay man (at a time when homosexuality in a man was a crime) he was to become ostracized and persecuted rather than praised. In 1952 he was found guilty of acts of gross indecency and was threatened with gaol. He opted to be injected with large doses of female hormones that were claimed to reduce his urges, and this 'chemical castration' was agreed by the court as an alternative to imprisonment. But his career was effectively destroyed; he lost his security clearance and his government position. Turing retreated into himself and became distressed. Within two years he was found dead in bed from cyanide poisoning. He had often said how much he liked the Walt Disney film *Snow White*, particularly the scene where the Wicked Witch poisons a red apple ... and a half-eaten apple was found on his bedside cabinet. Had it been used to deliver the fatal dose? We cannot know; the apple was never tested by the police.

So much of what we accept as today's truth is a distortion of reality. It is almost as though these most secret of schemes have acquired a new reality all of their own. The Enigma machine was not a secret device that was known only to a few. Over 100,000 Enigma machines were manufactured, and they were widely sold all over the world. It is an astonishing total. These encoding machines remained in use long after the end of World War II. Thousands were

Britain's leading cryptographer and brilliant mathematician Alan Turing. While he was a huge boost to Allied progress during the war, he was persecuted because of his homosexuality, and died of cyanide poisoning in 1954. (© The Granger Collection/TopFoto)

captured, intact, by the Allies as they advanced across Germany. And what was their fate? They were sold, in large numbers, to the governments of many of the newly emergent nations. So ingenious was the German design that Enigma continued to be used in peacetime for many years after the end of World War II. None of the purchasers knew anything of the code-breakers of Bletchley Park, so they were none the wiser; and Enigma lived on for a decade or more.

COMPUTERS – A LEGACY OF WAR

The first design for a computer was, of course, a mechanical device with gears and levers designed by the British mathematician Charles Babbage. He first wrote down the idea in a letter to Sir Humphrey Davy in 1822. His design could not be manufactured at the time (machining tolerances were not sufficiently advanced) but in 1991 a version was manufactured and was shown to work at the Science Museum, London. Babbage envisaged using a mechanical computer to calculate the odds on a horse race, since he was an inveterate gambler.

GERMANY, 1938

The first person actually to construct an electromechanical computer was a German aircraft technician and amateur enthusiast, Konrad Zuse. He used punched paper tape to input data and developed the first programming language, Plankalkül (plan calculus). His first machine, the Z1, was able to use binary floating point numbers, which allows for large calculations, and a form of programming based on the work on the Victorian English mathematician George Boole. Boole derived the form of analysis that combines terms (using 'and') or splits them into alternatives ('or') and Boolean logic, as we now call it, is essential in writing software. This early computer had no relays and a single electrical unit to give a clock speed of 1Hz. The Z1 could be programmed using punched tape and a tape reader. Zuse built it with his own (and his family's) money between 1936 and 1938, using part of the family living-room as his laboratory. This pioneering computer embodied most of the components we would recognize in a present-day machine, including a control unit and simple computer memory. He went on later to construct more advanced prototypes and hoped to make them commercially available. However, although he made several attempts to interest the German military in the possibilities offered by his computer, no-one there was interested. All his machines, and the documentation, were destroyed during the Allied bombing raids on Berlin in December 1943.

ENGLAND, 1944

The first programmable electronic computer was named Colossus, and was produced specifically to crack the Lorenz codes used by the German High Command, since these codes were more complex than those generated by Enigma. Colossus was designed and built by a team led by Harold Thomas Flowers who began working on the idea in the late 1930s. As a young engineer, Tommy Flowers had the idea of using thermionic radio valves, or vacuum tubes, as programmable switches. He fed data in using punched tape, like a ticker-tape machine. His original idea was to automate the British telephone exchanges, but as the war took hold news reached him of the need to decode German messages that were being intercepted by the intelligence service as part of the Ultra project. Tommy Flowers began work in 1941 and took just six months to demonstrate a prototype machine, and – unlike Zuse – he found the British authorities were becoming interested in what his computer could do.

In February 1943 construction work on the revolutionary computer began at the Post Office Research Station in Dollis Hill, North-West London. The computer was running successfully by December that same year, so it was disassembled and driven to Bletchley Park on 18 January 1944. It was fitted together again and worked perfectly, and was given its first message to decode on 5 February 1944. This Mark 1 Colossus was such a success that a further nine of the giant computers were ordered. The design and specifications were

George Boole invented Boolean logic. Born in 1815, he published many philosophical papers and has the rare distinction for a mathematician of being commemorated in a stained glass window in Lincoln Cathedral. (Getty Images)

Charles Babbage, mathematician and pioneer of machine computing, photographed in 1860. He designed the first computer so he could calculate the odds on horse races, but never saw it built. His ideas anticipated today's computers. (SSPL/Getty Images)

improved, and in June 1944 the Mark 2 went into full production. Colossus Mark 1 contained an astonishing 1,500 electronic tubes developed for radios, whilst the Mark 2 was fitted with 2,400 of these valves making it both simpler to use and five times faster. These Colossus computers could process nearly 10,000 characters per second, but the paper tape soon became shredded. The punched paper tape could pass safely through the readers at a maximum speed of 27.3mph (12.2m/s) so they settled on 5,000 characters per second as the optimum rate of operation. Trials were also held where two Colossus computers were used simultaneously on the same problem, thus proving the value of parallel computing.

It was the use of the Colossus machines by the War Department in London that allowed the British to considerably reduce the ability of German Admiral Karl Dönitz to make unexpected raids upon the convoys crossing the North Atlantic, and thousands of lives must have been saved. These Allied victories turned the course of the war.

AFTER THE WAR

The Americans stationed at Bletchley Park were highly impressed, and encouraged John Mauchly and J. Presper Eckert to press ahead with the design of a more advanced version at the Moore School of Electrical Engineering of the University of Pennsylvania. Their design

Colossus Mark 2 – the control panels of Colossus, the world's first electronic programmable computer, which was installed at Bletchley Park during World War II. (SSPL/Getty Images)

The EDSAC 1 computer (Electronic Delay Storage Automatic Computer), photographed in 1949. The designer of this machine was English physicist Professor Maurice Wilkes, who died as this book was being written. Wilkes went to see the American ENIAC computer in Maryland and built the Cambridge University digital computer EDSAC. (SSPL/Getty Images)

and development was code named Project *PX* and their prototype machine, ENIAC, was unveiled after World War II was over, on 14 February 1946. It had cost some $500,000 to build, worth $6 million today, a huge sum of money for such a project. This state-of-the-art computer was intended to make artillery calculations, but was soon being utilized for work on the development of the first hydrogen bomb.

Meanwhile, in Britain, even the very existence of Colossus was covered by the Official Secrets Act and it all remained a state secret well into the 1970s. The British authorities have always been sensitive about classified information, and the staff at Bletchley Park refused to talk about their work even into the 1990s. Although all of the ten Colossus computers survived into the 1980s, they were broken up and their records destroyed. The teams remained silent.

RECLAIMING HISTORY

The historical importance of the early Zuse computers became increasingly apparent in the post-war years, and in 1986 Konrad Zuse resolved to rebuild his original Z1 computer. It remains an important historical device for it embodies all the essential components we recognize in present-day computers. The task took him three years, and it was shipped to the Deutsches Technik Museum in Berlin-Kreuzberg where it is on display, in full working order, to this day.

Turing's name has been widely celebrated in the decades that have elapsed since his untimely death. There are institutes, buildings, prizes, award schemes and mathematical principles all devoted to his name. *Breaking the Code* was a play about Turing's life by Hugh Whitemore that was first performed in 1986, and was a success both in London's West End and on Broadway, where it received three Tony Award nominations. Another successful drama about Turing's life was screened by BBC television in 1996, and Turing's story featured in a television documentary, *Dangerous Knowledge*, in 2008. There are commemorative plaques at his birthplace in London and his former home in Wilmslow, Cheshire, and in March 2000 a set of stamps with his portrait was issued in the Caribbean. In 2001 a statue of Turing was unveiled in Manchester and three years later a bronze statue by John Mills was unveiled at the University of Surrey, Guildford, to mark the 50th anniversary of his suicide. Another statue was unveiled in 2007 at Bletchley Park. The costs were paid by Sidney Frank, an American philanthropist.

By 1994 it was realized in Britain what a priceless piece of scientific history had been lost by the destruction of the Colossus machines, so the (by now) Sir Harold Thomas Flowers with a team of fellow-enthusiasts unearthed the original drawings for the prototypes and discovered that large parts of the computers had been hidden away by enthusiasts from Bletchley Park. They set to work to rebuild a working Colossus computer, and now that Bletchley Park has become a museum, the computer is on permanent display there, a testimony to the vital role it played in the Allied victory.

The Colossus code-breaking computer was recently rebuilt at Bletchley Park and has been restored to full function. This photograph was taken in the late 1990s. (SSPL/Getty Images)

And what of the Bomba Kryptologiczna, the all-important Bombe? The remaining components were found at Bletchley and a replica was reconstructed by a team of enthusiasts led by John Harper. This complete and working replica was built at the Bletchley Park museum and was officially switched on by the Duke of Kent, patron of the British Computer Society on 17 July 2008.

When the 50th anniversary of the commissioning of ENIAC loomed in 1996, the University of Pennsylvania and the Smithsonian Institution in Washington DC marked the event with special publications and a huge exhibition involving senior American statesmen. Although ENIAC was designed to be physically rewired to change programming, it remains an inspiring step in the slow but steady progress of computers from Charles Babbage's imagined machine, to the massive mainframe computers of the present day.

In today's world, computers are everywhere. We need to recognize that – although the components were available – it took the urgency of war and the need to defeat a highly organized foe that gave the impetus to the design of Colossus and ENIAC. When you contemplate your desktop computer, just reflect: it would certainly have arisen anyway in the fullness of time – but, as it is, even your computer is a legacy of the secret science of World War II. Be cured by antibiotics; write with a ballpoint pen; travel in a jet plane; watch space rockets on television … and just reflect that it was World War II that brought them to reality. In our modern era, everything takes so much time to change and bureaucracy weighs us down. It was very different then, when survival depended on science and time was of the essence. In my view, we could usefully embrace some of those enthusiasms in facing our present-day problems, which (like global pollution and climate change, starvation and water shortage, political expediency and scientific illiteracy) affect everyone in the world. If ever we needed to learn the lessons of that wartime sense of dynamism and purpose, it is now.

FURTHER READING

BOOKS

Annas, G. J. and Grodin, M. A., *The Nazi Doctors and the Nuremberg Code*, New York: Oxford University Press, 1992

Barenblatt, Daniel, *A Plague upon Humanity: the Secret Genocide of Axis Japan's Germ Warfare Operation*, New York & London: HarperCollins, 2004

Barker, Ralph, *The RAF at War*, Alexandria, Va: Time-Life Books, 1981

Barnaby, Wendy, *The Plague Makers: The Secret World of Biological Warfare*, London: Frog Ltd, 1999

Barnes, Harry Elmer, *Perpetual War for Perpetual Peace: A Critical Examination of the Foreign Policy of Franklin Delano Roosevelt and Its Aftermath*, Caldwell, Idaho: Caxton Books, 1953

Beecher, H., *Research and the Individual Human Subject*, Boston: Little Brown, 1970

Beyerchen, Alan D., *Scientists under Hitler*, New Haven: Yale University Press, 1977

Blackett, P. M. S., *Military and Political Consequences of Atomic Energy,* London: M W Books, 1948

Boyne, Walter J., *Clash of Wings*, New York: Simon & Schuster, 1994

Bracher, Karl, *The German Dilemma*, London: Weidenfeld and Nicholson, 1974

Breuer, William B., *Secret Weapons of World War II*, New York: John Wiley and Sons, 2000

Bury, J. P. T., *France 1914–1940*, London: Methuen, 1960

Camarasa, Jorge, *Mengele: The Angel of Death in South America*, San Juan, Puerto Rico: Gerente Editorial Norma, 2008

Craig, Gordon, *Germany 1866–1945*, Oxford: Clarenden Press, 1978

Davidson, Eugene, *The Trial of the Germans,* New York: MacMillan Co, 1966

Emsley, John, *Molecules of Murder*, London: Royal Society of Chemistry, 2008

Endicott, Stephen and Hagerman, Edward, *The United States and Biological Warfare: Secrets from the Early Cold War and Korea*, Indiana: University Press, 1999

Ethell, Jeffrey L., *The Messerschmitt 163*, London: Ian Allan, 1978

Flower, Stephen, *Barnes Wallis' Bombs: Tallboy, Dambuster and Grand Slam*, London: Tempus, 2004

Ford, Brian J., *Allied Secret Weapons, the War of Science*, New York: Ballantine Books, 1970

Ford, Brian J., *German Secret Weapons, Blueprint for Mars*, New York: Ballantine Books, 1969

Gannon, Paul, *Colossus – Bletchley Park's Greatest Secret*, London, Atlantic Books, 2006

Gardner, Robert, *From Bouncing Bombs To Concorde*, Stroud: Sutton Publishing, 2006

Gimbel, John, *Science Technology and Reparations: Exploitation and Plunder in Postwar Germany*, Stanford: University Press, 1990

Goodman, Steve, *Sonic Warfare, Sound, Affect, and the Ecology of Fear*, Massachusetts: MIT, 2010

Green, William, *Rocket Fighter* (Ballantine's *Illustrated History of World War II*, Weapons Book No. 20), New York: Ballantine Books, 1971

Green, William, *Warplanes of the Third Reich*, London: Macdonald and Jane's, 1970 (fourth impression 1979)

FURTHER READING

Grunden, Walter E., *Secret Weapons and World War II, Japan in the Shadow of Big Science*, Lawrence: University of Kansas Press, 2005

Haining, Peter, *The Flying Bomb War*, London: Robson Books, 2002

Haining, Peter (compiler), *The Spitfire Log*, Souvenir Press, 1985

Harris, Robert, *Enigma*, London: Arrow Books, 1995

Harris, Robert and Paxman, Jeremy, *A Higher Form of Killing: The Secret History of Chemical and Biological Warfare*, London: Random House, 2002

Harris, Sheldon H., *Factories of Death, Japanese Biological Warfare and the American Cover Up*, London: Routledge, 1994

Hinsley, F. H. and Stripp, A., *Codebreakers: The Inside Story of Bletchley Park*, Oxford University Press, 1994

Hitler, Adolf, *Mein Kampf*, London: Hurst & Blacketts, 1939

Hodges, Andrew, *Alan Turing: The Enigma*, London: Vintage Books, 1992

Holloway, David, *Stalin and the Bomb*, Yale University Press, 1994

Irons, Roy, *Hitler's Terror Weapons: The Price of Vengeance*, New York: HarperCollins, 2003

Johnson, Brian, *The Secret War*, London: Arrow Books, 1978

Jones, R V, *Most Secret War*, London: Hamish Hamilton, 1978

Judt, Matthias and Ciesla, Burghard, *Technology Transfer out of Germany after 1945*, Luxembourg: Harwood Academic Publishers, 1996

Jurod, Marcel, *Warrior Without Weapons*, Geneva: IRC Publications, 1982

Lehmann, Ernst A. and Mingos, Howard, *The Zeppelins, Development of the Airship, with the Story of the Zepplins Air Raids in the World War*, New York: J. H. Sears, 1927

Lewin, Ronald, *Hitler's Mistakes*, London: Secker & Warburg, 1984

Ley, Willy, *Rockets Missiles and Men in Space*, New York: Viking Press, 1968

Morpurgo, Jack, *Barnes Wallis: A Biography*, London: Ian Allan, 1981

Morris, R. (ed.), *Breaching the German Dams: Flying Into History*, London: RAF Museum, 2008

Nichol, John and Rennell, Tony, *Tail-End Charlies – Last Battles of the Bomber War 1944–45*, London: St. Martin's Press, 2006

Norris, Robert S., *The Manhattan Project*, New York: Black Dog & Leventhal, 2007

Overy, Richard, *The Air War 1939–1945*, Washington: Potomac Books, 2005

Pawle, Gerald, *The Secret War 1939–45*, London: George Harrap & Co Ltd, 1956

Prange, Gordon, *At Dawn We Slept, the Untold Story of Pearl Harbor*, New York: McGraw-Hill, 1981

Rhodes, Richard, *The Making of the Atomic Bomb*, New York: Simon & Schuster, 1995

Shapira, Shmuel, Hammond, Jeffrey and Cole, Leonard (eds), *Essentials of Terror Medicine*, New York: Springer, 2009

Smith, Michael, *Station X: The Codebreakers of Bletchley Park*, London: Channel 4 Books, 1998

Späte, Wolfgang, *Top Secret Bird: Luftwaffe's Me-163 Komet*, Missoula, Montana: Pictorial Histories Publishing, 1989

Stinnett, Robert B., *Day of Deceit: The Truth about FDR and Pearl Harbor*, New York: Free Press, 2000

Terrell, Edward, *Admiralty Brief*, London: George Harrap & Co Ltd, 1958

Winter, Frank H., *The First Golden Age of Rocketry: Congreve and Hale Rockets of the Nineteenth Century*, Washington and London: Smithsonian Institution Press, 1990

Young, Richard Anthony, *The Flying Bomb*, London: Ian Allan, 1978

Zaloga, Steven, *V-1 Flying Bomb 1942–52*, Oxford: Osprey Publishing, 2005

Zeldin, Theodore, *France 1848–1945*, Oxford: Oxford University Press, 1980

ARTICLES

Alexander, L., 'Ethics of Human Experimentation', *Psychiatric Journal of the University of Ottawa*, 1: 40–46, 1976

Changnon, Stanley, and Ivens, Loreena J., 'History Repeated – the Forgotten Hail Cannons of Europe', *Bulletin of the American Meteorological Society* 62 (3): 368–375, March 1981

Chen, Y. F., 'Japanese Death Factories and the American Cover-up', *Cambridge Quarterly of Healthcare Ethics*, 6: 240–242, 1997

Drayton, Richard, 'An Ethical Blank Cheque', *The Guardian*, 10 May 2005

Dvorak, Petula, 'Fort Hunt's Quiet Men Break Silence on World War II', *Washington Post*, 6 October 2007

Fisk, Robert, 'Poison Gas from Germany', *The Independent*, 30 December 2000

Ford, Brian J., 'Chemical Warfare', *History of the Second World War*, 7 (6): 2845–2850, Bristol: Purnell, 1976

Ford, Brian J., 'Doctors at War', *History of the Second World War*, 7 (6): 2851–2856, Bristol: Purnell, 1976

Ford, Brian J., 'The Rocket Race', *History of the Second World War*, 7 (6): 2837–2844, Bristol: Purnell, 1976

Garth, John, 'The Great Panjandrum Rolls Again', *The Daily Mail*, 5 June 2009

Glines, C. V., 'Top Secret World War II Bat and Bird Bomber Program', *Aviation History*, 15 (5): 38–44, May 2005

Goddard, Robert H., 'A Method of Reaching Extreme Altitudes', *Nature* 105: 809–811, 1920

Hasan, M., 'Fathul Mujahidin' in Sultan, *Journal of the Tipu Sultan Research Institute and Museum*, 3: 1.13, 3.12, 3.31, India: Mysore, 1986

McLellan, Dennis, 'Obituary of Kermit A. Tyler', *Pittsburg Post-Gazette*, 28 February 2010

Meitner, Lise and Frisch, Otto, 'Disintegration of Uranium by Neutrons: a New Type of Nuclear Reaction', *Nature*, 143 (3615): 239–240, 1939

Ruane, Michael, 'Army Destroys Spring Valley Munitions', *Washington Post*, 16 April 2010

Simmonds, Deborah, 'Chemical Weapons Cleanup Blast Set to Go in D.C.', *Washington Times*, 15 April 2010

Tanaka, Yuki, 'Poison Gas, the Story Japan Would Like to Forget', *Bulletin of the Atomic Scientists*, 16–17, October 1988

Turing, Alan, 'On Computable Numbers, with an Application to the Entscheidungsproblem', *Proceedings of the London Mathematical Society*, 2 (42): 230–65, 1937

Turing, Alan 'On Computable Numbers, with an Application to the Entscheidungsproblem, A Correction', *Proceedings of the London Mathematical Society*, 2 (43): 544–6, 1937

Uttley, Matthew, 'Operation Surgeon and Britain's Post-war Exploitation of Nazi German Aeronautics', *Intelligence and National Security*, 17 (2): 1–26, June 2002

OTHER SOURCES

Air Raid Precautions, An Album to contain a Series of Cigarette Cards of National Importance (Wills, H. D. and Wills, H. O., a branch of the Imperial Tobacco Company, undated)

Air Raid Precautions Training Manual No.1 (1st Edition): Basic Training in Air Raid Precautions, (His Majesty's Stationery Office, 1940)

The Protection of Your Home Against Air Raids (Home Office booklet, His Majesty's Stationery Office, 1938)

'Veteran Memories', www.bletchleypark.org.uk/content/hist/history/Veterans.rhtm

Employment of German Scientists and Technicians, Denial Policy, National Records Office ref: AVIA 54/1403, 1945

INDEX

INDEX